WALDORF EDUCATION

THEORY and PRACTICE

A Background To The Educational Thought of Rudolf Steiner

Richard J.S. Blunt

NOVALIS PRESS

CAPE TOWN

EDUCATION SERIES

Copyright ©1995 R.J.S. Blunt.

All rights reserved.

No part of this publication may be reproduced, stored in a retrieval system or transmitted, in any form or by any means, electronic, mechanical, photocopying, recording or otherwise, without the written permission of the copyright owner.

Published by Novalis Press, P.O. Box 53090, Kenilworth 7745, Republic of South Africa.

Cover painting by Sonja Shepherd.

Copyright on the photographs in this book is held by Philosophisch–Anthroposophischer Verlag, Goetheanum, CH-4143, Dornach, Switzerland.

Typeset in 9.5pt Times Roman by Prototype Graphics & Documents, Cape Town.

Printed and bound in the Republic of South Africa by Mills Litho (Pty) Ltd., Cape Town.

First published 1995.

ISBN   0–9583885–4–7

This book was originally submitted as a thesis for the M.Ed. degree to the Department of Education, Rhodes University, Grahamstown, South Africa.

Publisher's Foreword

The publication of this book by Richard Blunt is in response to numerous requests for information about Rudolf Steiner education. Initially used as substance for a Master's thesis, the depth and breadth of this work make it an ideal source book on Rudolf Steiner's educational impulse.

Seventy-five years have elapsed since the inauguration of the first Waldorf School for children of factory workers in Stuttgart, Germany. Established by Rudolf Steiner at the request of the Managing Director of the Waldorf Astoria factory, "Waldorf" has become the largest and most progressive independent school movement in the world. Not confined only to First World countries, Waldorf education has also taken root in distressed socio-economic areas. From Romania to Brazil, from Soweto to black ghettos in Milwaukee, and from Moscow to Guguletu in Cape Town: communities in these areas have recognised the relevancy of Steiner education.

In South Africa alone not only are there many private Waldorf Schools and initiatives, but more than 2 000 state school teachers have been introduced to the creative impulse of Waldorf methodology and perspectives through teacher enrichment programmes and courses.

Major recognition of the value of Waldorf education has recently come from UNESCO, whose International Commission on Education for the 21st Century has issued a *Brief* (see Appendix 2) in which it sees Waldorf education as the education for the future.

This then begs the question: why has Steiner's work been overlooked, especially when so much academic attention has been given to courageous alternatives — such as A.S. Neill's Summerhill and other similar educational experiments — which are however heavily dependent on the charisma and talents of the founder? Surely in a world where education at large is in a recognised process of decay (see *The Closing of the American Mind* by Allan Bloom, published by Simon Schuster, N.Y. 1987, and *A Nation at Risk*, the report of the National Commission on Excellence in Education in the United States) Steiner education deserves attention, particularly when development of Waldorf schools has reached the point where well over a million parents from totally divergent cultures, languages and religions support the movement world-wide.

The publication of this book recognises that the tide is turning and that Waldorf education is beginning to be seen for what it is: an excellent schooling for life based upon the needs of the child, and relevance to the social demands of the times in which we now live. It goes further than this, for it respects the humanity of children and offers an education tailored to their growing and changing needs, instead of trying to fit the children to the requirements of various interest groups in society. It is able to do this because it recognises that human beings have a spiritual component — and it is this that all real education serves.

Ralph Shepherd

The Novalis Institute would like to thank the Embassy of the Japanese Government in South Africa for their assistance in meeting the costs of publishing the Novalis Education Series.

Their generous contribution towards this project is an expression of the support of the Japanese Government for teacher education in South Africa.

THE
NOVALIS
INSTITUTE

A Note On The Author

Richard (Bill) Blunt first developed an interest in Rudolf Steiner while studying Philosophy of Education for the B.Ed. degree at Rhodes University, Grahamstown, South Africa. One of the options of the course was to investigate any educational thinker. He had heard about Waldorf Education from friends who sent their daughter to Michael Mount School in Johannesburg. Their comment on the school had been that it provided a wonderful education, but that Steiner's philosophy was strange. Bill decided to use the B.Ed. opportunity to find out more about Steiner.

Two months later and well behind schedule with his other assignments, Bill handed in a forty page paper which seemed to him only to scratch the surface of the subject. He was baffled that, although much had been written on Steiner, no attempt had ever been made to draw together his philosophical and educational thought in a comprehensive and accessible way. His own search had begun with strong scepticism, which developed into grudging respect, and then became a sense of awe at the intense energy and sincerity of Steiner the man, and wonder at his seeming temerity in confronting the world with a view of reality that was altogether at odds with orthodoxy.

Bill was determined to pursue his interest for a Master's degree thesis, a project which led him into the world of Anthroposophy — the name given by Steiner to his world conception — and Waldorf Education. His experiences convinced him that there was a need for his study, and when he completed it he sent copies of the thesis to the institutions he had visited. The present book is an attempt to make it more widely accessible, but it is also one of very few works on Steiner written by someone who is outside the Anthroposophical movement.

Bill went on to teach Philosophy and Sociology of Education at Rhodes, and then spent several years at the University of Fort Hare in Alice, where he taught English for academic purposes and Applied Linguistics, and became involved in Academic Development. At present he is Deputy Director of Instructional and Organisational Development at the University of Port Elizabeth.

Acknowledgements

I gratefully acknowledge the assistance of all those who have willingly gave their time and knowledge to guide me in compiling this book.

Dr Arthur Clark promoted this work with constant interest and encouragement, at all times guiding my attention towards considering the needs of the reader when dealing with a body of material of such magnitude. His awareness of the importance of clarifying concepts and rationalizing the structure of Steiner's thought has been invaluable.

I am indebted to many of the staff and pupils of the following schools for allowing me to visit them, and to observe and discuss their work: Michael Mount Waldorf School in Johannesburg, South Africa; Michael Hall in Forest Row, Sussex, England; Bristol Waldorf School in England; Wynstones School, Gloucester, England; Michael House near Shipley, Derbyshire, England; and the Rudolf Steiner School of Edinburgh, Scotland. The lecturers and students of Emerson College, Forest Row, Sussex also received me generously.

The following people, many of whom have spent much of their lives studying and practising Steiner's thought, have been especially helpful and influential: Zelia Roelofse, Eddie Dawes, Brigitte Wegerif, Jacky Gordon, Ben Kleynhans, Dr Maghiel Hogerzeil, Francois Maritz, Susanne Hotz, Bill Day, John Thompson, Norman Davidson, Leslie Smollen, Carter Nelson, Graham Kennish, Dr Rudi Lissau, and Mike Caris.

Charles Abbott, who prepared the proofs of the book, contributed not only the presentation but also many stylistic and factual recommendations and additions which have improved the text. Ralph Shepherd of The Novalis Institute in Cape Town, who approached me about publishing my thesis in the form of a book, also read and made factual corrections to the text. Their role in updating and improving the text has been encouraging and valuable. However, I take full responsibility for any errors and misinterpretations of Steiner's work.

I owe special thanks to Professor Michael Ashley for first giving me the freedom to discover Steiner for myself, and then for his subsequent mature insights in support of my interest.

Finally, I wish to thank my friend Ken Durham for all his help over the years of my research. His support and deep insight into Steiner's thought constantly encouraged me, and ensured that the work reached completion.

Richard Blunt

CONTENTS

Publisher's Foreword   iii

A Note on the Author   v

Acknowledgements   vi

Notes on Presentation   xi

Introduction   1

1 Rudolf Steiner   3
1.1   **His Life**   3
1.2   **Steiner's View Of His Times**   10
1.2.1   Introduction   11
1.2.2   Philosophy   13
1.2.3   Science   14
1.2.4   Politics   16
1.2.5   Education   18
1.2.6   Religion   21
1.2.7   Technology   22
1.3   **Character Analysis**   23

2 Review Of The Literature   27
2.1   **Steiner's Books And Lectures**   27
2.1.1   The Selection of Books and Lectures   27
2.1.2   The Nature of the Books   28
2.1.3   The Nature of the Lectures   29
2.1.4   The Esoteric Lectures   30
2.1.5   Management of the Material   30
2.2   **Works On Steiner**   32
2.2.1   Biographical Works   32
2.2.2   Works on Education   32
2.2.3   Works on Philosophy   36
2.2.4   Works on Spiritual Science   38

3   The Foundations Of Educational Thought : Steiner's Concept Of Man   45

3.1   Steiner's Spiritual Science   46
3.1.1   Introduction 46
3.1.2   Spiritual Science and Natural Science 47
3.1.3   Method of Investigation 47
3.1.4   Proof in Spiritual Science 50
3.1.5   Access to Spiritual Science 52

3.2   The Structure Of Man   53
3.2.1   Body, Soul and Spirit 53
3.2.2   The Physical and Soul Bodies and the Ego 54
          Etheric Body   55
          Astral Body   55
          Ego   56

3.3   The Relationship Between Body And Soul   57
3.3.1   Analysis of the Physical Body and its Relationship to the Soul   58
          Nervous System   58
          Rhythmic System   59
          Metabolism and Limb System   59
3.3.2   The Senses 60

4   The Stages Of Development And Their Implications For Education   63

4.1   The Life Before Birth   64
4.1.1   Reincarnation. 64
4.1.2   The Law of Karma 65
4.1.3   Incarnation 66

4.2   Birth To The Change Of Teeth   67
4.2.1   Development 67
4.2.2   The Process of Imitation 68
4.2.3   Educational Implications 68

4.3   The Change Of Teeth To Puberty   72
4.3.1   From Imitation to Authority 73
4.3.2   Developments in Thinking 73
4.3.3   The Three Substages 74
          The First Substage   74
          The Second Substage   75
          The Third Substage   76
4.3.4   Educational Implications 76

4.4	**From Puberty To Adulthood**	**79**
4.4.1	Developments in Thinking	80
4.4.2	Educational Implications for Adolescence	81
	Preparation	82
	From Authority to Freedom	82
	The Development of the Intellect	83
	Moral Education during Adolescence	84
	The Social and Economic Life	86
4.5	**The Education Of The Whole Child**	**87**
4.5.1	Thinking	89
4.5.2	Feeling	91
4.5.3	Willing	93
4.6	**Education Towards Individuality: The Temperaments**	**96**
4.7	**Education Towards Freedom**	**98**

5	**The Aims, Principles And Methods Of Education**	**103**
5.1	**Aims**	**104**
5.2	**Principles**	**107**
5.3	**Methods**	**109**
5.3.1	The Teacher	109
	Practice	109
	The College of Teachers	115
	Preparation and Training	116
	Authority and Discipline	119
5.3.2	Subject Methods	123
	Kindergarten	123
	Writing and Reading	124
	Home Language: Speech, Poetry, Grammar and Writing	126
	Foreign Languages	128
	Eurythmy and Gymnastics	129
	Mathematics: Arithmetic and Geometry	132
	Science	136
	Geography	141
	History	143
	Art	145
	Drawing and Painting	147
	Sculpture and Modelling	148
	Music	150
	Handicrafts and Technical Subjects	151
	Religion	153
	Economics and Accountancy	155

6	Steiner's Educational Teachings In Practice	157
6.1	The Schools	158
6.2	Kindergarten (4-6 years old): Imitation	163
6.3	Class One (6-7 years old): From Imitation to Authority	165
6.4	Class Two (7-8 years old): A Main Lesson in Arithmetic	167
6.5	A Foreign Language Lesson with Class Two	169
6.6	Class Six (12-13 years old): Mineralogy	170
6.7	Educating the Will	173

7	Rudolf Steiner : A Modern Perspective	177
7.1	Steiner and Ancient Greek Thought	177
7.2	Steiner and the Child-Centred Theorists	179
7.3	Steiner and more recent Educational Thought	186
7.4	Summary and Conclusions	193

FOOTNOTES		199
BIBLIOGRAPHY		229
APPENDIX 1 :	The Von Hardenberg Foundation (Novalis Institute)	237
APPENDIX 2 :	*Brief:* UNESCO International Commission on Education for the Twenty-first Century	241

Notes on Presentation

Certain special forms of presentation have been consistently adopted for this book. Firstly, Steiner's terminology is given capital letters and is not italicised or placed in inverted commas. This has been done even for common terms such as Soul, Spirit, Thought, Feeling and Will, which Steiner uses in his own way.

Secondly, citations of Steiner's works in the text are dated according to when they were first published, or, in the case of lectures, the year they were delivered. Full details of the texts used may be found in the Bibliography.

Finally, in order for the style of the text to be in keeping with Steiner's expression, in the first five chapters the conventions of representing children and adults of either sex by the personal pronoun "he", or the nouns "man" and "mankind" are used. It is hereby acknowledged that, today, these conventions may be considered unacceptable.

INTRODUCTION

Rudolf Steiner's name is widely known especially in connection with education, yet few know much, if anything, about his philosophy. He was a deep thinking man whose educational ideas were founded on his unique analysis of man's being, developed in the course of a lifetime's experience of teaching.

A survey of Steiner's life reveals him to have been a man of exceptional energy, talents and intellectual ability, whose life demonstrated the moral qualities that he advocated for others[1]. This conclusion strengthens the argument that his unorthodox views ought to be examined more closely.

The literature which is presently available on Steiner contains only one formal study of his thought[2]. This concentrates on his vision of Man and the Cosmos, and says little about his educational beliefs.

Steiner's teachings on education were given almost exclusively in lecture form which were recorded by stenographers. These lectures form the basis of what has become the largest independent school movement in the world. Many books have been written on the subject, but never before has a formal attempt been made to synthesise and structure the content of the educational lectures.

Perhaps the strongest reason for this omission has been the extent of the task. Steiner had a holistic view of reality which was not a variation of, but an alternative to, more materialistic conceptions. Any attempt to describe his educational thought must therefore be founded on his analysis of Man.

For Steiner, the needs of the growing child can only be answered by finding an artistic way of presenting each subject of the curriculum. To this end, the teacher himself must develop an artistic perception of his subject.

Steiner's thought resists reduction to a set of principles, and it pleads for a less abstract and more human approach to education. It is the thought of a man of perception and compassion who had close experience of children and profound insights into Man's deeper nature. Sympathy as much as objectivity is necessary to allow its value to become evident.

---

1 *Footnotes will be found at the end of the book, starting on page 199.*

Rudolf Steiner (1861–1925), photographed in 1879 aged 18.

1

RUDOLF STEINER

1.1   HIS LIFE[1]

Rudolf Steiner was born on 27 February 1861 in Kraljevo[2] Croatia, which was then a province of Austria and is now in Serbia, Yugoslavia. His father was born in Geras, his mother in Horn, both in the lower Austrian forest area[3].

His father was a railway telegraphist. He was interested in politics and a "free thinker" although as a boy he had been closely associated with the Premonstratension Order. Steiner's mother was a devoted and loving housewife[4]. Steiner recalled the strong imitative urges he felt as a child, which focused on his father's work[5] and the interests of the townsfolk[6]. He had a strong and inquisitive interest in the world around him[7].

Moving to Neudorfl, Steiner found school to be boring, with the mechanical dullness of copying letters from the board. However it was here that he encountered a book on geometry and was thrilled to discover an inner world of the mind:

> "That one can live within the mind in the shaping of forms perceived only within oneself, entirely without impression upon the external senses – this gave me the deepest satisfaction." [8]

He grew to admire the teacher who owned the geometry book, and this man introduced him to "the element of art" through the piano, violin and drawing[9]. He also developed a sense of awe for the priest at Neudorfl whose powerful sermons, and the solemn liturgical music of church services became a "profound experience" for the young boy[10]. Steiner's father enrolled him at the Realschule, which had a curriculum of Science and Modern Languages, as opposed to the Gymnasium which had a Curriculum of the Classics. This was because his father wanted him to become a railways engineer[11].

When he was eleven he felt a great need for adult authority in his life, and found that his Mathematics and Physics teacher fulfiled his ideal:

> "His teaching was wonderfully systematic and thorough-going. He built up everything so clearly out of its elements that it was in the highest degree beneficial to one's thinking to follow him." [12]

By the age of fifteen he was already deeply involved with the inner world of the mind, an interest illustrated by his enthusiastic attempt to read Kant's Critique of Pure Reason [13].

He became friendly with the doctor at Neudorfl who awakened in him a love of literature.

"In the atmosphere of this lovable Doctor, sensitive to everything beautiful, I learned especially to know Lessing." [14]

He read Rotteck's History of the World, Tacitus and Johannes von Müller and did home study courses in analytical geometry, trigonometry and differential and integral calculus[15]. Regarded as a "good scholar" he was chosen as a tutor when only fifteen.

"I owe much to this tutoring. In having to give others in turn the matter which I had been taught, I myself became, so to speak, awake to this .... The development of what had thus been received in a half-waking state was now brought about by the fact that in the periods of tutoring I had to vitalize my own knowledge." [16]

"... this experience compelled me at an early age to concern myself with practical pedagogy. I learned the difficulties of the development of human minds through my pupils."[17]

Starved of the classics in the Realschule, Steiner bought his own texts and studied them[18]. He read Fichte's Theory of Science, Traugott Krug's Transcendental Synthesism, and Thilo's history of Philosophy while preparing to enter the Technische Hochschule (University) in 1879[19]. Once there, he studied literature since Goethe and Schiller's life and work under K.J. Schroër. He worked on the theme "To what extent is man in his actions a free being?" His philosophy lecturers were Robert Zimmerman and Franz Brentano, both of whom stimulated him[20], and he also had to study Mathematics and Natural Science[21].

It was at this time that he was developing full awareness of the spiritual world, but found that everyone he spoke to considered it to be "spiritistic" and he was intensely repelled by this[22]. A chance meeting with an elderly man who was quite "uneducated", but who clearly had direct experience of the spiritual world, strengthened Steiner's own perception[23].

Steiner chose to keep secret the name of this man, but he was subsequently identified as Felix Koguzki (1833-1909) who was a herb-gatherer and whose spiritual life was not evident in his public life. They met in 1879[24]. Felix introduced him to another, even more mysterious man, whose name has never been discovered. This man completed Steiner's spiritual training and gave him his life's mission as an "Initiate" :

"To reunite Science and Religion. To bring back God into Science and Nature into Religion. This to fertilise both Art and Life." [25]

He was instructed to begin his mission by understanding contemporary ma-

4

terialistic science, and then to confront it and face the inevitable consequences of public opinion.

"It is in the extremity of distress that thou wilt find thy weapons and thy brothers in the fight. I have shown thee who thou art, now go and be thyself!" [26]

At university he was studying Geometry, Space and Time[27] and the work of Hegel[28], Darwin[29], Keppler and J.R. Mayers[30]. He was "deeply stirred" by Schiller's letters on the "aesthetic education of man" in which "the coming to life in men of the true human being" was seen as the development of harmony between the life of the senses and the life of logic and reason, in which moral instinct and feeling for beauty would be realised.[31]

His lecturer in Literature, K.J. Schroër, became an increasingly important influence in his life. He introduced Steiner to Goethe's work, and influenced his thinking on education.

"In regard to education and instruction he spoke often against the mere imparting of information and in favour of the evolution of the full and entire human being." [32]

Steiner's experience with teaching underwent an important development. He was given charge of a family of four children, one of whom was hydrocephalic[33]. This developed in him, in his early twenties, belated insights into play:

"In the life I led before coming into this family I had little opportunity for sharing in the play of children. In this way it came about that my 'play-time' came after my twentieth year. I had then to learn also how to play, for I had to direct the play, and this I did with great enjoyment." [34]

The ten year old hydrocephalic child was a greater challenge:

"I had to find access to a soul which was, as it were, in a sleeping state, and which must gradually be enabled to gain the mastery over the bodily manifestations. In a certain sense one had first to draw the soul within the body. I was thoroughly convinced that the boy really had great mental capacities, though they were then buried. This made my task a profoundly satisfying one. I was soon able to bring the child into a loving dependence upon me. This condition caused the mere intercourse between us to awaken his sleeping faculties of soul. For his instruction I had to feel my way to special methods. Every fifteen minutes beyond a certain time allotted to instruction caused injury to his health. To many subjects of instruction the boy had great difficulty in relating himself.

This educational task became to me the source from which I myself learned much. Through the method of instruction which I had to apply there was laid open to my view the association between the spiritual–mental and the bodily in man. Then I went through my real course of

5

study in physiology and psychology. I became aware that teaching and instructing must become an art having its foundation in a genuine understanding of man." [35]

The child made dramatic progress. He caught up and completed his schooling and eventually became a medical doctor[36]. This experience had great significance for Steiner's later educational thought:

"For through this means I developed in vital fashion a knowledge of the being of man which I do not believe could have been developed by me so vitally in any other way." [37]

The first and most astonishing sign of Steiner's intellectual promise came in 1884 when he was only 23 years old. K.J. Schroër recommended him to Joseph Kurschner to edit Goethe's scientific writings, with an introduction and accompanying interpretative notes, for an edition of Deutsche National – Literatur [38]. This was a resounding vote of confidence in the young Steiner's ability, and of his insights into Goethe's thought.

Steiner believed that Goethe had found the secret for bridging the gap between nature and human concepts of nature[39]. Concepts which were appropriate for inorganic nature had to be vitalised; they had to develop a life of their own:

"... he (Goethe) sought to hold fast in his mind an ideal image of a leaf, which was not a fixed, lifeless concept but such a one as might present itself in the most varied forms. If one permits these forms in the mind to proceed one out of the other, one thus constructs the whole plant. One re-creates in the mind in ideal fashion the process whereby nature in actual fashion shapes the plant." [40]

Steiner saw such idealism as the gateway "into the world of real spirit". His work on Goethe was to be relevant for all his future thought.

"To me this idealism seemed the noble shadow, not cast into man's soul by the sense world, but falling into his inner being from a spiritual world, and creating the obligation to go forward from this shadow to the world which has cast it." [41]

In 1888, after completing his work for Kurschner, he was appointed editor of *Deutsche Wochenschrift* (German Weekly) but he was unable to write his weekly article on public affairs with any enthusiasm[42]. Confronted by contemporary socialist belief that material economic factors were the primary forces at work in man's evolution[43] and philosophical beliefs in the division between the world of nature and human concepts[44], Steiner realised how far removed his thoughts were from modern intellectual life.

In 1891 he was invited to work as a collaborator at the Goethe-and-Schiller Institute in Weimar, and he was there for seven years[45]. During this time he was awarded his Ph.D. by the University of Rostock with a thesis entitled Truth and

Science[46]. His aim in this was "to reduce the act of cognition, by analysis, to its ultimate elements and thus to discover a correct formulation of the problem of knowledge and a way to its solution." [47] This work was published together with an extended version entitled The Philosophy of Spiritual Activity (1894). Both works had much to do with contemporary philosophers, including Kant and Hegel. While at Weimar he published 95 titles, among them seven volumes of Goethe's scientific writings, a book on Nietzsche, and work on Fichte and Haeckel[48].

At Weimar he continued tutoring boys and girls, and learned "how different were the ways that the two sexes grow into life." [49]

In 1897 he went to Berlin where he became joint editor of *Magazin für Literatur*[50]. He married Anna Eunike in 1899[51]. In this same year he began lecturing at the Workers' Educational Institute at night[52], which he continued to do until 1905[53]. During this time he was fully absorbed and active among the artistic, literary and philosophical leaders in Berlin, but met opposition to his ideas among them[54].

In 1900 Steiner was invited to address the Theosophical Society, and began with lectures on Nietzsche and Goethe. This developed into a course of 27 lectures, subsequently published in a volume entitled Mysticism at the Dawn of the Modern Age, and its Relation to Modern World Philosophy[55]. In 1901–1902 he gave the society a further 25 lectures which were published under the title Christianity as Mystical Fact[56]. A further series of lectures, ending in 1903, was published as From Zarathustra to Nietzsche. The story of the development of Man as reflected in world philosophies, from the earliest oriental times up to the present, or Anthroposophy[57]. This was his first use of the term Anthroposophy. It was originally coined by one of his tutors at the University of Vienna, Immanuel Herman, the son of J.G. Fichte[58].

He did not only lecture to the Theosophists, but was invited to speak by a variety of groups. When the Theosophical Society opened its German branch in the presence of Annie Besant, and asked Steiner to be its Secretary General, he made it quite clear that he would retain his independence of thought and actions:

"I did not subscribe to any sectarian dogma; I remained someone who expressed what he believed himself to have the power to express about his own experiences of the spiritual world." [59]

He saw the period at the turn of the century as being a profound testing of his soul wherein he became aware of the incarnation of Christ as the centre-point of human history.

"The evolution of my soul rested upon the fact that I stood before the mystery of Golgotha in most inward, most earnest joy of knowledge." [60]

For Steiner the incarnation of Christ had implications far beyond those of religion. In addition, the Gospels could only be understood properly when it was realised that they were written by spiritual Initiates who were writing from occult points of view[61]. Many of his lectures were concerned with the subject of Christianity, and its relationship to "Spiritual Science."

7

He was emphatic that, from the outset of his teachings on spiritual matters, he was not intellectualising from his studies of other teachings, Gnostic or Theosophical. In 1903 he wrote to a friend,

"You write that I make manifest the Spirit in my life. In one respect, I assure you, I strive to do so: I never speak of anything spiritual that I do not know by the most direct spiritual experience." [62]

In 1904, he published Theosophy [63] on the basis of his spiritual research, and began a series of articles which were eventually completed and published in 1909 as Knowledge of the Higher Spheres. How is it achieved?[64]. In 1910 he published the third major work on Anthroposophy An Outline of Occult Science. This introduced a "general cosmology", including a chapter on the development of the world and man[65].

During this time he started other activities within the society. He and Edouard Schuré began to write "Mystery Dramas" and to produce them. He edited the Theosophical journal Lucifer – Gnosis with Marie von Sivers, an activity that he had to give up in 1908 because of the pressure of lecture engagements. A first lecture on Education was given and published as a booklet, a work which was seminal to all his later thought on education. In it he wrote,

"If called upon to develop a system of education, spiritual science will be able to impart everything that falls under this head, even down to instructions about individual necessaries and luxuries. For it is realistic in its approach to life, not vague theory, although perhaps owing to the aberrations of many theosophists it is made to appear so." [66]

This practical education was to be based directly on the development of the child:

"We shall not set up demands nor programmes, but simply describe the child-nature. From the nature of the growing and evolving human being, the proper point of view for Education will, as it were, spontaneously result." [67]

As in his spiritual instruction, so in its application to various disciplines, Steiner wished the teachings to be judged by their fruits.

"Only when it is perceived, in anthroposophical circles everywhere, that the point is not simply to theorize about the teachings, but to let them bear fruit in the most far-reaching way in all the relationships of life – only then will life itself open up to anthroposophy with sympathy and understanding. Otherwise people will continue to regard it as a variety of religious sectarianism for a few cranks and enthusiasts. If, however, it performs positive and useful spiritual work, the Anthroposophical Movement cannot in the long run be denied intelligent recognition." [68]

From 1907, Steiner's lecturing engagements took him throughout Europe. He was invited to speak in Germany, Austria, Switzerland, France, Italy, England,

8

Czechoslovakia, Norway and Denmark[69]. Already he was referring to his own teachings as "Anthroposophy", and it was clear that he considered them to be quite independent of the Theosophical teachings.

Galbreath shows that Anthroposophy was not a new term, having been used by Steiner's Philosophy lecturer, Robert Zimmerman, as well as Thomas Vaughan, Troxler and J.H. Fichte[70]. The term was sharply distinguished from "Theosophy".

> "... Steiner's use of the term shifts responsibility for attaining such wisdom ('sophia': divine wisdom) from divine revelation from beyond to man's own thinking processes, elevated to a higher level and brought into contact with 'sophia'." [71]

His break with Theosophy came when Annie Besant and Bishop Leadbeater proclaimed that Christ had returned to earth in the body of a young Indian boy, Jeddu Krishnamurti. They began an élite group within the Theosophical Society called the Order of the Star of the East. Steiner considered their beliefs preposterous, expelled members of the Order from the German branch and, between 1912 and 1913, established the Anthroposophical Society as a new and independent movement[72]. Steiner's action was considered outrageous by the Theosophists, but he justified his actions and was unrepentant[73].

His first wife, Anna, died in March 1911, and in December 1914 he married Marie von Sivers, who had been involved in the development of Eurythmy and was an elocution teacher[74].

In 1913 a building called the Goetheanum (in recognition of Steiner's esteem for Goethe) was begun in Dornach, Switzerland. It was to be the centre for Anthroposophical activities – lectures, festivals, drama and other artistic projects – and Steiner designed it himself. Built of wood on a concrete foundation it was an arresting sight, consisting of a huge, double dome. The cost of seven million Swiss francs was met entirely by donations[75].

In 1914 Steiner published an encyclopaedic treatise on Philosophy, placing Anthroposophy within its context. He called it The Riddles of Philosophy. During the Great War he lived alternately in Dornach and Berlin, continuing his lecturing and writing and the work on the Goetheanum[76]. In 1919 he became widely known for his book The Threefold State in which he described the principles necessary for the development of a spiritually healthy state.

Also in 1919 he was asked by the Director of the Waldorf-Astoria cigarette factory in Stuttgart, Emil Molt, to found a school for the children of his factory workers. Steiner responded enthusiastically to the opportunity. A remarkably accomplished group of people – five of them doctors – agreed to join his staff, and in August he began three courses of lectures to prepare them to start an educational programme based on Spiritual Science[77]. He was now 58, and in the next six years he gave 15 courses of lectures on education in Germany, Britain, the Netherlands and Switzerland[78].

From this time onwards his applications of the teachings of Spiritual Science mushroomed into almost every area of human interest.

In 1920 he gave lecture courses on Education, Physics, Medicine, Philology and on Thomas Aquinas[79]. In 1921 he spoke on Astronomy, Scientific experiment, Therapeutic Eurythmy, Theology, Medicine and Education[80]. In 1922 there were courses on Political Economy and Education[81] and the "Christian Community" was founded to "renew the religious life of the Christian church." [82] At the end of this year, the first Goetheanum burnt to the ground, a devastating event since the building symbolised so much for the movement[83].

The following year was one of renewal for Anthroposophy, culminating in "The Christmas Conference" of 1923[84]. Preparations were made for founding a General Anthroposophical Society for Germany, Norway, Switzerland, Britain, the Netherlands and Austria. He gave lecture courses on Education in Switzerland and England, and he began to publish weekly instalments of The Story of My Life in the Society's journal, *Das Goetheanum*[85].

Despite an extremely painful illness, described only as a "disorder of the digestive system" [86] Steiner maintained and even increased his activities in 1924. In the first nine months before becoming bedridden he presided over the planning and early building of the new Goetheanum – a gigantic concrete structure – lectured in Dornach, Prague, Stuttgart, Berne, Breslau, London, Arnhem and Torquay on Education and on Karma, gave courses on Eurythmy, Agriculture, Elocution and Theology, as well as regular lectures for the workers at the Goetheanum[87]. He died on 30 March 1925, and was active with his reading and writing to the end[88].

He left a strong, rapidly expanding educational movement. At his death there were two schools in Germany (the Stuttgart school had 800 pupils and over 40 teachers[89]) and one each in Britain and the Netherlands. In 1962 there were 26 schools in Germany and 40 in the Netherlands, Britain, France, Switzerland, Scandinavia, the United States, Mexico, Brazil and Argentina[90]. In 1978 the Waldorf Movement incorporated 150 schools spread over 20 countries. With more than 50 000 pupils it was then the largest independent educational movement in the world[91]. A 1994 UNESCO *Commission on Education* Report (Appendix 2) indicated the significant growth of the Movement in the years since 1978: with more than 600 schools, 1000 kindergartens and 500 institutions for remedial education and social therapy world-wide, its status as the largest independent educational movement appears unchallenged.

1.2   STEINER'S VIEW OF HIS TIMES

The following account of Steiner's views of his times has been written to supplement the above brief sketch of his life. It indicates something of the range of his interests, not as a thinker who withdrew from the world, but as one who had a lively interest – albeit from his own point of view – in world events. The intention is to portray, not to interpret, in order to reveal his thought, which is sufficiently clear and vivid in itself. His views are related, wherever appropriate, to education.

1.2.1 Introduction

Perhaps most central to his concerns was alienation between man and man, and man and his world.

"Everyone talks today of social impulses, yet none but anti-social urges are to be found among men. Socialism ought to have its roots in the new esteem men should gain for one another. But there can only be mutual esteem when people really listen to one another." [92]

The "grim and terrible world-war" had made many realise that there was something desperately wrong, that there was "something which the deepest soul of Germany is yearning for". Steiner identified this as being influences from the Middle Ages which gave rise to such a man as Goethe, but from which modern man had been isolated[93].

Steiner believed that since the time of Galileo and Copernicus men had been striving to see the world in a wholly material way, uninfluenced by religious and other preconceptions. However, until the fifteenth century, man's mind was alive with imagination, and his thought moved the whole of his soul. It was in the course of the fifteenth century that a major change took place in the thought-life of man. His thinking became increasingly a product of the physical brain, and less an activity of the soul. It was only as this change in man occurred that he became ready to look at the world in a different, material way, with the appropriate instrument, the physical brain.[94]

This change, which made possible the development of materialistic natural science, "... misleads man into regarding the sense-perceptible, physical existence as the one and only reality, thus shutting himself off entirely from any kind of outlook into a spiritual world." [95]

Materialism resulted in a mechanistic view of the universe[96], a mechanistic view of man, after Lamettrie for example[97] and a mechanistic view of man's soul as combinations and associations of thoughts, after John Stuart Mill's idea of imagery[98].

Modern materialistic conceptions even like to trace a man's spiritual qualities to inheritance from his ancestors[99], and in the field of public welfare, man's economic and material needs are considered to be the essential ones[100].

Steiner considered that this growth towards materialism was essential to emancipate man's spiritual life:

"Little by little the human being has lost the connection he had in olden times with the spiritual world. This was inevitable because he had to develop full freedom in order to shape all that is human out of himself. This has been the challenge since the fifteenth century, but it was not really felt until the end of the nineteenth and particularly in the twentieth century." [101]

It was only when man looked into his own soul and found emptiness that a "tension of dissatisfaction" [102] would encourage a striving for the spiritual life again. Steiner considered that the necessity for materialism was now past and man ought to be given true, spiritual-scientific insights[103].

Materialism not only led man to feelings of despair, but rendered him "a hindrance to the evolution of the entire world in which he lives" [104] because it blinded him to the tasks which were necessary for this age[105].

Steiner characterised the tasks of the modern age in terms of two principles (or principalities, since they existed for him as real beings in the spiritual world) which he named Lucifer and Ahriman. Lucifer lived in religious fantasy and mysticism, while Ahriman manifested through the objective, rational spirit of science. Man contained the potentialities of both principles within his soul, and he had to learn to develop them in harmony with one another, and balance his tendency to become obsessed with either extreme. This could be achieved through Art, although Art itself was subject to control from both sides[106].

Modern materialistic science moulded man's thinking to an Ahrimanic extreme, persuading him to throw off his "unscientific" heritage of past ages:

"In the foundations of the spirit life of the world it is as though a chain were there, reaching from the past over into the future, which must be received by each generation into itself, must be carried forward, re-forged, perfected. This chain has been broken in the age of intellectualism." [107]

In the interests of Science, thinking became based on sense experience alone, and personal feeling was deliberately driven out of it in order to achieve logic and objectivity[108]. As this was done, man lost his inner feeling for truth, he could no longer feel close to his fellow man in his social life, and his speech became devoid of soul, empty and cliché-ridden[109]. At the same time, calls for social reform became frenzied:

"The louder the call for social reforms, the more is it a symptom of the fact that men have become unsocial. Because they no longer have any feeling for what is truly social, they cry out for social reform." [110]

A crust of ice closed over the souls of the modern generation, and only the young still experienced warmth of heart in their thoughts[111]. The youth decided to form their own movements, to break free from the guidance of their elders and rely on their own guidance[112] so that a great chasm developed between the younger and older generations. They spoke "entirely different languages of the soul."[113] The older generation lost their authority over the young, and instead of looking into their own empty souls to see why this had happened, they began to look to the young for guidance and adapt themselves to the wants and demands of youth[114]. The youth for their part drifted towards the search for salvation in solitariness, isolated from their fellow man, so completing the disintegration of the social order as a real expression of man's soul[115].

"Human beings must again be capable of feeling not weakly but strongly:

beautiful–ugly, good–evil, true–false. They must be capable of feeling things not weakly but strongly, so that they live in them with their whole being, that their very heart's blood flows into their words."[116]

"In our time the soul must strive beyond empty phrase, convention and routine; beyond the empty phrase to a grasp of truth; beyond convention to direct, elementary warm-hearted relation between man and man; beyond routine to the state in which the spirit lives in every single action, so that we no longer act automatically but that the Spirit lives in the most ordinary everyday actions." [117]

1.2.2 Philosophy

Steiner's philosophical work – or that part of it which is of a more orthodox philosophical character – centres around three publications. They are Truth and Science (1891), The Philosophy of Spiritual Activity (1894), and The Riddles of Philosophy (1914).

In The Riddles of Philosophy he traced man's attempts "to solve the riddle of world and life"[118] and showed that modern philosophy was seeking for a way to overcome man's alienation from his world.

"Many of the most recent schools of thought prove to be attempts to search within the self-conscious ego, which in the course of philosophical development feels itself more and more separated from the world, for an element that leads back to a reunion with the world." [119]

This was the problem to which all his philosophical work was addressed, an epistemological problem which had to involve a marriage of Philosophy and Science. In his Preface to Truth and Science, he wrote,

"The sciences are seen in their true value only when philosophy explains the human significance of their results. To make a contribution to such an explanation was my aim. But, perhaps, our present-day science scorns all philosophical vindication! If so, two things are certain. One is that this essay of mine is superfluous. The other is that modern thinkers are lost in the wood and do not know what they want." [120]

Steiner's epistemological thought is outlined by Owen Barfield (see 2.2.3). In developing it, Steiner discussed the thought of Kant and his followers, J.G. Fichte and Hegel[121]. He also analysed the theories of knowledge of many of the contemporary schools of philosophical thought such as Critical Idealism, Naïve Realism, Metaphysical Realism, Monism, both Materialistic and Spiritualistic Dualism, Ethical Individualism, Evolutionism, Optimism and Pessimism[122].

Long after he left the fold of orthodox philosophy he was to relate all his occult thought to his early philosophical work, showing that both placed man at the centre of knowledge:

"I have repeatedly said that man, and the soul of man, is the stage upon which world events are played. This thought can be expressed in a philosophical abstract form. And in particular, if you read the final chapter about spiritual activity in my book Truth and Science, you will find this thought strongly emphasised, namely: what takes place in man is not a matter of indifference to the rest of nature, but rather the rest of nature reaches into man, and what takes place in man is simultaneously a cosmic process; so that the human soul is a stage upon which not merely a human process, but a cosmic process is enacted. Of course certain circles of people today would find it exceedingly hard to understand such a thought." [123]

This view of knowledge contrasted sharply with the philosophy of his time wherein through "external philosophy, which is derived from Anglo-American thought, man is reduced to being a mere spectator of the world[124].

Steiner's philosophical work is of such breadth and depth that it marks him as a man of exceptional intellectual ability, and transforms his occult work into something more than a body of esoteric teachings. The philosophy gives the occultism a framework amenable to human reason, forging a link between the known and the unknown. This helps to bridge the gap between orthodox educational thought and Steiner's teachings on education which are based on an occult analysis of man (see Chapters 3 and 4).

1.2.3 Science

Steiner advanced a comprehensive critique of reductionist science. Natural Science, he believed, should neither be over– nor under–estimated[125]. However, it only concerned itself with the physical world, ignoring the soul and spirit, so that in effect it was dealing with a fraction of reality[126].

"What it offers is not the world, it is rather a spectre of the world. Everything that scientists have thought out and that has become popular education, all this – much more so than is imagined – is belief in a spectral world; actually superstition." [127]

The physical sciences reduced matter to atoms and molecules[128]; the human sciences reduced man to specimens of a genus[129]. Both served to narrow man's vision for truth[130].

In its study of man, science had become obsessed with the physical – the part which was only a corpse without the soul and spirit[131]. Scientific concepts, such as those of the elements, were rigid and devoid of all inner feeling[132]. Instead of forming concepts out of the real nature of the world, materialistic science imposed its preconceived assumptions about reality onto its judgements of the world[133].

In many experiments, scientists spent time and ingenuity on research which was trite, or else "old established knowledge as far as common sense is concerned[134]. Having lost their inner insight, experiment was the only way they could find conviction. In education, for example, children were subjected to all kinds of experiments which should never be done to them[135]. The statistical methods used in social science were fallacious because their quantitative nature could not reflect the qualitative part of man[136].

Steiner saw these characteristics of natural science as having enormous influence over the whole of European civilisation:

"There can be no doubt whatever that the habit of thought derived from natural science is the greatest force in modern intellectual life, and it must not be passed by heedlessly by any one concerned with the spiritual interests of humanity." [137]

The alternative to materialistic experiment was a kind of research which involved the whole human being in "observation" of phenomena, and then analysis of what was experienced[138]. On this basis, postulates could be set up.

"You ought only to set up postulates, and not to give definitions which claim to be universal." [139]

Experimentation was useless in Educational research since it revealed only what was of the nature of the animal in man[140]. In order to understand man himself, man had to be the instrument for research.

"We must learn to observe our children; we must grow into them with our feeling. We must not be making all manner of experiments upon them from outside, but be ourselves within them, be right within them." [141]

The concepts of man's nature developed by science should be altogether different from the coldly logical conceptions of materialistic science. They should be artistic concepts, capable of capturing man as a living being, not merely as a physical body.

"The scientific outlook of the present day has not been able to approach the human being because it has not taken into account that when nature rises from the mineral kingdom, to the plants, animals and finally to man, at each step its creation is not such that it can be grasped by logical concepts, but can only be grasped in an increasingly artistic way. What lives in the human being has many aspects in the last resort, it is tremendously varied. And because the science of spirit seeks the inner harmony between knowledge, religious devotion and artistic creation, it is also able to grasp with the spiritual eye the mysterious but remarkable being of man and how it is integrated into the world." [142]

Only artistic concepts could bridge the gap successfully between the living whole and its analysis into parts:

"If we want to come near to reality, especially the reality of human nature,

15

we must be clear that all separation proceeds from unity: if we were only to recognise an abstract unity then we should learn to know nothing whatever. If we never differentiated, the whole world would remain vague ...." [143]

It is because Steiner analysed the Soul and Spirit, developing their commonly vague and general meaning and relating them to the physical body, that he was able to formulate a complete educational theory. In Chapter 3 the concepts he uses will be introduced, and in Chapter 4 their educational implications will be shown.

1.2.4 Politics

Steiner had little truck with what is usually seen as "political reality" :

"The fascination of intellectualism is now in the life of very many persons. They easily adapt themselves to thought which is quite unlike their own. But whoever possesses a world of vision, such as the spiritual world must be, such a person sees the correctness of various 'standpoints'; and he must be constantly on guard within his soul not to be too strongly drawn to the one side or the other." [144]

"The various intellectual 'standpoints' repudiate one another; spiritual vision sees in them simply 'standpoints'. Seen from each of these the world appears differently. It is as if one should photograph a house from various sides. The pictures are different; the house is the same."[145]

He was more interested in the deeper attitudes of soul that resulted in the external appearances of politics. After the Great War his book The Threefold State[146] aroused widespread interest and this analysis of the social system in Europe was directly related to education in a series of lectures[147]. Both of these were hard statements made at a tragic time, and both merit study in themselves. Only a simple sketch is possible here, and no more will be necessary, for though Steiner described the kind of social structures that ought to be aimed for from the spiritual point of view, he made it clear that children in Waldorf schools were not to be prepared for an ideal society, but for life as it was.

"The point is so to educate the child that he remains in touch with present-day life, with the social order of today. And there is no sense in saying: the present social order is bad. Whether it be good or bad, we simply have to live with it." [148]

In the search for an answer to the problems of the times, Steiner warned that to simply look at external social realities was an illusion and must prove useless[149]. It was in the soul life of the working class masses that the source of social dissatisfaction was to be found. This soul life was characterised by a pervasive mode of consciousness: the scientific mode of thought[150].

"Scientific thought" should not be conceived of as an intellectual discipline — such as when science is studied formally — but as a tendency to live through the intellect, divorced from deeper feeling or will[151]. The development of this tendency to a restricted consciousness of the intellect was initiated not so much through exploitation in itself (which was blamed for social ills) but because in the process of industrial development, the worker was not given anything to satisfy and sustain his soul[152].

Whereas the "upper classes" retained a connection with the spiritual life through their old traditions, they passed on only the "scientific point of view" to the working classes, whose circumstances had divorced them from their heritage of traditions[153].

It was thus that the theories of Marx and Engels found an enthusiastic reception among the proletariat, not so much through their content but because of their intellectual character[154]. The modern workers flocked to the socialist movement because in their deepest souls they hoped to find something there that they felt was lacking[155], but they found only ideology. They came to believe that their life of thought was all unreal ideology[156].

"As a consequence of his thought being thus fashioned on scientific lines, not only science itself, but art, religion, conventions, justice, are turned for the worker into departments of human ideology." [157]

Modern man was blind to the inner spiritual forces that were the only source of healing for the deep unhappiness caused by the belief that everything in his life was ideology[158].

"But the essential thing remains: it will not enter the head of anyone who today is thinking on strictly socialist lines to say: 'Supposing we find anywhere signs that there is a life of the soul, having its source in the spirit of the times, bearing mankind up and on with it as it goes, and rooted in a spiritual reality, then from this soul life may radiate the force which shall give the right impulse to the social movement also.' " [159]

In order to find this "life of the soul", one had to return to "primal conceptions" of man's life in the world, and to do so was not to deal with "unpractical generalities", but on the contrary, it was the only way to find the practical life again[160].

There were three primal conceptions which formed the basis for man's actual life. Firstly, there was the regulation of his material life in the material world. This could be called the Economic life. Secondly, there was his relation to his fellow man. This could be called his Political life, or the life of Rights. Thirdly there was the life of individual expression which reached into social life. This could be called the Spiritual life[161].

In order for the state to be healthy, clear distinctions had to be made between these three areas of human life, in spite of their intermingling in reality. He likened this to seeing the nervous system of the human body as an integrated yet independent structure[162].

The Economic life had to do with commodities, their production, distribution and consumption. The life of Rights had to do with human relations according to purely human principles. The Spiritual life had to do with the natural aptitudes of the private individual[163].

The central principle for the Economic Life should be free association between men for the furtherance of their economic interests; for the Life of Rights it should be equality through democracy, and parliament should only have power in matters of men's rights; for the Spiritual Life it should be freedom[164].

In The Threefold State, Steiner argued that the real causes of the First World War lay in the chaos and confusion which arose in "one-fold states" when the three natural divisions of human life were not clearly separated[165].

Education was at the core of the Spiritual and Cultural life and as such had to be free. It was education that could introduce the impulse which could work into the whole of life and renew it[166]. But for this to happen, theories such as those of Marx were quite useless. Men would have to learn the joy and love of work done with devotion to their fellow men in the social organism. The new social order had to come through men themselves, not through theories, and men would only develop the strength to achieve this when they learned to listen to the true spiritual leaders[167].

One of the important features of the times following the Great War was the rise of Nazism, and this should perhaps not go entirely unmentioned. Steiner's opposition to Nazism is illustrated by his expulsion of Nazis from the Anthroposophical Society[168] and by the banning of the Society for ten years in Germany while Hitler was in power[169]. However, to say more would lead this investigation into a complex side of Steiner's occultism in which he spoke about the spiritual background to such movements. Two such lectures are entitled Behind the Scenes of External Happenings[170].

1.2.5 Education

The following account of Steiner's view of the education of his day is included at this juncture rather than in the later analysis of his educational thought. This is done for two reasons. Firstly, it is more relevant to his views of his times than it is to Waldorf Education, which differed considerably from orthodox education; and secondly, it would disrupt the progressive development of the analysis if it were introduced later.

Nonetheless it must be said that Steiner made his criticisms of orthodox education in order to highlight the alternatives advanced by Waldorf Education. His teachings on education therefore attempt to answer the failings which he identified in the education of his time.

Steiner avoided condemning efforts which were being made to improve education. He saw his contribution as deepening, not opposing, such developments.

18

"Just because the science of spirit values modern science it has every reason to advise the excellent things that have been introduced into the world by the great educators and educational movements of the 19th and early 20th century. It does not seek to oppose any of this, but takes its own stand on the basis of modern educational thinking by deepening and broadening what has been done, by making use of what can be studied and discovered by Anthroposophy." [171]

What prevented modern education from finding this depth was that it was trapped in intellectualism.

"The most wonderful ideas can be thought out and made the principles of large movements for reform, and so on. But in life all this is not so important. The important thing in life is to look at life itself, to see the living human being who does what is possible and necessary, in whatever conditions exist." [172]

One such example was Froebel, whose system arose out of "true inner love for children", and who understood that imitation was "part of the very nature of the child". Because Froebel did not properly understand how imitation worked in the child, he used it wrongly by permeating all activities with intellectual structure and content for the child to copy. This destroyed everything of value in imitation, which was not intellectual but an active, pictorial process[173].

Man had lost his understanding of his soul: he did not know what took place within him when he was thinking, feeling and willing[174], and when he spoke of developing individuality his words were empty because he did not know what individuality was[175].

"If I want a house properly built, I must go to an architect who knows in detail how the plan must be drawn, how the bricks are to be laid, how massive the girders must be to bear the weight on them and so on. The essential thing is to know in detail how the human being is constituted, and not to speak vaguely about human nature in general as one speaks about a house being weatherproof, comfortable and beautiful to look at." [176]

Steiner maintained that man had also lost his conception of the developmental unity of the whole of his life. Therefore the child was educated for the present and a little of the future, not in such a way as to prepare for the unfolding of the whole of life[177]. The concepts which were given to children were rigid and abstract and were made so with the deliberate intention that they should never change, but remain static throughout life.

"We teachers must see to it that we give the children feelings and impressions that live on further, as truly as the limbs of their bodies live on and develop. Human beings are not built up bit by bit, so that, for example, when they are three years of age two arms are added, which remain as they are. Human beings grow. And we must convey to the children concepts and ideas and feelings that will also continue to grow." [178]

All modern education achieved was that our external lives would be orderly and mechanical; it gave nothing to the feeling, the will or the body[179]. From the earliest entry into school the child's admiration and wonder was treated in such a way as to render him apathetic and insensitive. And in later life he was unable to find beauty in the world because he did not learn to do so as a child[180].

Setting aside one lesson a week for music, religion, gymnastics and art was typical of the modern curriculum and proved its intellectual bias. Even when these subjects were taught they were done in an intellectualistic way[181]. The curriculum was broken up into isolated units and had no unifying spirit, so children had to constantly change their mental orientation for each new lesson[182].

The curriculum was plagued by influences that did not meet the needs of children. On the one hand modern education – especially that of the Gymnasium – was not born out of our own age, but out of the Greco-Latin age, and at its foundations it was inappropriate to the present time[183]. On the other hand, each of the modern political orientations were trying to get control over education. The tendencies from the socialists were to enshroud education with regulations[184] and to destroy the natural and essential authority relationship between adult and child:

"The educational programme developed in Russia murders all true socialism. But also in other regions of Europe the educational programmes are actually cancerous evils, particularly the socialist programmes of education, because they proceed from the almost unbelievable principle that schools must be established after the pattern of adult life in the social organism. I have read school programmes whose first principle is the abolition of head-masters; the teachers should stand in a relationship of absolute equality with the students, the entire school should be built up on comradeship." [185]

Democracy was being brought into everything, even schools[186]. The fact that Governments had taken over schooling from the old churches was a good thing, but now the state wanted to make the school its servant[187]. Education had to be free:

"And what is important to realise today is that the real cultural and spiritual life that humanity needs can only be one that makes the children of the future into free beings, who can create an existence worthy of the human being .... People from every country who realise that education must be based upon a free and emancipated cultural life should be united in a world association of schools .... Such an association of human beings that would be fostered spiritually in a world association of schools would bring the peoples of the whole earth together to engage in one great task." [188]

Steiner ascribed great power to education. Modern schools did not educate children to be men, "but a finished product leading a well defined and circumscribed

20

existence." It produced automatons[189]. Such a situation could only be worsened when democratically elected people were given the power to make decisions about education[190] because this simply continued to plough back the same problems into the education of the younger generation. Social conditions were not directly products of the state, but of the education men and women received as children[191].

The Anglo-American view of education differed fundamentally from the German one. Steiner characterised the Anglo-American view as being the belief that if the child was taught in an external way then his inner abilities and qualities would emerge in response to it. Logic and morality was not directly cultivated.

"And the teacher feels sure that if he has sufficiently educated the whole physical being of the child that surrounds this centre, then the forces he has developed will make their way inwards, will dissolve the surrounding walls of the little casket, and lo, intellect, morality, religion will come showering forth, of themselves." [192]

A discussion of Steiner's educational thought is only appropriate after his theory has been outlined. However the brief outline above reveals Steiner's concern for the return of human values to education. Intellectualism, dilettantism and political manipulation in education had to be done away with if education was to develop strong human values with right regard to the spiritual, social and economic life.

1.2.6 Religion

From the time of the publication of <u>Christianity as Mystical Fact</u>[193] Steiner's teachings were centred on the Christ incarnation, which marked the emancipation of the Mysteries and man's ascent in his spiritual life from the experience of spiritual knowledge to that of faith[194].

Education was not a specifically religious process, but a preparation for a healthy spiritual life[195]. The Waldorf Schools were not sectarian — no dogma was taught[196] — and Steiner strongly objected to suggestions that it ought to be more explicit about its Christian character:

"Why have people in recent times become so irreligious? For the simple reason that what is now preached is far too sentimental and abstract. People are irreligious now because the Church pays so little heed to divine commandments. For instance there is the commandment: Thou shalt not take the name of the Lord thy God in vain. If you heed this and refrain from mentioning the name Jesus Christ after every fifth sentence or talking about God's universal order, you are immediately criticised by those so-called church-minded people who would prefer to hear you mention Jesus Christ and God in every sentence. These church-minded circles are the very ones who regard as an irreligious attitude the meek and quiet spirit that seeks to be inwardly penetrated by the divine and avoids uttering 'Lord, Lord' at every moment. And if what is brought to human beings by teachers is permeated by this quiet, inwardly working godliness that is not carried sentimentally on the top of the tongue, the cry, resulting from wrong up-bringing, is heard on every side: Ah, yes, he ought to speak far more about Christianity..." [197]

Steiner rejected the widely held "simple belief in the attainment of salvation through Christ" as the extreme egotism of souls who wanted to be passively transported to heaven. Modern man was lazy within his soul, and though he did not cherish inner activity, this was what was needed for salvation[198].

"Concerning the most intimate spiritual life, the religious life, the world of the future will demand of man that he work for his immortality; that he let his soul be active so that it may receive into itself, through activity, the Divine, the Christ-impulse." [199]

1.2.7 Technology

Steiner was dismayed that the specialisation which permeated all modern life began in school, just where children ought to be forming an interested attitude towards everything that was happening in their lives. The result of this specialisation was that many people could not form the vaguest notions about the phenomena of technical and social life, so that a deep insecurity and weakening of the will affected their assurance about life[200].

When man was able to understand a machine and was put to work on it in a factory, he found that the machine was transparent; there was nothing in it to which his soul could relate and it debilitated his soul to work with it[201]. It was the machine that did the work, and so human will was not used but rendered useless. The work of a machine was of no value to the human soul.

"When a man plows his field with his horse – man and beast straining themselves in labour – this work in which natural forces are involved has a meaning beyond the immediate present; it has a cosmic meaning .... Through modern industrialism we have abandoned cosmic value. In our kindling of electric flames there no longer lives any cosmic significance. It has been driven out. A completely mechanised factory is a hole in the cosmos, it has no meaning for cosmic evolution."[202]

The senselessness of man's activity of the will when he worked with machines was anaesthetizing his soul[203]. Modern man could work well enough if told what to do with a machine or follow instructions, but he could no longer find the strength of will to act out of himself. His will, which was what enabled him to relate to the world, was not developed in education and was therefore weak[204].

Those men who considered themselves the most practical of our age were really completely impractical. The commercial and industrial men and bankers were absorbed in a life of thought which was devoid of feeling and will.

"The 'Practical life' today is absolutely impractical in all its forms." [205]

With all man's theories so bound up with materialistic science, even the earth was beginning to be destroyed by the narrow, chemical approach of the agriculturalists[206]. And the economy was plagued by chaos through the ever expanding, random production of goods without thoughtful direction[207].

Steiner was therefore justifiably concerned about the materialistic world that children moved into from school. He realised that unless education helped them to be strong in their thought, feelings and will, their individualities would be submerged by modern life. If children were to find the world meaningful and fulfilling, they had to be given a firm foundation for their spiritual, their social, and their economic lives.

1.3   CHARACTER ANALYSIS

Despite the brevity of this account of Steiner's life and his views of his times, it is possible to construct from them a fairly comprehensive description of him, and additional material will be introduced to give a closer view of his character.

An assessment of his character is important for a study of Steiner's educational thought, not only because education is a sensitive subject of profound social, economic and personal interest, but more so because Steiner's teachings were drawn from his Spiritual Science. As will be made clear, Spiritual Science (by Steiner's own teaching) depends on extraordinary qualities of character (see Chapter 3.1) which Steiner would have to measure up to in order to be credible.

As a child he seems to have been hard working and appreciative of clear or aesthetically refined thinking in his teachers. He extended himself beyond the demands of his schools and had wide interests, including the arts, history, mathematics, science and religion.

Steiner's tutoring activities reveal an abiding interest in teaching from the age of fifteen. He seems to have been a conscientious, interested tutor, ready to search for new insights.

The work on Goethe was the result of K.J. Schroër's belief in his ability to interpret a man of great literary stature for an important publication. This editorial work, together with a Doctor's degree in philosophy and subsequent philosophical publications, document his considerable intellectual ability.

The philosophical writings, newspaper editorships, and his job as a lecturer at a Working Man's College (which he held for six years) show that Steiner was very much involved with the social and intellectual life of Germany at the turn of the century.

Even after developing Anthroposophy he maintained an influential interest in public life (for example with The Threefold State).

The extraordinary speed and facility with which he developed his occult writings and lectures strongly suggest that, as he claimed, he had indeed received occult training as far back as 1879. Furthermore, a study of his philosophical and occult work in retrospect shows so direct a bond between them that it seems to be clear that his philosophical arguments were motivated by private spiritual experience.

After 1900 he was increasingly in demand as a lecturer on occultism in Germany and then internationally. The success of his publications, as well as the vast sums of money given towards the financing of the two Goetheanums, suggest that Steiner had a large and dedicated following which included appreciable numbers of professional people.

His lectures may be mysterious to the newcomer, but once the terms of reference are grasped they can be seen to be deeply thought out and logically consistent. Even in print they are colourful, showing a range of moods, feeling for his audience, and frank and penetrating criticism of his times. He offered his teachings with complete conviction, answering criticisms and arguments against his teachings convincingly.

Steiner was fearless in public life, stating his beliefs while fully aware of the scepticism they would draw. The break with Theosophy and his forming of the Anthroposophical Society reveal great self assurance, and a refusal to be constrained in his convictions.

The enormous volume of recorded lectures and writings[208] of great variety are indisputable evidence of his extraordinary energy. The fact that in education alone his influence is still expanding rapidly, not among the ignorant, but among intelligent and well qualified people, says much for his work.

Despite openly expounding controversial teachings, he had a secret side to his life. He never spoke or wrote of his private married life and we hear little about his own family. He said almost nothing about his occult "master" and though he described the spiritual worlds minutely he never related experiences within them. This suggests that he was a man of exceptional inner qualities.

By examining the opinions of some of the people who were close to Steiner, one gains an altogether more intimate, personal look at him.

There are, for example, testimonies of his behaviour under the most stressful and saddening circumstances. Wachsmuth's account of the silence with which he watched the burning down of the first Goetheanum, and of his only comment, "Much work and long years", reveals that his sense of loss was in human rather than materialistic terms[209].

Towards the end of 1924 when he was suffering from his final, unnamed illness[210], which sounds every bit as devastating as cancer of the stomach, he continued to work with extraordinary strength. His wife, Marie Steiner, bears witness to the period of September 1924 when he was running three courses of lectures, for artists, theologians and medical practitioners:

"Every day, three courses manifesting an inexpressible power of ascent of the spirit, of an astonishing plenitude in integrated composition and practical instruction. In addition, at least three lectures every week about Anthroposophy and magnificent lectures for those working on the building. One dared not utter a word about sparing him. Pleas to spare himself constituted a hindrance. Thus destiny had to take its course.

He himself said to us many times that what brought him to his sick bed was the numerous private conferences. The lectures he could divide into parts according to his forces, so he thought, and there was also a sustaining force in them. The rest, yielding to the pleas, he could no longer control, could no longer adapt to the residue of his strength. The door-keepers counted four hundred visitors during the time that he was daily giving four lectures. There had for a long time been no moment of rest remaining to build up what was destroyed in the forces of the organism."[211]

Retiring to his sickbed after his final course of lectures, given, Wachsmuth remembers, "with terrible physical distress", he continued to write his autobiography[212]. This is a work of clarity, detail and quality as great as any of his earlier books, betraying no hint of suffering except, perhaps, in the last few pages when he must have known that he no longer possessed the strength to record the most complex years of his life. In addition, Steiner handwrote two articles each week[213] and did a "tremendous amount of reading", numbering dozens of books every few days[214].

"When he studied the tremendous pile of books lying on the right side of the bed, in the midst of all his other work, and in spite of his illness, is a puzzle, but chance remarks on the next occasion of the delivery of books indicated that he had in the meanwhile taken thorough account of their contents." [215]

Nor was this kind of energy brought on by his final illness. Dealing with the year 1920, for example, Wachsmuth writes:

"The impression of such conversations remains vivid in my mind as they occurred in the midst of his manifold burden of work. After one had waited in the anteroom of his place of residence together with other friends more or less patiently for the opportunity of a personal conversation, when he himself opened the door with a friendly invitation to enter, it would have seemed perfectly natural to many persons if there had been in the expression of friendliness, the gesture, the conduct of the conversation on the part of this person so overburdened, so terribly under the pressure of events, any symptom of weariness, of reduced attentiveness in conversation, or of an early inclination to shorten the interview. For many were still waiting outside; in the next hour he had to give a lecture, to take part in conferences, or arrive at important decisions. Nevertheless, nothing of weariness, disinclination, impatience was to be discovered; on the contrary, in this atmosphere of calm,

25

goodness of heart, patiently listening understanding which radiated from Rudolf Steiner, one became free from the excitement and inner restlessness with which one had entered the room." [216]

These sorts of testimonies are by no means rare, and their mention seems to be essential in order to alert the reader to Steiner's exceptional character. His work betrays so little of his qualities of personality that it is all too easy to imagine that they are the product of superficial thinking. It is only when one studies his works with the awareness that they were given from "the most profoundly moving inner experiences of my soul" [217] that one can begin to approach an understanding of what Steiner's work was about.

One further testimony, this time of his manner with children, comes from the editor of his series of lectures entitled Curative Education[218] during which he dealt with problems such as epilepsy, kleptomania, hysteria and depression. A note at the end of the volume states,

"Wonderful, above all, was the example Rudolf Steiner set us in the whole way in which he met the children, entering with loving and devout interest into every single detail of their condition." [219]

As hasty as we are in the modern world to pour scorn on spiritual teachers who reveal defects in their characters, so equally hasty are we, it seems, to ignore their good qualities. How true this is of Rudolf Steiner, who shows himself to be beyond personal reproach, and indeed has a worthy character for an educational thinker.

2

REVIEW OF THE LITERATURE

2.1   STEINER'S BOOKS AND LECTURES

2.1.1   The Selection of Books and Lectures

The books and lectures referred to in this thesis represent a small fraction of Steiner's work. Hemleben lists 41 books[1] and cites a survey which identifies about 6 000 of Steiner's[2] lectures and addresses as well as numerous articles.

Steiner believed that the renewal and development of every lecture was essential to enliven teaching[3].   Therefore every lecture is to an appreciable extent unique and holistic in both content and organisation. Accordingly any course of lectures omitted from this account may contain certain fresh information and associations of ideas not otherwise examined.

Recognising this limitation, lecture courses representative of the whole period of Steiner's work were examined. The lectures on education were delivered to Waldorf teachers as well as to the public[4]. Certain other courses of lectures[5] which were thought to contain important information, have also been used.

Since this account is based on English translations from the German, a number of translation problems arise which will be dealt with in the course of the text. Experienced Anthroposophists emphasise that language imparts a definite flavour to Steiner's work. This study is therefore a reflection of the way Steiner's work is translated into English.

The books referred to[6] for the philosophical and Spiritual Scientific foundation of the theory of education were revised several times in the original German by Steiner himself, and have undergone revisions of translation. These books are the basis of all Steiner's Spiritual Science. He regarded the earlier philosophical work as indispensable for a secure foundation to the study of Spiritual Science[7].

27

2.1.2 The Nature of the Books

When Occult Science was published, Steiner was aware that its content rendered it "... a venture of some temerity." [8] He knew it would be met with widespread philosophical and scientific scepticism, but counted on the need and longing for knowledge of the world of spirit to prevail against the leadership of the Natural Sciences, and draw sufficient readers to justify the book. He was not mistaken despite the demanding nature of his writing, which served the dual purpose of both informing and developing the consciousness of the reader.

> "The books Theosophy and Occult Science have been widely read, though they count not a little on the reader's good will. For it must be admitted, they are not written in an easy style. I purposely refrained from writing a 'popular' account, so-called. I wrote in such a way as to make it necessary to exert one's thinking while entering into the content of these books. In so doing, I gave them a special character. The very reading of them is an initial step in spiritual training, inasmuch as the necessary effort of quiet thought and contemplation strengthens the powers of the soul, making them capable of drawing nearer to the spiritual world." [9]

Steiner claimed that the content of Occult Science, despite using the terminology of other schools of thought, was based entirely on his own spiritual research and drew nothing from these other sources. It was therefore "... an epitome of Anthroposophical Spiritual Science as a whole... " [10]

To the criticism that the statements of Spiritual Science betrayed an ignorance of modern philosophy and science, Steiner answered that he adhered to the principle never to speak or write about anything from the spiritual scientific point of view that he was not adequately conversant with from the orthodox standpoint [11].

Steiner conceded that language and terminology imposed great limitations on Spiritual Science. He admitted to being "... painfully aware of the inadequacy, the excessive rigidity of the only available means of presenting the revelations of supersensible research." [12]. Steiner described how he first clarified his spiritual perception of the thing to be described, and only then did he express it in words. Where terminology was borrowed from other sources its previous meanings were consciously excluded, with the result that Steiner's use of terms is different to their former uses. The reader who has an acquaintance with terms such as "Astral" or "Etheric" from elsewhere should not assume that they correspond to Steiner's use of the words [13].

Steiner claimed that his revisions of his books never changed their content, but only added further elaboration [14], or improved his original wording [15].

Steiner asked his readers to approach his books with, "... unprejudiced logic and a healthy feeling for truth." [16] He challenged that, "... reasoned thinking can and must be the touchstone of all that is here presented. Only those who will apply to the contents of this book the test of reason — even as they would to a description of natural-scientific facts — will be in a position to decide." [17]

The argument used in Steiner's philosophical and Spiritual Scientific work is obviously too detailed and lengthy to reflect here. However he answers seemingly every position that may be taken against the idea of a Spiritual Science. The argument in his books is more thorough, logical and incisive than that of the lectures.

One feature of the books that is rather disturbing to the newcomer is the impersonal objectivity with which Steiner writes. Galbreath comments that,

> "His writings project an aura of remoteness and distance which, no matter how much contradicted by the statements of Anthroposophists who found him a vital presence and a being of great compassion and humanity, an outsider cannot penetrate." [18]

Galbreath suggests, rightly it seems, that this was a deliberate strategy to avoid adulation:

> "... his discoveries were, in his opinion, empirical, objective and repeatable. He was anxious, therefore, not to have disciples who would depend upon his authority for their own spiritual sustenance, but rather colleagues of critical temperament who would investigate the supersensible realms on their own. Accordingly, he downgraded his personal experiences to remove a potential source of distraction and to forestall the possible formation of a cult centered on himself." [19]

In his autobiography, Steiner hints at his approach:

> "... it has always been my conviction that in many provinces of life the personal element gives to human action a colouring of the utmost value; only it seems to me that this personal element should reveal itself through the manner in which one speaks and acts, and not through conscious attention to one's personality." [20]

Steiner distinguishes between his books and lectures. The books, he says, responded to what was "... present in the striving of this age for knowledge." [21] The lectures, by contrast, were given in response to " ... whatever was manifested in the membership (of the Anthroposophical Society) as the need of their souls or their longing for the spirit." [22]   These two forms of expression were initially separated, with the lectures being withheld from publication.

2.1.3   The Nature of the Lectures

Steiner would have preferred the lectures to never have been printed, but to have remained as spoken words. He describes the transcripts as "... really reports on the lectures more or less well made and which I, for lack of time, could not correct." [23] He allowed them to be printed, privately at first, publicly later, in response to demand.

However, he states, "Whoever reads this privately printed material can take it in the fullest sense as that which Anthroposophy has to say .... Only it will be necessary to remember there are errors in the lectures which I did not revise." [24]

This warning covers all but the first[25] lecture on education, and adds weight to the need for basing Waldorf Education on the lectures as they integrate with Steiner's written work. The establishing of recurrent themes will also establish accuracy and authenticity of lecture material.

In their first attempt to read one of Steiner's lecture courses, most people will be bewildered by the unfamiliar terminology and ideas. This is because they were given (with the exception of some public lectures[26]) to people who were fully conversant with Spiritual Science. They therefore assume considerable knowledge on the part of the reader.

> "These premises include, at the very least, the Anthroposophical knowledge of Man and of the Cosmos in its spiritual essence; also what may be called 'Anthroposophical history', told as an outcome to research into the spiritual world."[27]

Steiner saw his lectures as being artistic expressions, rather like pieces of music[28], as opposed to obeying the laws of intellectual orderliness. He felt that some people were unaccustomed to this manner of presentation and therefore thought that the content itself was difficult to understand. It is true that some lectures appear to pursue a theme whose relevance seems quite unrelated to the matter at hand, and then quite suddenly Steiner reveals his purpose in pursuing it. This demands attentiveness and patience on the part of the reader.

Another feature of many of the lectures, which emerges even from the printed form, is their inspirational character. Steiner considered this to far surpass mere emotional excitement. For him the lectures had something of the character of prayer[29]. Like the books, therefore, the lectures were intended to both inform and uplift the consciousness of the audience[30].

2.1.4   The Esoteric Lectures

Some of Steiner's lectures were initially withheld from publication and circulated only among Anthroposophists, who would have had the background knowledge necessary to understand them. However, these are now available. For the purpose of preserving a measure of objectivity with respect to this research, the author remained officially independent of the Anthroposophical Society[31], and did not have access to the esoteric lectures.

2.1.5   Management of the Material

Some Waldorf School teachers and Anthroposophists[32] objected to the author's plan of collating all the material from the books and various courses of lectures and analysing it. They felt that the context of each point made was essential to its meaning. This objection is certainly justified and supported by the paragraph under 2.1.3 above in which it was shown how Steiner considered each lecture an

artistic unit. Since each lecture is too complicated to allow for a description of
the context of each point made, an alternative approach will be adopted in which
the interrelatedness of the concepts and practices referred to will be shown. Considerable attention will be given to this feature of the account. In Steiner's work
the "whole" is very much greater than the sum of the "parts"; it is in fact essential
to understanding Steiner.

> "Whoever is ready to look into all that I have said and done will discover
> harmony, where by not looking at the whole he only finds contradictions." [33]

In spite of the efforts to present the theory as an organic whole, some Anthroposophists may still argue that Steiner's presentation of spiritual knowledge,
artistic as it was, had something of the spiritual about it which tends to be destroyed
in the heavy hands of the analyst. This may be true, but is, arguably, essential if
Steiner's teachings are to become better understood. Steiner's own work in Occult
Science, Theosophy, and Knowledge of the Higher Worlds is an outstanding
example of the analysis of otherwise whole experiences into order and structure.
This is the unique feature of his work that has attracted so many intelligent students.
In Steiner's own words,

> "Disregard for strict forms is shown only by those who do not know that
> the internal must come to expression in the external. True, it is the spirit
> of a thing that matters, not the form; but just as the form without the
> spirit is null and void, so would the spirit remain inactive if it did not
> create a form for itself." [34]

The account given here will therefore pay attention to the concepts and their
interrelatedness in the body of the theory. It will not attempt to show how the
theory evolved[35] except in the broadest sense of drawing the theory of Education
out of Spiritual Science. It would be extremely complicated and would serve very
little purpose to trace the evolution of Steiner's teachings, since they are so
interwoven that the later ideas can be found in germinal form in his earlier works,
and every idea would have to be individually traced.

However, an unorthodox approach has been adopted to the system of footnotes.
Steiner's works have gone through several publications, revisions, translations, and
revisions of translations. The publications studied are mostly recent, and it seemed
to serve no useful purpose to record the dates of these publications in the footnotes.
On the other hand the recording of the date when the book was first published, or,
in the case of lecture courses, the date when the course was given seemed much
more valuable, particularly for the reader who is unfamiliar with the subject. This
will enable an examination of the introduction and evolution of concepts to be
easily achieved without referring the reader to the Bibliography.

Full details of the publications drawn from and to which the page numbers
refer are given in the Bibliography.

This unusual approach is used only for Steiner's own works. All other
references record the date of the publication.

31

2.2   WORKS ON STEINER

2.2.1   Biographical Works

Four sources have been used for biographical references. The first is Steiner's autobiography which he was prevented from completing by his death on March 30, 1925. In this he dealt with the period up to the turn of the century in detail, but laid only an introductory foundation with little specific mention of his activities in this century.

He called his autobiography The Story of My Life, and it was first published in book form in 1928. Although reflecting the natural characteristics of hindsight, it is a remarkably consistent and coherent account, especially since it was written in separate, weekly instalments in the last fifteen months of his life[36].

The continuation of The Story of My Life has been written by Guenther Wachsmuth[37]. He was a student and close companion of Steiner's. His account is full of reverence for Steiner, but is nevertheless exhaustively researched and factually written.

The third book used is Hemleben's[38]. This provides a clear, simplified perspective of Steiner's complex life, and emphasises his most important and influential work.

Fourthly there is Galbreath's account[39]. This concentrates on Steiner's life as an occultist and is deeply researched.

Hemleben[40] lists 22 works on Rudolf Steiner's life and work besides his own, most of them written by people who knew Steiner. There is therefore an abundance of material available in this regard.

The account of his life provides only what is considered to be an appropriate framework for the purpose of an overall view of his educational work.

2.2.2   Works on Education

This section is intended to indicate the uniqueness of purpose and content of the present work, not to provide a guide of all available literature.

A beautifully illustrated and fascinating volume is Frans Carlgren's Education Towards Freedom. A Survey of the Work of Waldorf Schools Throughout the World[41]. This gives a modern perspective of the whole range of Waldorf Education and reveals the extent to which Steiner's principles have been developed. It is an introduction to modern practice, and though it contains quotations from Steiner it is not an examination of his work in itself. The Bibliography gives a selection of books by Steiner and others on general and specialised aspects[42]. This is an authoritative publication, and of interest to laymen and experts.

Two publications which are especially suitable for newcomers to the subject are Francis Edmunds' Rudolf Steiner's Gift to Education – The Waldorf Schools[43] and A.C. Harwood's The Way of the Child[44]. Both of these communicate the

32

authors' perspectives of the practice of Waldorf Education. Neither volume is a direct study of Steiner's work but rather an expression of each one's personal assimilation of it.

A much larger work is A.C. Harwood's The Recovery of Man in Childhood. A Study in the Educational Work of Rudolf Steiner.[45] This book probably comes closer in purpose than any other to the present work, except for the great difference that, like his smaller volume, it reveals Harwood's own mastery of Waldorf Education. From time to time he measures its ideas against those of other thinkers, which gives it the character of an academic study, but the sheer volume of information about the practical application of ideas makes it primarily a personal statement. Steiner's writings and lectures are not dealt with directly.

Numerous short articles have appeared on Waldorf Education. These are of two sorts, the first being by people within the movement, such as Davies, J. Child Centred Education. The Ideas of Rudolf Steiner, which was first published in the *Times Educational Supplement*[46]. Four more recent papers from a symposium on Waldorf Education at Teachers College, Columbia University appear in the journal *Teachers College Record*[47]. They are: Barnes, H. An Introduction to Waldorf Education; Howard, A. Education and our Human Future; Davy, J. The Social Meaning of Education; and Leichter, H.J. A Note on Time and Education. The lecturers concerned are each recognised authorities on Waldorf Education and respected within the movement, and as such their statements are not examinations of Steiner's work in itself but descriptions of modern practice and thought.

The second kind of article on Steiner is by people outside the movement. This sort of account is nowhere better illustrated than in an article in *New Society*[48] by Rosemary Dinnage. Cheekily entitled Benign Dottiness: The World of Rudolf Steiner, it reveals with what ease a writer can make Steiner's thought appear ludicrously inappropriate to modern society. Thrown together with a smattering of Steiner's autobiography and a few quotations from authorities in the field, the only positive statements smack of condescension.

> "There is undoubtedly dottiness to be found in it, but this is, it seems, a benign dottiness, untainted by authoritarianism, guru-worship or brain-washing. What it offers is a scheme – one of the more amazing ones – for making sense out of the whole mess: we came from somewhere, we are going somewhere." [49]

The editor of *New Society* decided to illustrate the article on the front cover by portraying Steiner with a drawing of the Goetheanum changing into a tree. The symbolic relevance would obviously be lost on the layman.

Books by pupils of Steiner on child development are most interesting and reveal considerable independent thought on the part of his followers. Two such publications are König, K. The First Three Years of the Child[50], and C. Von Heyderbrand, Childhood: A Study of the Growing Soul[51].

Numerous books exist on specialised aspects of Waldorf Education[52]. Some of these are: Lund, K.A. Understanding our Fellow Man[53] which is a lucid and penetrating account of the temperaments written in layman's language with a completely practical approach; Raffé, M. *et al.,* Eurythmy and the Impulse to Dance[54]; McAllen, A.E. Teaching Children to Write[55]; and Whicher, O. Projective Geometry. Creative Polarities in Space and Time. Many of these books develop ideas which go beyond Steiner's teachings, indicating the extent to which Steiner's broad insights now exist as a foundation to the Waldorf School Movement.

The English journals for the Waldorf Schools Movement are *Child and Man,* which is published in England, and *Education as an Art,* published by the Anthroposophical Society in America. Both appear twice yearly and contain articles and book reviews, lists of Steiner Schools, Editorials and advertisements. They are of a high standard, with colour plates, and the articles are generally well written and informative.

Writing as they do for a restricted audience, students of Steiner's work generally produce material of an extremely high standard. An example of a well researched topic, drawing extensively on Steiner's works, is Hilde Boos-Hamburger's The Creative Power of Colour. Rudolf Steiner's Approach to Colour and Art[57]. Such works are far beyond the brief of this book in their specialised fields, and are works which lead the student well past what could be expected to be achieved in schools.

An example of empirical research done on Waldorf Education is E.J. Ogletree's doctoral thesis for Wayne State University, entitled A cross-cultural exploratory study of the creativeness of Steiner and state school pupils in England, Scotland and Germany [58]. This project decided in favour of the Steiner School pupils. However the overwhelming weight of opinion encountered among Waldorf School teachers by the present author was in favour of longitudinal rather than latitudinal studies. As will become clear, Steiner considered that education ought to integrate with the whole of human life and not merely act as a springboard, so that the individual's progress after school is as important to the Waldorf system as his progress in school.

An influential author among Waldorf School teachers and newcomers to the movement is Roy Wilkinson. He has written an introductory volume called Commonsense Schooling Based on the Indications of Rudolf Steiner[59]. This has been stripped of "occult" concepts and presented as a lucid and structured account of Waldorf Education. It is supplemented by an extensive series of booklets, some of which are entitled The Curriculum of the Waldorf School (1975), The Temperaments in Education (1977), Physical Sciences I and II for Age Groups 12-14 (1977 and 1978), Teaching Mathematics to Age 14 (1978), Teaching English (1976), Nutrition/Health/Anthropology for Classes 7/8 (Ages 13/14) (1978), Teaching History. The Ancient Civilisations of India, Persia, Egypt/Babylonia (1973), Plant Study – Geology for the Age Groups 11 and 12 (1977), Teaching Geography (1973), and Studies in Practical Activities, Farming, Gardening, Housebuilding for the Age Groups 9 and 10 (1975).

The practical nature of these booklets is obvious from the titles and they are

34

widely used by teachers. Wilkinson himself has studied Steiner's work for forty years, and taught in Waldorf Schools for thirty years[60].

Two Curricula (apart from Wilkinson's) are published. They are by E.A.K. Stockmeyer: Rudolf Steiner's Curriculum for the Waldorf Schools (1969), and C. Von Heydebrand: The Curriculum of the First Waldorf School (1977). Both of these must be adapted to suit local and modern conditions[61].

These Curricula are not so much records of the material to be taught, as chronicles of "readiness"; records of the ages at which pupils are ready to tackle certain subjects, in particular ways.

"Yet, if the Curriculum is vague as to content of lessons, it is in another sense, rigorous indeed. It is absolutely obligatory upon every teacher that the way in which each subject is treated in every lesson shall be in strict accordance with the degrees of incarnation indicated by the ages and characteristics of the children in the class." [62]

It is this which gives meaning to the curriculum; the content alone is the outer form for the expression of the approach.

One of the interesting features about the literature on Waldorf Education is that very little of it exists from sources independent of the movement.

Encyclopaedia Britannica gives a single column to Steiner[63] and a brief mention in the Macropaedia[64], but nothing on Waldorf Education. Blond's Encyclopaedia of Education[65] gives short passages on Steiner and on Waldorf Education. The Year Book of Education carried an article on Steiner schools, but it was by A.C. Harwood and as long ago as 1957 [66].

E.P. Cubberley's Readings in the History of Education (1920) and W. Boyd's History of Western Education (1921), obviously could not be expected to mention Steiner. However, there is no mention of him in R.R. Rusk's History of Infant Education (1933), nor in E.H. Wild's The Foundations of Modern Education (1936), nor in A.E. Meyer's The Development of Education in the Twentieth Century (1939). It may be argued perhaps that these publications are too general in scope to mention Steiner, but it may be equally contended that many educationists of lesser achievement are included in them.

C.V. Good's (ed.) Dictionary of Education, (1945) classifies everything from Abacus to Zygote, but no mention is made of Steiner or Waldorf Education. J.S. Ross' Groundwork of Educational Theory, (1942) mentions progressives such as A.S. Neill but not Steiner. He is also ignored in A.D.C. Peterson's A Hundred Years of Education, (1952); R. Skidelsky's English Progressive Schools, (1969); R.J.W. Selleck's English Primary Education and the Progressives, 1914-1939, (1972); and J. Bowen's History of Western Education (Vol. I. 1972 and Vol. II. 1975).

It is doubtful that this silence is any sort of conspiracy! It probably springs from a combination of factors: The Waldorf Schools Movement is very isolated from other school movements and guards its independence jealously, so that even in physical terms the gap is not easily bridged. It seems reasonable to suggest, therefore, that most authors are quite simply ignorant about Waldorf Schools.

Many people seem to have heard of the schools, even if they associate them vaguely with the separate institutions which are for the mentally handicapped, but in the course of his research the author found extremely few people who have any accurate ideas about Waldorf Education, even among experienced educationists.

This raises the important questions of how and whether educational theory becomes recognised, disseminated and practised, but these problems extend far beyond the present task.

It follows from this review of the literature that the purpose of this book is to fill an extremely large gap; firstly as an objective study of Steiner's books and lectures, independently of modern developments; secondly as a structured analysis of the principles involved, fully integrated with "Spiritual Science"; and thirdly as a record of the way in which Steiner's thought contrasts and connects with several other major western educational thinkers, in order to indicate his context in the modern educational world. Without such a study, no movement, least of all a movement outside mainstream modern thought, can lay claim to academic credibility. Moreover, Steiner's books and lectures are much more difficult to study than orthodox educational theory, and consequently Waldorf teacher training is more arduous, especially with its emphasis on the development of artistic abilities. This attempt to synthesise a wide range of Steiner's work into a single theoretical structure aims to enhance both the accessibility of the whole as well as the perspective of the parts within their context. It also aims to clarify the concepts involved.

2.2.3 Works on Philosophy

Galbreath gives an interesting, thorough account of Steiner's philosophical work[67]. However it is too detailed to summarise here. Rather Owen Barfield's article[68] which captures the essence of Steiner's epistemology will be described, ending with a quotation to demonstrate Galbreath's impression of this area of Steiner's thought.

This section is of value to an analysis of Steiner's thought on education because it establishes the philosophical foundation for spiritual knowledge[69]. This spiritual knowledge is gained through Spiritual Science, and Steiner uses it as a basis for his educational thought. No other occult teaching offers such a philosophical justification, even if it were "radically opposed to almost all major philosophical currents of the late nineteenth century." [70]

Barfield's essay comes at the beginning of a collection of centenary essays on the work and thought of Steiner. The volume consists of nineteen essays by people of academic distinction on the main aspects of Steiner's thought. His concepts of Mind, Time and Consciousness, Evolution, Christ, History, Psychology, Science, Self Development, Space and Counter-Space, Colour, Architecture, the Mongol Child, Education, the Handicapped Child, Medicine, Agriculture and Sociology are covered.

Barfield's article provides a sketch of Steiner's epistemology uncomplicated by references to the philosophical context in which he was writing. Its purpose – like that of this section – is to provide a foundation for the subsequent articles.

Barfield says that, in Steiner's epistemology as laid out in The Philosophy of Spiritual Activity, it is argued that the act of thinking is our own activity[71] and is anterior to both conceptualisation and perception[72]. Steiner differs from Hegel, therefore, in his assertion that thinking as an (albeit unnoticed) act, must be distinguished from thought as a concept[73]. Therefore if thinking, as the instrument of knowledge, is taken as the starting point of the theory of knowledge, then we begin without any suppositions at all, because thinking is anterior to any attempt to think about anything else (conceptualise)[74]. Steiner believed that many philosophical errors were caused by attempts to investigate knowledge before it was established what was meant by knowing.

Steiner showed that pure concepts (such as the concept of a triangle) are identical in all the minds that think them[75]. These, together with Percepts, which do not refer to the process of perception but to the object of the process[76] constitute the building blocks of which all human knowledge is constructed[77].

To show how Steiner bridges the gap between the picture of the world as given (percept), and the picture of it which our cognitive activity unfolds (concept) Barfield contrasts the existence of the "net Given"[78], which is the act of thinking, with the "specious Given", the world as normally perceived and which is "qualified by predicates"[79]. Positivism treats the "specious Given" as the ultimate starting point for all reliable knowledge[80], but Steiner rejects this as incomplete and unreliable because it may be tainted with subjectivity and error. He postulates instead that thinking itself provides the only proper empirical basis for knowledge; that "truth is an ideal reproduction of some given object". Barfield likens this to Gabriel Marcel's conclusion that "all knowledge is contingent on a participation in being, for which it cannot account because it continually presupposes it"[81]. It follows that,

> "If we are determined to eliminate all subjectivity and to be uncompromisingly empirical, if we insist on verifying from experience at all points, from the start onwards, our only course is to find some way of penetrating with full consciousness into that unconscious no-man's-land (or should one say 'every-man's-land'?) which lies between the net Given and the specious Given. This is the realm where thinking performs the function of Coleridge's 'primary imagination', or what Susanne Langer calls 'formulation'." [82]

Thinking must therefore become the tool whereby man "inserts himself spiritually into reality" [83], and all Steiner's later work is concerned with the way in which the act of thinking can be refined and strengthened to the point at which it experiences higher levels of consciousness in the spiritual worlds[84].

Galbreath suggests rather strangely that analytical philosophers may be best

37

able to judge the soundness of this argument, which Steiner calls "Objective Idealism" [85]. It is of immense importance to the rest of Steiner's work.

"Its scope is impressive, and Steiner's willingness to attack established orthodoxies and academic philosophies merits respect. The system as a whole is certainly plausible and, for many later Anthroposophists, convincing. It reveals his Goethean outlook and, from the perspective of his occultism, it provides Anthroposophy with a philosophical foundation which could be examined without embarrassment by many spiritually thirsty intellectuals of the turn-of-the-century." [86]

2.2.4 Works on Spiritual Science

An excellent overall view of Steiner's work has been written by A.P. Shepherd[87], a man who came to study Steiner from an orthodox academic background. It is probably the best introduction to Steiner's work.

However, Galbreath's thesis deals with Occultism at a much more profound level, tracing its history and complexity. This will be summarised as briefly as possible in order to indicate something of the context of Steiner's thought. It emerges not as an isolated teaching, but as part of a gigantic web which extends deeply into the main stream of intellectual thought of the turn of the century.

There is a vast literature on Occultism, Magic, Mysticism, Spiritualism and Theosophy. With specific reference to Steiner, Hemleben lists a selection of 45 books written by his pupils[88] and there are many more. The following summary therefore encapsulates an extremely complex field.

Galbreath recognises Steiner's diligence in outlining his methods and his efforts to make occultism appeal to the modern mind. He was exceptionally well prepared for this by his philosophical and editorial experience[89]. Steiner ought not to be underestimated:

"It is far too easy to laugh at occultism and dismiss it as absurd. Scorn, however, almost always denotes a lack of understanding .... I have concluded on the basis of broad reading in general occultism and detailed consideration of Steiner's works and activities that although charlatanry, deception, credulity and ignorance are endemic to the occult field, some few figures and movements stand out by virtue of their patent sincerity, intelligence and openness. Rudolf Steiner, in my estimate, possesses these latter characteristics in full measure. I have encountered no evidence of any sort that he knowingly deceived anyone about his occult abilities." [90]

Galbreath contrasts the aims of "Mysticism" and "Occultism". They share certain broad similarities. Both reveal forms of literal and symbolic rebirth or regeneration, both claim that man is able to experience higher states of being, that

all people possess "latent capacities or faculties" for experiencing higher consciousness and that these faculties can be "activated through rigorous training" [91]. Although both aim ultimately at union with God, or Oneness[92] occultism disassociates
itself from this goal if it is seen as a selfish or emotional desire[93].

Whereas mysticism is concerned with Oneness in a broad sense, occultism
seems to be always focussed on specifics. Oneness is achieved with a specific
level, being or phenomenon of the higher worlds, rather than as the unity of the
whole[94].

The occultist tries to penetrate the secrets of nature by investigating the
spiritual dimensions. He sees the forces he is dealing with as neither good nor
bad in themselves, but neutral[95]. The motives of the occultist place him on the
Right-Hand or the Left-Hand path. The Right-Hand path requires "strict discipline,
personal morality of a high order, and thorough purification of the self", whereas
the Left-Hand path is that of selfishness, personal gratification and vanity[96].

Although occult organisations may espouse teachings on a variety of religious
questions, they do not claim to be religions or sects, and do not practise worship[97].
Instead, occultism is seen as a science:

> "... the primary basis for the scientific claims of occultism is its insistence
> that it is experiential, although not necessarily experimental, in its ac-
> tivities. That is to say, the content of occult science has been acquired
> through the direct observations of the initiates and empirically verified
> by their disciples." [98]

The most sophisticated, or "higher" forms of occultism strive to synthesise
Science, Mysticism, Religion, Philosophy and Psychology in their highest forms[99].
Galbreath concludes with a definition:

> "The spiritual variety of occultism, then, in contrast to a concern with
> the occult arts and magic, may be regarded as the belief in the existence
> of dimensions of reality beyond the range of the ordinary senses and the
> methods of orthodox scientific procedure, and the study of such phenom-
> ena (laws, planes, beings, forces, events and purposes) through the moral
> purification of the individual and the unleashing of latent faculties under
> the stimulation of exercises, rituals, or initiation, leading to experiences
> of oneness with the higher dimensions and an awareness of the essential
> spiritual unity of the cosmos. Rudolf Steiner's science of the spirit was one
> of the leading representatives of this tradition in the twentieth century. [100]

Higher forms of mysticism and occultism are not kept secret[101] for selfish
reasons, but rather to protect them from the scepticism of those who do not have
a sufficiently refined consciousness to understand them. The real secrecy of higher
spiritual knowledge lies in its inaccessibility to grosser levels of consciousness:

> "It is because enlightenment or initiation or mystical consciousness con-
> note a condition of being that the secrets of the Mystery rituals cannot

be revealed and that occult knowledge is truly 'hidden'. Intellectual or conceptual statements about undifferentiated unity, the evocation of forces, or the perception of the astral planes do not truly communicate or reveal anything of importance to the uninitiated." [102]

Examining German Occultism from Romanticism to Rudolf Steiner, Galbreath shows that Steiner's work can be viewed as the culmination of more than a century of interest throughout Europe in occultism, magic, theosophy, spiritualism and mysticism. This fascination with the occult was not peculiar to Germany[103]. Steiner's "... occult teachings can by no means be considered an isolated and therefore periph eral and unessential phenomenon in the course of recent intellectual history."[104]

The late eighteenth and early nineteenth century revival of interest in the occult constitutes "... one of the most vital currents of anti-Enlightenment thought, as well as one of the most decisive in the growth of Romanticism." [105] The most comprehensive study of the relationship between mysticism, occultism and Romanticism is Auguste Viattels Les Sources occultes du romanticisme: Illuminisme – Theosophie 1770-1820[106], but the connections are widely documented and certainly not novel. Galbreath shows that what is often not appreciated is that ultimately Romanticism is mysticism:

> "The subject-object distinction drawn by earlier rationalistic and empiricist philosophers is overcome in both Romantic and mystical theories of cognition. In the philosophies of Fichte and Schelling, for example, emphasis is placed on the superiority of intuitive cognition *(intellektuelle Anschauung)* in grasping ultimate reality." [107]

Once he is able to overcome the habits of "customary thinking, the lower self, or the understanding *(Verstand)*", the idealist philosopher is able to experience a higher self with his higher intuitive faculties. This self-knowledge is claimed to be an experience of true reality because it is "an immediate, direct possession of the knower. The knower knows the real by becoming real himself." [108]

Developments in German scholastic and artistic life were stimulated by the infusion of Oriental and Occidental streams of mystical and occult thought during the latter half of the eighteenth century. These included Neoplatonism, Gnosticism, Hermetic philosophy and alchemy, Medieval German mysticism, Pietism, Freemasonry, Rosicrucianism and Indian Mysticism. Jacob Boehme, Swedenborg, Saint-Martin and Mesmer were also influential[109].

Such men as Fichte, Goethe, Herder, Lessing and Mozart were attracted to Freemasonry, and Baader, Hamann, Mesmer, Novalis, J.W. Ritter, Schelling, G.H. von Schubert and Zacharias Werner to Rosicrucianism. These movements had their own rituals and teachings but were strongly influenced by Swedenborgianism, Martinism, Saint Martin and Mesmerism. They wielded powerful influences over the religious revival of the late eighteenth century[110].

In the early nineteenth century some Romantic literary men and philosophers followed the revival of interest in the medieval mystics that had been initiated by Protestant and Catholic theologians. Hegel, for example, developed a profound interest in Meister Eckhart (c. 1260-1327/8)[111].

Occultism encouraged a complex interaction between mysticism, religion, philosophy, science and literature[112] and many of the German Romantics were interested in the investigation of hypnotic, magnetic and mediumistic phenomena[113].

Impetus was added to interest in spiritualism from America with Andrew Jackson Davis' book of 1847 claiming to contact the spirits of Galen and Swedenborg[114] and by the Fox family drama in 1848[115]. In the same year Alphonse Cahagnet emerged as a French counterpart of Davis[116].

Allan Kardac devised French Spiritualism[117], in 1882 the English Society for Psychical Research was started[118] and in 1875 the Theosophical Society was founded in New York[119]. The Theosophical Society, with its famous and controversial characters in Madame Blavatsky (1831-1891), Colonel Henry Steel Olcott (1832-1907), Annie Besant (1847-1933) and Charles Leadbeater (1847-1934), has affected modern occultism more than has any other movement. It has an enormous literature and an immensely complex body of teaching, complicated further by attempts to develop Madame Blavatsky's teachings[120].   W.B. Yeats belonged to Madame Blavatsky's London section of the society for a short time[121].

Galbreath's survey of Neo Romanticism and the twentieth century reveals a mushrooming of occult interest. Publications on occultism, occult fiction, astrology, magic and Atlantis thrived. H.G. Wells and Jules Verne incorporated these interests into their work, and Yeats was also involved with the Theosophist movement called the Hermetic Order of the Golden Dawn and other societies[122].

Christian Science, New Thought, Gurdjieff, Vivekenanda, Ramakrishna, Ralph Waldo Trine and O.S. Marden came into prominence. Nietzsche, Julis Langbehn, Rudolf Otto and Schopenhauer all expressed themselves on occultism. The scandal of racialism entered the fray with the Prana Group of Leipzig, deliberately irrational in outlook, preaching the creation of the Aryan Man. Volrath, subsequently a Nazi, was expelled by Steiner from the Theosophical Society for his racism, and Ludendorf and Hans Hörbiger combined racism and pseudo occultism in their scheme of things[123].

Bruder Johannes, Johannes Muller, Bô Yin Râ and Count Herman Keyserling were all well known for their work. Galbreath considers Keyserling and Steiner the two most influential occultists[124], and notes that many textbooks point to their large followings as evidence of the growing irrationality of Weimar Germany. However Galbreath rejects this as an oversimplification because of the strength of occultism since the 1880's.

Galbreath considers diverse points of view in his analysis of the popularity of occultism: the sense of mystery, the thrill of doing something forbidden, faddishness, intellectual fashion, the imitation of scientific respectability and the practice of magic as a desire to relieve tension and anxiety may all provide motives. However, he rejects cynicism as a valid approach:

"Still another method of 'explaining' occultism is that of denigrating it as the mental turbulence of the illiterate or degenerate. Mysticism is an escape from the world, Theosophy is a mishmash of pseudo scholarship and religious eclecticism for the half-educated, magic is merely the infantile effort of the deprived to assert themselves, astrology mirrors the uncertainty of the times. Most of these points are simply clichés of journalism which imply that occultism is one of the growing pains which industrial mass society must endure. The heuristic value of such explanations is decidedly limited." [125]

Galbreath also rejects the idea that occultism is a revival of Gnosticism, although the influences of this, as well as immanenticism, secularism, Romanticism and a reaction to materialism are all considerable. Secularism reveals an important reason for the influence of occultism – the modern search for authority: occultism offers a unified and intensified body of knowledge which seems appealing in the face of the moribund and distant appearance of traditional philosophy and theology. Occultism gains strength in its combination of the authoritative disciplines of History, Science and Revelation[126].

Galbreath sees Steiner's occultism as offering a satisfying extension of modern knowledge into the spiritual. It does not divorce man from modern life, yet tries to arouse his consciousness of his ancient origins and his spiritual destiny[127].

Galbreath's description of Steiner's life gives an intensive survey of Steiner's extraordinary spectrum of activities. He notes how little Steiner reveals of his personal, private life such as his occult experiences and initiation, his family life and marriages, his final illness or personal conflicts with others. Steiner distances himself from these and treats them objectively, or omits them altogether, expanding only on what develops into his "mission" in life.

"That he recorded his life at all is testimony only of his desire to refute those who failed to detect a thread of consistency running through his life and work." [128]

Galbreath's account searches out in particular that which is relevant to Steiner's occult life, bringing together information from diverse sources to form an unique picture. Insofar as this is relevant, it has been incorporated into the account of Steiner's life in Chapter 1.

The remainder of Galbreath's thesis consists of an account of Steiner's philosophical exposition (Objective Idealism)[129], Spiritual Science[130], the process of Initiation[131], and the spiritual structure of Man and the higher worlds (in a chapter entitled Microcosm and Macrocosm)[132]. These will not be summarised because they explore areas of Steiner's work which are not necessary for a book on his educational thought. The author's own accounts of Spiritual Science and the spiritual structure of man in the following chapter will cover what he considers to be essential.

Galbreath's final chapter attempts to assess the status of Steiner's Spiritual

Science as a "Science"[133]. Although his discussion has implications for all Steiner's work, it is regarded as the province of Galbreath's thesis rather than the present book, and will therefore be omitted here.

Galbreath sums up Steiner's occultism as being directly based on his philosophical work, "Objective Idealism". It is a rationally and systematically ordered body of knowledge which is, to Steiner, empirical knowledge. It rejects materialism as an ontology, neo-Kantianism as an epistemology and mechanism as a model of explanation beyond the physical realm. It asserts that there are different levels of being and activity each with their respective laws which are inherent in the phenomena of each level and independent of human consciousness. It is broadly focussed and is concerned with all human experience[134].

It points to the presence of spiritual faculties in man by which higher worlds can be known. This epistemology has two corollaries. Firstly, it is dependent on the moral development of the investigator (a condition unheard of in orthodox science), and secondly the knowledge attained is part of an integrated whole of the cosmos. Man is not master of nature, but part of it[135].

Steiner indicated the role of the spirit in both modern and ancient thought, clearly differentiating spiritual from orthodox science:

"He rejected amoralism and agnosticism, and insisted on the inadequacy of relying solely on matter without spirit, physics without metaphysics, scientific reason without intuition, sense organs without spiritual faculties, control of nature without integration with it, and mechanism without organicism. Simply to list these differences reveals Steiner's strong affinities with Romanticism, as well as to traditional occultism and to many elements of the pre-Copernican world view .... He draws too upon Christianity, Oriental Mysticism and Goethe. There is, moreover, a strong archaic flavour to his thought ..." [136]

C.S. Lewis labelled Anthroposophy "medieval" after his initial acquaintance with it. However, it is folly to entertain simplistic notions about it.

"It is indeed medieval but it is also much more. It is both archaic and Modern, it combines both science and religion, it accepts the present and looks to the future, it operates within a matrix of secularisation to establish resacralisation. Such combinations need not be paradoxical. Steiner has attempted, like so many of his contemporaries, to construct a more satisfying philosophical framework for man and his destiny." [137]

For Galbreath, "eclecticism constitutes both Steiner's strength and his weakness, his originality and his obscurity ..." But it succeeds in challenging modern materialism and faith in sense data[138], and its assimilation of polarities into a dynamic synthesis is appealing[139]:

"... conflict and opposition are overcome within the framework of a higher perspective." [140]

43

Steiner's work is in harmony with many of the advanced intellectual currents of the turn of the century: opposition to both standard Marxism and Positivism; Durkheim and Weber's view that the source of the modern crisis is the conflict between Science and Religion; Nietzsche's warning of the fallacies and cultural dangers of any system of normative ethics based on standards external to man; the many systems of Idealism; explorations into cosmic evolution by Bergson and Teilhard de Chardin, and the concern among artists and thinkers with inner psychic experiences — the French symbolists, Post Impressionist Art, Bergson, Freud and Jung[141].

Galbreath identifies many noteworthy people who were either Anthroposophists, interested observers, or critics of it[142]. He analyses the reasons that it has not attracted still more interest. It seems, for example, to have had none of the impact on modern values that Jung's work has had, even though Anthroposophy has a membership of about 60 000 and uncountable other students, whereas by comparison there are only some 250 trained Jungian analysts in the world[143].

Galbreath attributes this to several factors: the reputation of occultism; the form of Steiner's occultism (the difficulty of its presentation and its inherent difficulty); its popular rather than academic appeal may prejudice intellectuals against it[144]; it does not have the immediate impact, interest or evident relevance to everyday life that Freud or Marx have[145]; Steiner's writing exhibits very little passion, unlike the humanizing, moral concerns of other thinkers; it may be seen to parallel or represent a revival of other streams of thought[146]; and its mixture of science and myth may be unacceptable to many[147].

Galbreath himself remains intrigued, enlightened, stimulated but unconvinced at the end of his research[148]. He finds that the rational grounds for Steiner's work are not sufficient to overcome the scepticism of a materialist perspective, and he has not gone beyond the material into the spiritual. The brief outline of Spiritual Science which follows will indicate something of the territory which he explored.

3

THE FOUNDATIONS
OF EDUCATIONAL
THOUGHT

STEINER'S CONCEPT
OF MAN

Steiner's educational thought rests on one of the deepest and most complex occult analyses of man, and uses terms which may be foreign to the reader who is unfamiliar with occult teachings. Even those who are familiar with such terms will find that Steiner uses them in a way which is peculiar to his own holistic thought and not analogous to their use elsewhere.

The term "Soul", for example, is used by Steiner in a different sense from that of orthodox Christian teachings. Similarly, his use of the term "Ego" is different from Freud's and the terms "Etheric" and "Astral" seem not to be the same as in Theosophy. Comparisons of Steiner's concepts with these others would be irrelevant to the present analysis of his thought, since the author's aim is to be accurately descriptive.

An introduction to these conceptions is necessary because Steiner draws his educational thought directly from his concept of Man. This will be shown in the chapter on The Stages of Development. Moreover, concepts such as "pictorial thinking" and the "temperaments" can be fully understood only with reference to Steiner's analysis of Man. These will be dealt with in due course.

A description of the Spiritual Worlds has been omitted from this section because they are alluded to, insofar as is necessary, under 4.1.1 and 4.1.3. Further description would be unnecessary and inevitably complex[1].

For the present, the Spiritual foundations of the theory have been divided into three sections: Spiritual Science, which sketches the method by which the structure of Man is perceived; The Structure of Man, which describes the essence of Steiner's analysis of Man's nature; and The Relationship between Body and Soul, which reveals the way in which man's Soul is bound up with the physical body, whereby it becomes amenable to Education.

In this chapter and throughout the analysis of Steiner's thought the relationships of his ideas to those of other thinkers have been ignored. This is to avoid confusing an already complex and extensive body of thought. Such relationships, parallels as well as differences, are so numerous that they require analysis in themselves. At the end of this book some of the stronger links to Steiner's educational thought are traced.

3.1   STEINER'S SPIRITUAL SCIENCE

3.1.1   Introduction

Steiner considered that Waldorf Education should not be separated from Spiritual Science[2]. The necessity for Waldorf teachers to become familiar and involved with Spiritual Science will be increasingly evident as this book progresses.

The first step that the student must take is to realise the absolute sincerity of the subject. It is concerned with all that is most sacred and most central to human life.

> "Spiritual Science must be taken in deep earnestness, for only so can it
> be rightly understood. It is not the outcome of any sectarian whim but
> something that has proceeded from the fundamental needs of human
> evolution." [3]

Steiner is uncompromising in stating that if human beings find the teachings of Spiritual Science "overwhelming", the fault lies not in Spiritual Science, but in themselves[4]. The student of Spiritual Science must work to understand it, for its teachings are not only concerned with the physical but also with the spiritual life[5].

Spiritual Science seeks for the sources of all existence in order to understand Man's being and destiny[6]. It takes nothing from written records of any sort, but from direct observation of spiritual realities alone[7]. Only after this is achieved can the attempt be made "... to rediscover these results in the outer records." [8]

The process of development of the faculties by which one can perceive spiritual realities has been practised from time immemorial. Attempts to devise new ones inevitably go astray and lead to paths of "boundless fantasy" [9]. The method that Steiner describes is the safest for most people, although he concedes that shorter, simpler paths may be successful for the few who already have considerable psychic gifts[10].

Spiritual Science is defined as "... the study of the spiritual processes in human life and in the cosmos. " [11] It is not a body of new teachings, but rather an "instrument" for studying Man's universe[12].

3.1.2 Spiritual Science and Natural Science

Spiritual Science does not conflict with the principles of Natural Science, except where these are not clearly understood[13]. The principles of Science are often confused with its subject-matter:

"How a pursuit comes to be a science cannot in the nature of the case be ascertained from the subject-matter to which it is devoted, but only by recognizing the mode of action of the human soul while engaged in scientific endeavour." [14]

Spiritual Science speaks of Spiritual phenomena in the "same mood" as Natural Science speaks of sense perceptible phenomena [15]. Spiritual Science serves as a continuation of Natural Science[16] and aims to make all sciences more fruitful, stimulating them and bringing forward what flows from the basic assumptions of Natural Science but which it does not strive for itself[17].

Spiritual Science investigates the spiritual causes behind physical evolution. "The material" evolved out of "the spiritual", like ice from water, and originally the earth was a spiritual entity[18]. The physical world cannot be properly understood in its relation to Man without access to "supersensible cognition."

"Just as we cannot see the physical objects around us until we have a light, so too, we cannot explain what goes on in and through the soul-life of man till we have knowledge of the supersensible." [19]

3.1.3 Method of Investigation

The student of Spiritual Science must be clear that his task has to do with the direct observation of life, not theories or ideas about life.

"We shall only be acting in the spirit of natural science if we study the spiritual development of man as impartially as the naturalist observes the sense world. We shall then certainly be led, in the domain of spiritual life, to a kind of contemplation ....

An investigator of this kind must also go beyond a merely historical examination of the documents relating to spiritual life .... When a chemical law is explained, it is of small use to describe the retorts, dishes and pincers which led to the discovery of the law .... Nor does the naturalist who is investigating the nature of man trouble about the origin of the word "man" .... He keeps to the thing, not to the word in which it finds expression. And in studying spiritual life we must likewise abide by the spirit and not by outer documents." [20]

Quoting from Goethe[21] Steiner shows that the research process is linked directly to the very nature of Man as body, soul and spirit. In his body Man apprehends sense-perceptible data, in his soul he responds with feelings and judgements to these data, but only with his spirit is he able to observe the world dispassionately, seeing its phenomena as things in themselves and in their relations to their surroundings and free of personal response to those data[22]. It is therefore the spirit which must be trained and developed by the spiritual researcher.

Steiner's descriptions of his findings through spiritual research are intended initially to appeal to the reader's thoughtful judgement, and then gradually to lead him into the "delicate and unwonted nature of the experience". The reader begins to realise that Steiner is not describing dogmas but states of consciousness, and now the training of the faculty of thought can be begun[23].

The faculties of the soul — thought, feeling, and will — must become absolutely firm and disciplined to the extent that even when normal waking consciousness is relinquished they remain under control[24]. In this process of training, our natural qualities are of little account. It is what we make of ourselves — the work we do — that is valuable[25]. The pupil's guarantee against self deception is his development of the power of thought[26]. This development and discipline of the soul leads the pupil to a sensitivity and richness of soul experience that is beyond the awareness of normal waking consciousness[27].

The exercises by which the faculties of the soul are disciplined and developed are described in <u>Knowledge of the Higher Worlds</u>. The exercises are progressive and are too extensive to describe or to generalise about because they are concerned not only with the different faculties but with their development through different stages of consciousness. Nothing can replace Steiner's own text in this regard. Suffice it to say that they require the student to apprehend a faculty (such as the Imagination) to learn to use it and control it consciously through exercises (such as Imagining various subjects) and then to be able to eliminate it from the mind, whereupon the next, deeper level of soul or spiritual awareness is revealed[28].

However, these exercises do not constitute the "method" of spiritual development. They are only one of the essential activities the pupil must practise. The "method" embraces every aspect of conscious life, even the physical life of the senses[29]. The growing dedication that this demands must go hand in hand with the development of moral strength.

Spiritual training is *ipso facto* moral training[30]. The pursuit of spiritual knowledge must be absolutely unselfish[31] and devoted to the service of humanity[32].

"This golden rule is as follows: for every one step forward that you take in seeking knowledge of occult truths, take three steps forward in the improvement of your own character." [33]

Steiner describes how moral qualities can be developed: judgement and criticism of others must give way to an attitude of mature respect, devotion and veneration towards all[34]. Courage, fearlessness[35], and a love of work in itself, not for the sake of success[36] must be developed. Some of the other qualities that are essential are calmness, patience, perseverance[37]. The pupil must overcome conceit[38], develop firm judgement, stable character and conscience[39], equanimity in the face of pleasure and pain and a positive attitude to the world[40].

Without these moral qualities, a pupil who reaches the spiritual world would be like a man in the sense-world who is in a stupor. His vision would be dim and erroneous[41].

Ethical behaviour may be subjective, but there are ethical laws which are of the spiritual world in the same way as physical laws are of the physical world[42]. As the pupil finds his way into the spiritual world, so he learns these spiritual laws with increasing directness and this learning furthers his development. The impulse for moral behaviour therefore comes from the spiritual world:

> "The Spirit-self brings to the 'I', from the world of the spirit, the eternal laws of the true and good. These link themselves through the consciousness-soul with the experiences of the soul's own life." [43]

Despite these spiritual laws and the difficulty of achieving them, the pupil must always be completely free:

> "True, the conditions are strict, but they are not rigid, because the fulfilment of them not only should be, but actually must be, a free deed." [44]

As the pupil progresses in self discipline and moral strength, spiritual "organs" of perception develop which enable him to perceive the spiritual world[45]. What the pupil sees and hears in the spiritual world is only so by way of analogy with the physical senses.

> "It must be explicitly emphasised that these 'colours' are not colours as seen by physical eyes. To apprehend 'blue' spiritually means to be aware of or to feel something similar to what is experienced when the physical eye rests on the colour blue." [46]

This analogy to "feeling" in spiritual perception does not imply that it is subjective. The pupil must learn to free his perception of all personal feelings or responses to what is perceived in order to find permanent truth[47]. All things being equal, different spiritual researchers "... reach no divergent views but come to the identical insight." [48] This requires more disciplined thought than is necessary for natural science[49] to the point where all sources of self delusion are dispelled[50].

The sort of knowledge thus obtained goes far outside what Kant, Herbart, William James, Schiller or Bergson would have considered admissable[51].

> "This kind of cognition shows itself from the first to be of quite a different character from the cognition that relates to the physical world. Here, we receive impressions through our senses and then proceed to entertain ideas and concepts about these impressions. The acquisition of knowl-

edge by means of Inspiration* [52] is not like that. The 'knowing' is achieved in one single act; there is no thought-process following the perception. What in the act of cognition by means of the physical senses is acquired only subsequently in the concept, is in the Inspirational cognition given simultaneously with the percept." [53]

In order to communicate the findings of spiritual thought at the level of normal consciousness it is necessary to use comparisons or analogies with things in the sense world[54]. The investigator must try to cast his perceptions "... in genuine forms of thought, without thereby depriving it of its "Imaginative** [55] character."[56] These "concepts" can be understood if approached with "... unprejudiced logic and a healthy feeling for truth." [57] They are formulated more accurately than in ordinary science or life[58], and their applicability can be readily seen:

"When rightly applied in life, knowledge of the supersensible worlds proves not to be unpractical but practical in the highest degree." [59]

3.1.4 Proof in Spiritual Science

When the natural scientist looks at spiritual science one of the first things he asks for is "proof". This is understandable since the proofs of spiritual science can never be as "tangible or compelling" as those of the sense-world[60].

Proof is not of course obtained by merely showing how spiritual findings are borne out by our knowledge of physical realities, (although they may be illustrated thus) because it could be argued that they were formulated from knowledge of the physical[61].

The proof which Steiner regarded as absolute could only be obtained by the actual practice of spiritual science:

"Anyone who really enters into the descriptions of Occult Science will presently perceive that in the process he acquires ideas and concepts he did not have before. He begins to have quite unexpected thoughts concerning what he formerly imagined to be the essence of a 'proof'.... Here, the activity which is applied to the proof in natural-scientific thinking, already lies inherent in the seeking for the facts. One cannot even find the facts without the path towards them carrying its own inherent proof. Anyone who really goes along this path will in so doing have experienced the proof, and nothing more can be achieved by any added proof from outside." [62]

---

* "Inspiration" is a special term used by Steiner to denote perception of, though not entry into, the spiritual world.

** "Imagination" here is quite different from the normal use of the term and refers to the first stage in the development of spiritual sight.

Proof is therefore an intimate, inner experience for the pupil of spiritual science[63] and it is attained most completely at the highest level of spiritual consciousness, called "Intuition" * [64].

There are, however, several ways in which normal thinking can come to some degree of conviction without following the method for developing spiritual sight. Many "facts" can be accepted on purely logical grounds[65], but the reverse is not always as true:

"... exception can never be taken to the facts themselves on merely logical grounds. Just as in the realm of the physical world one can never prove by logic whether or not a whale exists, but only by inspection, so it is with supersensible facts; they can be apprehended by spiritual perception and by that alone." [66]

One of the means of reaching conviction which Steiner considered most important was by studying the way in which spiritual truths mutually support one another[67] in a holistic sense: "... the core of the matter does not lie in one truth, but in the harmony of them all." [68]

The findings of different spiritual researchers ought to correspond, but of course this is not evidence in itself since mutual influence cannot be ruled out[69]. Much depends on the students' personal sense of truth to decide what is acceptable and what not. For example, with a concept such as Reincarnation, the revelations of former lives given by one with spiritual sight should be judged in the light of one's intimate knowledge of the person concerned.

"... the re-embodiment of the spiritual human being is, naturally, a process which does not belong to the domain of external physical facts, but is one that takes place entirely in the spiritual region. And to this region no other of our ordinary powers of intelligence has entrance, save that of thinking. He who will not trust to the power of thinking, cannot in fact enlighten himself regarding higher spiritual facts .... Anyone who ascribes to a so-called proof, constructed according to methods of natural science, greater power to convince than the above assertions concerning the significance of life-history may be in the ordinary sense of the word a great scientist; but from the paths of true spiritual investigation he is very far distant." [70]

Steiner also set great store by the proving of spiritual knowledge, not in itself, but through its application in practical life. In this respect the practice of education was only a part of his concern.

"... it is so important that the science of spirit can be cultivated at the Goetheanum in Dornach – although it is not yet completed – for then it enters into practical affairs in order that by means of them it can prove

---

* "Intuition" is a special term with no relationship to the normal use of the word.

its knowledge of the human being and its ability to deal with practical human matters." [71]

3.1.5 Access to Spiritual Science

Of importance to its status as a science is that spiritual science should be "... accessible to every human mind" [72],

"They (communications from the supersensible world) are however thoroughly comprehensible — and not alone to those whose thinking has been educated through spiritual training, but to every thinking person who is conscious of the full power of his thinking and ready to apply it." [73]

Every age requires new methods for the path of higher development to suit the outer forms of man's life, but the method described by Steiner is specifically suited to modern times[74].

"... it can be carried through no matter what one's situation is amid the typical conditions of our time." [75]

As a scientific method it is of course universally applicable:

"True, he must have the experience himself, just as everyone has to perceive for himself the proof of a theorem in mathematics. But the pathway by which the experience is reached, no less than the method of proving the mathematical theorem, is universally valid." [76]

The mere possession of spiritual sight does not make a person into a spiritual scientist. This requires an even greater intensity of training than is required in the physical sciences. Anyone trained in the hard schools of the physical sciences and philosophy (as was Steiner) would benefit from such training if he were to develop spiritual sight.

"Higher seeing makes a 'knower' in the spiritual as little as healthy sense-organs make a 'scholar' in regard to the realities of the senses. And because in truth all reality, the lower and the higher spiritual, are only two sides of one and the same fundamental being, anyone who is unlearned in the lower branches of knowledge will as a rule remain so in regard to the higher." [77]

With respect to the terms "Occult Science" and "esoteric training" Steiner is adamant that "occult knowledge is no more of a secret for the average human being than writing is a secret for one who has not learnt it." [78] The withholding of "knowledge" is really a withholding of an experience of inner consciousness until the pupil is prepared in terms of self discipline and moral consciousness to receive it[79]. Spiritual science is "occult" inasmuch as it is not evident to the physical senses as is natural science, but it is open to anyone who is prepared to "turn his inner life towards the spirit." [80] Only those who do so will be able to understand —

not only intellectually but as a holistic experience — the inner nature of the child as body, soul and spirit. This is the goal of the Waldorf teacher. When it is achieved he will be able to educate correctly from the depths of his own nature, and not merely from his intellect[81].

3.2   THE STRUCTURE OF MAN

The aim and value of this section will be to capture what constitutes an extensive and highly complex part of Steiner's analysis of man's non-physical self, in as concise and relevant a way as possible.

Several esoteric concepts are involved.   Though the terminology used may sound strange at first hearing, it should not prove an obstacle to understanding, since some form of terminology is necessary[82].   Anyone who is familiar with some of the terminology used, but whose knowledge comes from a source other than Steiner's, ought to put aside all preconceptions about the meanings, because Steiner based his formulations of the concept on his own spiritual research alone, not on that of other "seers".

"My knowledge of the spiritual — of this I am fully conscious — springs from my own spiritual vision.   At every stage — both in the details and in synthesis and broad review — I have subjected myself to stringent tests, making sure that wide-awake control accompanies each further step in spiritual vision and research." [83]

3.2.1 Body, Soul and Spirit

The physical body is, quite simply, that which remains after physical death: the corpse.   It is the "mineral" part of man[84].   When animated by the soul and spirit, the physical body is capable of receiving sense impressions from the physical world.

The most primary form of soul life is "sensation" which is the subjective response of the person to a physical sense impression[85].   Sensation is closely related to "feeling", which is a stirring of the soul, and to "will":

"Through the will man reacts on the outer world.   And he thereby stamps the impress of his inner being on the outer world.   The soul of man as it were flows outwards in the activities of his will.   The actions of the human being differ from the occurrences of outer nature in that they bear the impress of his inner life." [86]

The "content" of the soul is therefore sensation, feelings of desire and aversion, impulses, instincts and passions.   All of these are interrelated and dependent on the bodily nature[87].

53

A central function of the soul is "memory" which preserves the past in the form of conceptions which can then exist independently of the sense experiences that initiated them[88].

The soul is subject to influences from the sense world, but it is also subject to influences from the organising power of thought[89]. The brain is the bodily instrument of thinking which is the expression of "spirit" [90]. However the thought-life of man "is shadow, a reflection of the true, spiritual being to whom it belongs." [91]

"A man is more perfect, the more his soul sympathises with the manifestations of the spirit; he is the more imperfect the more the inclinations of his soul are satisfied by the functions of the body.

The spirit is the central point of man, the body the instrument by which the spirit observes and learns to understand the physical world and through which it acts in it. But the soul is the intermediary between the two." [92]

Soul and Spirit are general terms in Steiner's analysis. A more detailed description follows.

3.2.2 The Physical and Soul Bodies and the Ego

Besides the physical body, there are two non-physical "Soul Bodies" which inter-penetrate[93] both one another and the physical. These are the Etheric and Astral Bodies. Although Steiner's analysis of man's Soul and Spirit is more complex, for the purposes of education man may be seen as a fourfold being of physical body, Etheric and Astral Bodies (Soul) and Ego (Spirit).

As will become clear, these four bodies can never be correctly understood as isolated concepts since they interpenetrate one another in function as well as presence. Just as oxygen and hydrogen do not constitute water when they are separated, so the fourfold nature of man only comes into its own as a unity. Their interaction is therefore of central importance, and any attempt to separate them physically (for example by means of tables or diagrams, however subtle) distorts their real nature. Steiner's analysis must therefore also be seen as a unity.

The reader should take note especially of Steiner's associations of the Etheric and Astral Bodies with plant and animal life, because this makes the Bodies what they are, not abstract concepts but living elements of man's holistic nature.

In this respect it is well to remember Steiner's warning that the reader who approaches these concepts with only intellectual understanding may be able to formulate a rationally consistent understanding of Steiner's analysis of man, but he will not be able to conceive of the "Bodies" in themselves, as they are within man's own being. In order to truly understand them one would have to develop strongly, by means of Spiritual Science, the kind of awareness that is consistent with the inner nature of the Bodies. The intellect, which uses the physical brain, is only able to understand the physical body, not the other elements which give it life[94].

This analysis of man provides the foundation for Steiner's educational thought, and will be brought to fulfilment in subsequent sections, especially those on child development.

"It is on these four members of the human being that the educator works. Hence, if we desire to work in the right way, we must investigate the nature of these parts of man. It must not be imagined that they develop uniformly in the human being, so that at any given point in his life — the moment of birth, for example — they are all equally far developed. This is not the case: their development takes place differently at the different ages of a man's life. The right foundation for education, and for teaching also, consists in a knowledge of these laws of development of human nature." [95]

3.2.2.1   Etheric Body

"Etheric" has no relationship to the term "Ether" used in Physics, and "Body" should be not understood in the physical sense[96].

Just as man has a physical body in common with the Mineral world, he has an Etheric Body in common with the Plant world[97].   Everything living has an Etheric Body, so that it may also be called the Life Body[98].

The Etheric Body preserves the form of the physical body from disintegration which occurs when it separates from the physical at death[99].   Every organ in the physical body has an Etheric counterpart, except that the "Etheric organs" are far more complicated than the physical ones and they exist "in living interflow and movement." [100]   Since the Etheric Body works to preserve the forms of the physical, it may also be called the "Formative-Force-Body" [101].   The form which the Etheric Body gives to the physical originates archetypally in the Astral Body[102].

Perception of the Etheric Body can be achieved by developing a sense of form in a sculptural manner[103].   It appears to spiritual perception as an extremely fine and delicately organised, peach-blossom coloured structure, approximately the same size as the physical body[104].

The Etheric Body is bound up with pictorial thinking and Feeling (see 4.3.2) and with the Rhythmic System (see 3.3.1.2).   However pictorial thinking can only occur when the Etheric Body is connected with the Astral Body.   When they are disconnected (which happens in dreamless sleep) the pictorial thinking fades[105].

3.2.2.2   Astral Body

The use of the term "Astral" is justified because this "body" is of the same order of existence as the non-physical emanations of stellar worlds[106].

Man has an astral body in common with the animal world, which therefore has three bodies, physical, Etheric and Astral[107].   Animals, like man, have sensations, impulses, instincts and passions, but whereas animals respond directly to these, in man they are interwoven and intercepted by his thought life[108].

The Astral Body contains the "pattern forms or archetypes" for the Etheric and Physical Bodies[109], and these emanate originally from the highest levels of the Spiritual World[110].

To spiritual sight, the Astral Body is really a slightly different form to what is termed the Sentient Soul[111], but in function they are so closely related as to be considered a unity[112]. The Astral Body "awakens" the Etheric[113]. Together with the Etheric the Astral enables the pictorial or image forms of the soul to become conscious[114]. The Astral brings external sense impressions from the physical world to consciousness[115].

The Astral Body first serves to unfold the potentialities brought with the individual from the spiritual world. It then becomes enriched by all the experiences of earthly life, which it bears with it into the soul world after death[116].

An understanding of the Astral Body can only be reached by developing an inner feeling for the rhythm and melody of music[117]. To spiritual perception, the Astral extends beyond the physical body, on all sides[118]. The Astral Body is bound up with the Will (see 4.4) and with the Metabolic and Limb System (see 3.3.1.3).

The Etheric and Astral Bodies go to make up the Soul of man for the purposes of the present analysis. However, Steiner's full analysis is much more detailed and complex[119].

3.2.2.3   Ego

Steiner's use of the term Ego is best translated into English as "the I" [120]. It must be distinguished from any connotations of "egoism" which is "the pursuit of individual satisfaction" [121].

Only man has the Ego, which distinguishes him from animals. The Ego is what gives to life a sense of permanence, or memory[122] and what enables man to develop an inner life, independently of the external world of the senses[123].

> "... life is proper to the etheric body, consciousness to the astral body, and memory to the Ego." [124]

What is considered to be "memory" in animals is really of the order of sensation or impulse, and is quite different from memory in human beings. Whereas man's memory is an activity of thought, animals experience only needs and aversions with respect to past experience[125].

The Ego can exist independently of all external things and for this reason some religious faiths have come to see it as containing a portion of God. The comparison used is, "as the drop is to the ocean, so is the I to the Divine." [126] In the course of life the Ego becomes more and more "ruler of body and soul"[127].

> "... it is this which constitutes the special task of the Ego. Working outward from itself, it has to ennoble and purify the other members of man's nature." [128]

As the Ego "works on " the Etheric it changes from its primary function as a formative force in growth and reproduction and "becomes the vehicle of man's habits, of his more permanent bent or tendency in life, of his temperament and of his memory". [129]

As the Ego works on the Astral, its impulses, desires and passions become transformed into "purified sensations of pleasure and pain, refined wishes and desires." [130]

> "The work penetrates right down into the physical body. Under the influence of the Ego the whole appearance and physiognomy, the gestures and movements of the physical body, are altered." [131]

The activity of the Ego on the three Bodies creates three levels of Soul life:

> "The astral or sentient body, transformed through the Ego, is called the Sentient Soul; the transformed etheric body is called the Intellectual Soul; and the transformed physical body the Spiritual Soul .... From the moment when the Ego lights up, all three bodies are undergoing transformation simultaneously." [132]

The Astral Body receives "sensation"; the Sentient Soul gives it "permanence, duration" [133]. The Intellectual Soul transforms perceptions of external objects into an inner life of the mind, gradually liberating itself from external perception[134]. The Spiritual Soul develops a knowledge and awareness of self[135].

For general purposes, Steiner unites these three elements of soul life into the single concept of Ego[136].

The influence of the Ego on the three bodies goes to create the higher levels of spiritual consciousness[137], but these are not of primary concern for Steiner's educational thought.

The Ego is invisible to spiritual perception, but the results of the Ego's activity are evident in the other bodies[138]. It is brought into expression and awakened most powerfully in speech[139].

3.3   THE RELATIONSHIP BETWEEN BODY AND SOUL

In Steiner's view, modern Psychology had a naïve grasp of the way Man's soul faculties — Thought, Feeling and Will — related to the physical body. So much of modern theory consisted of empty words, devoid of any real understanding. Talk of the "interplay between body and soul", or "psycho-physical parallelism", told us nothing of value[140].

> "That a spiritual philosopher should consider firstly the development of the physical organism may seem to be a fundamental contradiction." [141]

However it was precisely in this way that Spiritual Science proved its value over the modern sciences, which were either wholly physical or else wholly theoretical.

> "For, you see, you may leave the physical body out of account, and perhaps you may attain to a high state of abstraction in your spiritual nature, but it will be like a balloon in the air, flying off. A spirituality not bound to what is physical in life can give nothing to social evolution on the earth." [142]

3.3.1 Analysis of the Physical Body and its Relationship to the Soul

Steiner analysed Man's body into three systems, each of which was related to Thought, Feeling and Will, with one of these predominating. His analysis was done by means of "spiritual sight," but he held that it could be confirmed in retrospect by normal human understanding if modern abstract preconceptions were put aside[143].

Feeling and Will were integrated with Thought in normal life, but were separate faculties in themselves. Modern Psychology tended to think of them as having a basis in Thinking, or a cognitive core, because they were apprehended by thinking. In reality the link was indirect, and they had separate expressions in the physical body[144]. When the soul underwent spiritual training, these three faculties became quite independent and had to be consciously ordered by the Ego[145].

The three systems in Man fully interpenetrated one another, and none acted in isolation from the others. The analysis therefore had to be understood in terms of its unity in the living man[146].

The three systems are the Nervous System, the Rhythmic System, and the Metabolic and Limb System[147].

3.3.1.1 Nervous System

Steiner also referred to the Nervous System as the Head System[148] or Head Man[149] in order to convey the concept of the nervous system pervading the whole Man, but dominating the Head area[150].

The Head contains parts of the Rhythmic System, in the form of the nose for breathing, and the Metabolic and Limb System, in the form of the mouth and jaw for eating[151]. The Head System of Man is more fully physically evolved than the other systems[152].

The physical body has stronger influence in the Head than the other bodies. The Etheric, Astral and Ego have progressively weaker activity in the Head[153].

The Head is responsible for thought, ideation and conceptualisation, but these are not autonomous processes. They are the results, or "reflections" of what occurs

58

in the other systems, where the Astral Body and Ego are more active[154].

The Head serves as a synthetic system for the activities in the lower organism[155] and it is through the Head that the formative forces of the Etheric Body flow into the lower organism. This activity is strongest in the first seven years (approximately) and is completed around the twentieth year[156].

3.3.1.2 Rhythmic System

Steiner also referred to the Rhythmic System as the Chest System[157] or Chest Man[158] in order to convey the concept of a centralised system which pervaded the whole body.

The rhythm of heart beat and breathing in their approximate four to one ratio, constitute the basis of the Rhythmic System.

"It is this inner interplay and relationship of pulse rhythm and breath rhythm, and its connection in turn with the more extended rhythmic life of the human being, that constitutes the rhythmic nature of man — a second nature over against the head or nerve nature." [159]

The Etheric Body is the most active body in the Rhythmic System[160], the physical, Astral and Ego having progressively weaker influence.

Feeling is bound up with the Rhythmic System[161]. It is this system which is most active between the time when the child changes his teeth, up until puberty[162].

Physical impressions are conveyed to the Head which then reflects them into the Rhythmic System where they are transformed into sense impressions such as sound[163]. Sensation is therefore an activity of the Rhythmic System and its conceptualisation in the Head is a reflection of this.

Similarly, mental processes which are bound up with feeling, such as the process of judgement which has feeling accompanying it, takes place in the Rhythmic System, and is only then apprehended and conceptualised in the Head[164].

Man is not aware of these processes because his feelings are not fully conscious experiences, but are only semi-conscious as in dream consciousness[165].

3.3.1.3 Metabolism and Limb System

Steiner also referred to this as the Limb System because he considered that "Metabolism is very intimately connected with movement"[166]. He also called it the Limb Man[167] in order to convey the idea that what was centralised in the limbs also pervaded the whole body.

The Will is bound up with the Metabolic and Limb System.

"The 'movement system' and 'metabolic system' I hold to be the third member of the human organism. And with this the will is immediately bound up. Every will impulse in man is accompanied by a particular form of the metabolic process which has a different mode of operation

59

from that of the nerve processes which accompany the activity of thinking." [168]

The Astral Body is most active in the Metabolic and Limb System.

"In regard to the head, man is mostly physical body. In regard to the chest organs, the organs of rhythm, man is mostly ether body. In regard to the metabolic organs he is mostly astral body. The ego has no distinct expression in the physical world as yet." [169]

The Ego's activity in the body only begins to take place from around the twenty first year[170]. The Ego rises as a force which "paralyses" the formative activity of the Etheric Body which is working down through the Head System[171].

The Ego "has its ground of support in legs and feet."[172] Together with the Astral Body, the Ego forms the Will, which uses muscles and blood as its organic instruments[173].

Like the Rhythmic System, the Metabolic and Limb System is closely bound up with the senses[174]. The Will and Limb System is also where mental processes involving decisions or conclusions originate. These are then conceptualised and made conscious by the Head system[175]. However, it is the Will which "directs the course" of the individual[176]; the concept is only a reflection of Will activity.

If, therefore, Logic is seen as a threefold matter of forming concepts, passing judgement thereon, and drawing conclusions[177], it is evident that only the first stage – forming concepts – is done in the Head. The whole body participates in the full process[178].

The reason that man is not aware of the contribution made by the Will to the logical process is that Will activity is unconscious, as if asleep. The whole process of Metabolism takes place unconsciously and automatically, without any need for conscious control. The Ego does manifest itself slightly through cognition in images, but otherwise only spiritual discipline will bring it into fuller consciousness[179].

These three systems are all an essential part of Education:

"Right regard and care for the three members of the threefold human being is the mark of true education. We have to see that each member plays its part, and we have also to see that all three interact rightly in and with one another." [180]

3.3.2 The Senses

Steiner identified twelve senses instead of the customary five[181]. In life these interweave in unlimited combinations and permutations, but in education, each one ought to be carefully developed[182]. Only a brief listing of them is possible here.

Firstly, there are the senses which are mostly to do with the Head System. These are the "Ego Sense" in which one senses not one's own Ego, but that of

60

others[183]; the "Thought Sense" through which one senses the thoughts of others through their whole demeanour, not only through speech[184]; the "Sense of Hearing" and the "Sense of Speech" in which one senses all that is expressed in the production of speech[185]. These senses are mainly connected with Thinking.

Secondly, there are the senses which are mostly to do with the Rhythmic System[186]. These are the "Sense of Smell", the "Sense of Taste", the "Sense of Sight", and the "Sense of Warmth" which should not be confused with the sense of touch[187]. Each of these is mainly connected with Feeling.

Thirdly, there are the senses mostly to do with the Limb System, which are penetrated by the activity of the Will. These are the "Sense of Touch"; the "Sense of Life" whereby one senses one's well being in the conditions of one's body; the "Sense of Movement" and the "Sense of Balance"[188].

This chapter has outlined the process by which Steiner achieved his insights into man's Soul and Spirit, has summarised his analysis of man's Bodies, and has traced his description of the ways in which the physical and soul bodies are related. The next chapter puts this analysis into the context of human development, and shows how Steiner extrapolated conclusions for education.

4

THE STAGES OF DEVELOPMENT AND THEIR IMPLICATIONS FOR EDUCATION

This chapter describes the main features of Steiner's perception of the way in which man's physical body, Soul Bodies and Ego develop during the first twenty years of life. This period sees the completion of the gradual process of "incarnation" in which the child grows to manhood, mature in thought, feeling and will. Although Steiner sees this development as a natural process, he considers it man's task to harmonise the child's body, Soul and Spirit through education, and that only a knowledge of man founded in Spiritual Science can reveal the way to achieve this effectively.

Approximately every seven years in the life of man "... certain powers not in operation before make their appearance or are forthcoming in greater strength." [1] These periods should not be interpreted crudely[2]. The seven year pattern may vary[3] and each change takes place gradually, reaching its culmination about that time[4].

By careful observation, and particularly spiritual perception, these changes can be seen taking place even in the later years of life[5]. Physical changes are more noticeable in childhood, but spiritual observation reveals that such physical changes are secondary phenomena, and are caused by deeper changes in the soul of man[6].

Each stage has relevance for every other stage:

"We must realise at the outset that life is essentially a unity. We cannot take a piece out of it and consider that piece on its own account without doing injury to life itself." [7]

Therefore it is out of an understanding of the developmental sequence of the whole individual, particularly during his early life, that an education ought to be drawn. One ought not to think up "the most wonderful programmes for what should take place in education"; the basis for education is not to be found in abstract ideas, but in what the inner nature of the child is found to be. Education is a concern of life itself and must be drawn from life to be practicable[8].

As Steiner had maintained more than a decade before the founding of the first Waldorf School:

> "We shall not set up demands nor programmes, but simply describe the Child-nature. From the nature of the growing and evolving human being, the proper point of view for Education will, as it were, spontaneously result." [9]

4.1 THE LIFE BEFORE BIRTH

The "spiritual kernel" of the human being may have existed for thousands of years, and entered into physical incarnation numerous times[10].

4.1.1 Reincarnation

Many erroneous ideas about Reincarnation exist, especially some from India which were spread by people who did not have proper spiritual insight into the process[11]. Reincarnation must be seen from a spiritual perspective:

> "The human spirit is its own species. And just as man, as a physical being belonging to a species, transmits his qualities within the species, so does the <u>spirit</u> within its species, that is, within itself. <u>In each life the human spirit appears as a repetition of itself with the fruits of its former experiences in previous lives.</u>" [12]

The reasons for reincarnation must also be understood from a spiritual perspective[13]. It is what the spirit wishes to bring to and learn from the physical world that impels it to reincarnate.

> "Thus the physical world is both the scene of his creating and of his learning. What has been learned is then transmuted, in the Spiritland, into living faculties of the spirit." [14]

The fruits of the spirit's earthly life are completely spiritualised in the higher levels of the spiritual world, so that before it reincarnates it has lost all connection with the physical world[15]. The spirit, or Ego, which then takes on new bodies, works from unconscious depths[16] and it is only present "in embryo" during earthly life[17].

With the help of Beings in the spiritual world, the Ego is invested with Astral, Etheric and physical bodies[18]. This process is impelled by the desire of the Ego to put right its former deeds on earth, in accordance with the spiritual law of Destiny, or "Karma", which is an expression of the Ego's own Will[19].

4.1.2 The Law of Karma

The Law of Karma "chains" man to the physical world[20]. The conditions that a man creates in one incarnation must be balanced in a subsequent incarnation, so that each man creates his own destiny, or Karma[21].

"Thus does the former life wield a determining influence upon the new; the deeds of the new life are, in a way, caused by the deeds of the old. In this relationship of law and causation between an earlier and a later life we have to recognise the real Law of Destiny — often denoted by a word taken from Oriental Wisdom, the law of 'Karma'." [22]

The circumstances in which the individual finds himself in each life are by no means accidental. They are carefully planned in great detail from the spiritual world[23].

"For the incarnating spirit brings its destiny with it from its previous incarnations. And this destiny determines its life. What impressions the soul will be able to have, what wishes it will be able to have gratified, what sorrows and joys shall grow up for it, with what individuals it shall come into contact — all this depends on the nature of the actions in the past incarnations of the spirit. Those people with whom the soul was bound up in one life, the soul must meet again in a subsequent one, because the actions which have taken place between them must have their consequences. When this soul seeks re-embodiment, those others, who are bound up with it, will also strive towards their incarnation at the same time. The life of the soul is therefore the results of the self-created destiny of the human spirit." [24]

Karma is also bound up with community life, and is not a purely personal matter[25]. Moreover what appears from our physical perspective to be a cruel fate, may be of the deepest value for the Ego of man:

"That which then, in the following earth-life, appears as painful destiny from the point of view of that life — nay, is perhaps deeply bewailed as such — is the very thing the man in this region of the Spiritland finds absolutely necessary for himself." [26]

However, this does not mean that the educator or doctor should not try to help a child suffering as a result of Karma. Curative education in particular is concerned with such intervention.

"Whenever we give treatment to a backward child, we are intervening in karma. And it goes without saying, we must intervene in karma in this way. For there is such a thing as right intervention." [27]

Such intervention aims to bring about in the child what "would otherwise be brought to fulfilment at a later time." [28] It requires a developed sense of respon-

65

sibility and courage to undertake such spiritual work[29]. In addition, whether or not a condition is a manifestation of Karma cannot be known except by spiritual sight, so that the teacher must approach every child with the assumption that he will follow the normal developmental process. The necessary experiences must be given at the appropriate ages.

> "The development of the human being is a mysterious matter, and in all that we strive for in teaching and education we should never reckon with the abnormal but always with the normal." [30]

4.1.3 Incarnation

Neither physical heredity nor environmental factors can account for the spiritual nature of individuals. Individuality expresses itself in something that reaches beyond these earthly influences[31].

> "It is a quaint and no doubt a trite comparison, yet to an open mind it is surely apposite: a man who has fallen into the water will be wet, but his wetness is no evidence of his inner nature." [32]

There are deeper laws governing the presence, or lack, of "innate talents" in a child than the law of physical heredity[33]. However, physical heredity is an enormously strong influence[34] and the incarnating soul itself affects the physical processes, thereby transmitting soul qualities into the physical body[35].

Physical heredity from the child's parents is a particularly strong determinant in the first stage of life, but after the change of teeth the Ego begins to assert itself[36]. The stronger the Ego, the greater will be its influence upon the inherited physical body. A weak Ego will result in a physical body which will be a "slavish copy" of the inherited one[37].

At incarnation the strongest formative forces from the spiritual world work on the head. The strongest influences of physical heredity work on the Rhythmic and Limb Systems. It is therefore the lower two systems that have closest contact with the physical world[38].

The Ego is working itself into the physical body and affecting its development even from the spiritual world. Usually incarnation involves a struggle on the part of the Ego to prepare the physical body, as the inherited characteristics may not be in harmony with its own nature[39].

Life in the spiritual world is altogether different from life in the physical world, and this must be understood if the correct prenatal educative environment is to be given to the child. In the spiritual world, the Ego lives within other beings and they within him. A condition of complete mutual sympathy exists. This attitude of spirit does not change at incarnation and the child in the womb is constantly suffused by the soul of his mother. This is the profound basis of the faculty of imitation which plays a central role in the first stage of the child's life[40].

"Hence a prenatal education cannot be addressed to the child himself. It can only be an unconscious result of what the parents — especially the mother — achieve. If until birth the mother behaves in such a way that she brings to expression in herself what is morally and intellectually right, in the true sense of the word, then of its own accord what the mother achieves in this continuous self education will pass over to the child." [41]

4.2 BIRTH TO THE "CHANGE OF TEETH"

The phrase "change of teeth" is consistently used by Steiner to refer to the time when the primary teeth are lost and the permanent teeth emerge. This stage of development lasts for approximately the first seven years after the child is released from the protective envelope of the mother's womb. Birth enables the child to exist as an independent physical organism[42].

The Etheric and Astral Bodies are not yet born and are held in Etheric and Astral "envelopes" which surround the physical body[43.]

4.2.1 Development

The Etheric Body which is held within the Etheric envelope works within the physical body as a shaping, moulding[44] and organizing[45] force which streams down from the Head into the lower organism.

The physical body is a wholly undifferentiated sense organ[46]. This is because the Etheric and Astral Bodies are not yet born and the three Systems of Head, Rhythm and Limbs are therefore not yet differentiated. Their development is gradual. The sense of Taste is experienced throughout the body so that, when feeding, the young child kicks his legs and waves his arms in the all pervading experience of Taste. The other senses work similarly[47].

The Astral Body, held within the Astral envelope, has no independent soul life yet. It works directly in the organs of the body[48].

The Ego is still largely outside the physical body, in the environment, but it is active in the limbs, particularly the legs[49].

The Etheric body therefore works down from the Head as a formative force. The Ego works up from the legs as an awakening force[50]. The child is disorganised in his limbs until the Etheric force begins to penetrate them, enabling him to begin to walk[51]. He is asleep in his head until the Ego begins to penetrate it, enabling him to become conscious of his environment[52], to begin to talk, and to become aware of himself as an Ego[53]. The first traces of memory begin with the purposeful use of the limbs when the child starts to walk[54].

4.2.2 The Process of Imitation

Because the Etheric, Astral and Ego are deeply absorbed in the development of the physical body, and because the physical body is at first an undifferentiated sense organ, the Spirit, Soul and Body are not separated in the young child. They operate as a unity[55]. Therefore whatever is experienced by the physical body in the form of sensation is drawn directly into the Soul and Spirit, and whatever is experienced by the Ego is drawn directly into the physical body[56].

The child is enormously receptive in his Senses, and whatever is observed or heard or tasted is drawn into his unity of Body, Soul and Spirit where it is reproduced[57]. Furthermore, the Ego, which has retained its tendency from the spiritual world to live sympathetically in its surroundings, absorbs the environment of Soul and Spirit in which it finds itself. This is drawn into the Soul and physical body where it is reproduced[58].

> "There are indeed such influences that pass from man to man, aroused by things which are almost if not wholly imperceptible to men today. These things occur in the intercourse between men and animals, and they occur also in man to an enhanced degree when the soul and spirit are not yet free of the body, namely in early childhood. The little child can really perceive the morality which underlies every look and gesture of the people around him, though this may be no longer possible for those who are older. It is therefore of the utmost importance that we should never allow ourselves to think ugly thoughts in the presence of the child, for not only will this live on in his soul, but will work right down into his physical body." [59]

The process of reproducing what is perceived within the Body, Soul and Spirit, is called Imitation[60]. Originating to a great extent in the child's life in the spiritual world, it has the character of complete and naïve trust. The child believes that everything in his environment is true, as it was in the spiritual world[61]. Similarly his impulse to imitate his surroundings is the continuation of his impulse to be one with his environment in the spiritual world[62].

4.2.3 Educational Implications

This stage is the most important one in the whole of life[63], and great respect must be paid to the being of the child. Just as the organs of the physical body are protected from the direct influences of the external world before birth, so the Etheric and Astral Bodies and the Ego must not be directly educated. At this stage their task is to work within the body as a unity, and the faculties which they give rise to later, such as thought, memory, feeling and will, must not be drawn from the child[64]. Premature or wrong influences on the child have a harmful effect on the whole of his later life[65]. The educator should not take advantage of the early awakening of thought before the change of teeth. External instruction which is imposed at an early age harms the child's development[66].

The Head System is unconscious and dreaming in early childhood, and its education should be indirect.

"All we have really to do is to develop the limb man and part of the chest man. For after that it is the task of the limb man and the chest man to awaken the head man. Here we come to the true function of teaching and education." [67]

The first influence in this educative process beginning in the limbs is milk, a product of nature, which has properties beyond those of physical nutrition. Milk has a direct connection with the Limb System.

"The milk producing organs can be said to be a continuation of the limbs, inwards. Both in the animal and human kingdoms milk is the only substance which has an inner connection with the limbs, which is, as it were, born of the limbs, and hence retains the power of the limbs within it. And as we give the child milk it works upon the sleeping spirit and awakens it — the only substance, essentially, which can do this. Here the spirit that dwells in all matter asserts itself in its rightful place. Milk bears its own spirit within it, and this spirit has the task of awakening the sleeping spirit of the child. This is no mere picture, it is a profound scientific truth that the genius in Nature, which creates the substance milk from out of secret depths, is the awakener of the human spirit in the child." [68]

With the earliest stirring of the Ego in the limbs, the first purposeful movements are made as the beginnings of "play" [69]. Thus Nature cares for the infant's "education", and the work of the educator is to continue the awakening process from the limbs. The essential principle is that the awakening forces and soul bodies are already within the child; they do not have to be implanted by the educator.

"We can awaken what is in the child, but we cannot implant a content into him." [70]

A child must not be forced to walk, but rather helped, with utmost respect for the inner mystery which impels it. Coercion exercises parts of the soul and spirit which ought to be left to continue their work on the development and strengthening of the physical body. The effects of this remain in the body and may result in diseases related to metabolism in later life[71].

Speech does not only arise from the upper part of the body; it involves the whole organism, and the developing control of the limb system is reflected in speech. As the child's impulse to walk is lovingly assisted, so will his control of speech strengthen.

"Speech arises from the entire motor-organism of the human being. How the child learns to walk, to orientate himself in space, to transmute the first erratic and uncontrolled movements of the arms into gestures definitely related to the outer world – all this is carried over by the mysterious processes of the human organism to the head, and manifests as speech." [72]

Imitation plays a much deeper role than is normally recognised. Not only are the outer forms of speech imitated, but its inner character of truthfulness is absorbed into the whole bodily organism of the child, particularly the breathing.

"A child whose teachers are filled with inner truthfulness will, as he imitates his environment, so learn to speak that the subtle activity constantly generated in the organism by the processes of in-breathing and out-breathing will be strengthened. Naturally, these things must be understood in a delicate and not in a crude sense. The processes are indeed delicate, but are nevertheless revealed in every manifestation of life." [73]

The babble of baby language should never be reflected back to the child. Instead, true, well formed, adult speech should be used. This will lay the foundation not only for sound speech, but also for sound thought. It is at these early stages that the foundation for healthy thinking is laid.

"Just as speech develops from walking and grasping, in short from movement, so thought develops from speech. In helping the child as he learns to walk we must be pervaded by love; in helping the child to gain the power of speech we must be absolutely truthful, and since the child is one great sense organ and in his inner physical functions also copies the spiritual, our own thinking must be clear if right thinking is to develop in the child from the forces of speech.

No greater harm can be done to the child than by the giving of orders, and then causing confusion by reversing them. Confusion that exists in the child's surroundings as the result of inconsequent thinking is the actual root of many so-called nervous diseases prevalent in our modern civilisation." [74]

Between the third and fourth years, elementary Eurythmy[75] and Dance[76] may be done with the child. However, excessive excitement in dancing should be avoided because it evokes the forces of the Astral Body and Ego too strongly, and "dazes" the developing consciousness[77].

The evolving "play" activities of the child must be strongly linked to Imitation:

"Thus we have gradually to learn that it is not so much a question of inventing, out of our own abstract thoughts, all kinds of things for little children to do .... His powers of soul must be aroused, and then he will imitate what the grown-ups are doing. A little girl plays with her doll because she sees her mother nursing the baby. What is to be seen in grown-up people is present in the child as the tendency to imitation" [78]

When the impulse to imitate is not fulfilled in early childhood, it emerges in adolescence as a harmful influence instead of the strengthening foundation for life that it is designed to be. Concerning the adolescent:

"If he has nothing within him that he has acquired through imitation and imagery, which can rise up into his thinking out of the depths of his soul, then, when his thinking should develop at puberty he will find nothing within himself to further his own growth, and his thinking can only reach into emptiness. He will find no anchorage in life, and just at the time when he ought really to have found a certain security in himself he will be running after trivialities; in these awkward years he will be imitating all kinds of things which please him ... and he imitates these things now because he has not been allowed to imitate rightly as a young child in a living way." [79]

Play involves many activities of the soul: joy, pain, sympathy, antipathy, and especially curiosity, a desire for knowledge, which is allied to the impulse to imitate. Play is spontaneous, not constrained into any form of work, and as such, the task of the educator is to watch and ensure that it satisfies the young child. If it does satisfy, then the child's metabolism, particularly his digestion, will be strengthened. If not, the physical results will not be only transitory, they may also affect his metabolic processes in later life, even into old age[80].

The Astral forces which flow upwards from the Limbs, through the Chest, into the Head, and the Etheric forces which flow downwards through the Head System, have a moulding, formative effect on the physical body (see 3.2.2.1). They also take in the living world — which is of a pictorial nature — around them. This is deeply absorbed and influences physical development[81].

The shaping, moulding or pictorial forces at work in the child's being must be correctly met by the educator if they are to be strengthened and not misused. One of the most harmful ways of misusing these inner forces is to give children toys which are too perfect replicas, such as dolls which do all kinds of realistic things. A child's inner nature is wounded by such toys. Far more valuable are simple rag dolls and wooden constructions. The inner Astral and Etheric forces can engage with these imaginatively, and the child can make them his own. Perfect reproductions are hideously inartistic and repel the child's inner nature[82].

The child's whole being can become imaginatively, inwardly alive and active if he is given things into which he can pour his inner forces with strong feeling. Rigid or abstract forms repel the imagination. This is especially true of story telling: the educator must fill his stories, legends and fairy tales with living images and feelings to evoke the child's imagination and awe. Story telling must be done with absolute conviction in order to engage the whole child, and not only his thinking and understanding which is of secondary importance[83].

"All that has to evolve in the etheric body before the seventh year — ideas, habits, memory, and so forth — all this must develop 'of its own accord', just as the eyes and ears develop within the mother-body without the influence of light." [84]

71

4.3   THE CHANGE OF TEETH TO PUBERTY

At about the age of seven the Etheric "envelope" which protects the Etheric Body falls away, and the Etheric Body is "born" [85].

This "second birth" [86] is the culmination of the process that has been going on in the first few years of physical life, that of formation of the physical body by the Etheric embryo. From this point onwards, forces within the physical body play the main role in growth[87].

The birth of the Etheric Body results in a major change in the physical body. The inherited organism is driven out and replaced gradually by another formed by the soul and spirit.

> "The spirit and soul lay hold of the physical body that has its origin in the stream of inheritance. The physical body becomes its model, and on this model an entirely new human organism is formed, and the inherited organism is thereby driven out." [88]

The change of teeth is the most obvious symptom of this, and what is important is not the physical event, but the inner changes of the life of the soul that it signals.

In this stage the child changes from being a unity of Body, Soul and Spirit, to being Body and Soul (Etheric) and a separate nature of Soul (Astral) and Spirit (Ego)[89].

The powers of the soul which emanate from the Etheric Body now become to some extent independent of the rest of the child's being. These powers of the soul are certainly present before this stage, but they only come to maturity and are ready to be developed after the birth of the Etheric[90].

The sense life, which was undifferentiated in terms of soul-life during the first stage, now also becomes more independent of the soul and more physical[91].

The role that Education can play in this stage is to assist the downward flowing Etheric forces and the upward flowing forces of the Astral and Ego to develop as they are meant to, harmoniously.

> "The task of education conceived in the spiritual sense is to bring the Soul-Spirit into harmony with the Life-Body. They must come into harmony with one another. They must be attuned to one another; for when the child is born into the physical world, they do not as yet fit one another." [92]

A knowledge of the way in which the Astral and Etheric Bodies interact enables the educator to work through the Rhythmic and Limb Systems to develop the child's imagination, feeling and will (see 3.3.1.2 and 3.3.1.3). This prepares the way for the awakening of the Head System after puberty (see 4.4.1) and constitutes the foundation for Waldorf Education.   It will be further explicated under 4.5.

4.3.1 From Imitation to Authority

During the course of this stage the child's powers of Imitation gradually diminish. The process by which the child's environment is absorbed by the Ego and transmitted into the Soul and Body, and the process by which sense impressions are absorbed into the Soul and Spirit, are disrupted by the separation out of the Etheric Body. The soul-life becomes increasingly independent of the physical body[93].

This separation changes the child from an Imitative being to one who feels the need for an authority in his life. Imitation is increasingly externalised as a desire for Authority[94]. The need for Authority must be satisfactorily fulfilled during this stage in order to lay the basis for correct development after puberty[95]. Indeed, the individual's sense of security for the whole of life is dependent on the proper fulfilment of this need[96].

It is absolutely inappropriate, therefore, to introduce ideas of *democracy* and *self-direction* into education during this stage[97].

Such ideas are typically based on abstract theory, and not on the actual nature of the child:

> "Although what is revealed in human life is spiritually under the impulse
> of freedom, it is just as fully subject to law as the life of nature. It is,
> therefore, not for us to decide according to our likes or dislikes what
> kind of education should be given to our children between the time of
> the change of teeth and adolescence. Education should rather be dictated
> by the needs of human nature itself." [98]

All education at this stage must be held under the sway of Authority in order to satisfy the child's longing which reaches into his innermost being[99], just as Imitation did before. It must not be an Authority which has to be enforced, but one which arises naturally from what the educator is himself[100]. The strongest and correct way for the educator to develop this Authority is through Art, and all teaching must be pervaded by an artistic approach[101].

4.3.2 Developments in Thinking

The release of the Etheric Body also releases the faculty of thought from the rest of the child's being[102]. The child's concepts become increasingly clear and he begins to form them actively. At the same time his natural memory declines and he starts to make deliberate efforts to note and remember things[103].

However, his thinking is not the abstract thought which is possible in adulthood. The Etheric Body creates thought of a pictorial character[104], and, dominating the Rhythmic System, it is bound up with Feeling[105]. The child's thought is therefore of an imaginative, artistic nature. It is also flexible and living, becoming involved especially with the images presented to it by those that the child deems to be authorities[106].

The word that Steiner used to express the "pictorial character" of the child's thinking was *bildlich*, which includes not only the pictorial, but also the idea of modelling, fashioning, creative industry[107].

Whereas before this age the child did not differentiate himself from the world, he now does so increasingly[108]. He no longer absorbs everything into his being so naïvely and innocently, but nor is he yet able to grasp abstract moral precepts. He is held instead in the sway of his feelings and images of the world.

> "... it is not yet the intellectual element that concerns him but the element of feeling. He takes it in as one takes anything from an accepted authority. Before puberty the child can have no intellectual convictions of right and wrong .... This is why all moral concepts that one brings before the child must be of a pictorial nature." [109]

4.3.3 The Three Substages

Development from the change of teeth to puberty is gradual, and Steiner discerns three substages.

4.3.3.1 The First Substage

This lasts until the child is about nine years old. Imitation is still strong[110] and the child does not yet differentiate himself from the world.

> "Until about the age of nine a child cannot distinguish himself from the world around him. We must only be careful not to apply such abstract concepts as some people do today who say: 'Well, of course, when a child bumps into the corner of a table he hits the table because he thinks that the table is also something living.' This naturally is nonsense. The child does not think the table is a living thing, but rather he treats the table as he would treat another child, because he cannot differentiate himself from the table. Whether it is a living thing or not is of no consequence." [111]

The child still absorbs his experience of the world into his unified being of Body, Soul and Spirit[112], and separation from the world must not be forced on the child since it occurs naturally with the birth of the Etheric Body[113].

The child receives his impressions in the pictorial form of imagination and fantasy[114] through which he is directly bound up with the world around him. This must be respected in education and the child must be given concepts which are pictorially related to the living world[115]. If abstract concepts are given to the child they force a premature separation of the child from the world which spoils the imaginative strength of his thinking in later life.

> "Although it is highly necessary, in view of the nature of our modern

civilisation, that a man should be fully awake in later life, the child must be allowed to remain as long as possible in the peaceful, dreamlike condition of pictorial imagination in which his early years are passed. For if we allow his organism to grow strong in this non-intellectual way, he will rightly develop in later life the intellectuality needed in the world to-day." [116]

The separation of this imaginative thinking from the child's whole being comes with the emergence of the new teeth[117].

4.3.3.2   The Second Substage

This substage lasts from about nine to twelve years of age. The child experiences his inner separation from the world in the form of a feeling of astonishment and wonder for the world. He has, as it were, woken up to the world[118].

If a child is pushed into school too early and forced to do inappropriate activities, the experience of astonishment which he should naturally have at this age is lost, and he is rendered apathetic and insensitive to the world that confronts him. This experience is the foundation for the individual's sense of wonder and beauty, and if it is lost it will affect the whole of his later life[119].

"It is indeed a striking characteristic of our times, that people find nothing in life, and all because they have not learned as children to find life lovely and beautiful. They keep looking all the time for something that shall increase their knowledge — in the most narrow and barren sense of the word. They fail to find the hidden secret beauty that is everywhere around them, and so lose gradually all connection with life." [120]

At this stage the child becomes able to conceptualise the world as a separate reality. He no longer requires only pictures of the world, but can receive simple descriptions of it[121]. However he cannot yet grasp the difference between what is living and what is dead in the world. To him even inorganic nature has life[122]. Education must respond to this by bringing the child an anthropomorphic view of the world[123].

The child must not be sharply detached from nature; his whole feeling must be that he is linked in a living way to the world around him[124].

The sense of wonder, and his feeling for what is alive are part of the need he experiences for a human authority that he can love and admire[125].

Another major feature of this stage is that, as the Etheric separates from the Ego and Astral Body, the Ego consciousness stirs. This Ego activity has important repercussions for the child's inner life. Up to this time the child's whole being has received the world with an indiscriminate and naïve trust. Now he experiences the stirring of his Ego (not intellectually but as a dreamlike feeling[126]) as an impulse to question whether the world is worthy of his trust[127]. It is essential that he receives reassurance from an adult who is able to meet the demand[128]. If the child's trust is not confirmed, a sense of insecurity develops which is rooted deeply in his soul and lingers there, expressing itself in his character, temperament and bodily health, even though he may be unaware of it[129].

The stirring of the Ego is also evident in the child's strengthened self awareness, which helps him to distinguish himself from his surroundings[130].

4.3.3.3   The Third Substage

This lasts from about eleven or twelve years until puberty, and is the culmination of the separation of the Etheric and its integration with the Rhythmic System.

By the age of ten the Etheric is working within the beat and rhythm of the blood circulation and breathing, building the Rhythmic System "in the way which corresponds to its inner disposition." [131] Through this it finds its way into the heart and gradually the rest of the muscular and bone system.

Up to the age of eleven the development of the skeleton is closely bound up with the development of the muscular system. However, when the Etheric Body penetrates this system the skeleton becomes more independent of the muscles and responds more to external demands which are made upon it from the physical world. Before the age of about eleven, movement was an expression of the child's impulses of Feeling and Will, with little heed to the demands of the physical world. By the age of twelve, movement becomes directed increasingly by the physical, mechanical laws of leverage and balance[132].

This has profound implications for the child's consciousness. Firstly, it is only once the Etheric reaches the skeleton, at approximately eleven or twelve years of age, that the child is able to conceptualise the difference between what is living and what is dead in the world[133]. The skeleton, which is of a more mineral, dead nature than the muscles, awakens in the Etheric Body an awareness of what is mineral and dead in the world. This enables the child to look at the world of nature more objectively[134].

Secondly, the child's growing awareness of the laws of mechanics — of leverage and balance — provides the foundation for his awareness of the laws of causality. The child only understands cause and effect properly when they arise out of his own inner experience[135]. This has wide implications for education, not only in science but also in subjects like history.

However, it is the child's concepts of objective phenomena, and their mutual influences and connections, that have developed, and not his ability to understand abstract rules and definitions. These must not be introduced to him until later[136].

4.3.4 Educational Implications

Education between the change of teeth and puberty must work with the Etheric Body in the Rhythmic System:

"In a child between the change of teeth and puberty it is the rhythmic system which preponderates, which has the upper hand .... Hence we must know here: the essential thing is to work with the child's rhythmic system, and everything which works on something other than the rhythmic system is wrong. But now what is it that works upon the rhythmic system? It is _art_ that works upon the rhythmic system, everything that is conveyed in artistic form." [137]

Moral education should not be given in terms of moral precepts, but as living pictures pervaded with feeling. This can be done by means of example, the natural authority of the teacher, or else with symbolic stories which capture the child's feelings. The teacher must never work on the child's intellect:

"We must not engraft moral judgement onto the child. We must so lay the foundation for moral judgement that when the child awakens at puberty he can form his own moral judgement from observation of life.

The last way to attain this is to give finite commands to a child. We can achieve it however if we work by examples, or by presenting pictures to the child's imagination: for instance through biographies or descriptions of good men or bad men; or by inventing circumstances which present a picture, an imagination of goodness to the child's mind. For, since the rhythmic system is particularly active in the child during this period, pleasure and displeasure can arise in him, not judgement as to good and evil — but sympathy with the good which the child beholds presented in an image — or antipathy to the evil which he beholds so presented. It is not a case of appealing to the child's intellect, of saying 'Thou shalt' or 'Thou shalt not,' but of fostering aesthetic judgement, so that the child shall begin to take pleasure in goodness, shall feel sympathy when he sees goodness, and feel dislike and antipathy when he beholds evil." [138]

The child's fantasy, not his intellect, predominates at this stage, and the teacher must meet it by developing his _own_ fantasy [139]. This fantasy is the teacher's means of creating artistic, living images for the child which must be presented with absolute conviction, untainted by condescension or scepticism for the images presented [140]. Where the teacher is unable to believe in his images an intellectual element enters into the telling of them, which the child responds to with the feeling that what the teacher is saying is untrue. This has a destructive, crippling effect on the child [141].

"Through Anthroposophy we ourselves learn once more to believe in the legends, fairy tales and myths, for they express a higher truth in imaginative pictures. And then our handling of these fairy tales, legends and mythical stories will once more be filled with a quality of the soul. Then when we speak to the child, our very words, permeated as they will be by our own belief in the tales, will flow over to him and carry truth with them .... " [142]

These are the images which, permeated with feeling, provide the aesthetic foundation for the development of morality later on. At this stage the child's morality must never be constrained by the compulsions of logic[143].

It is through art that the child's questioning of authority can be answered. As the child sees the teacher working as an artist he feels inclined to do what his teacher is doing; to follow his natural authority[144].

Writing is an activity that the child begins early on in his school life. The alphabet, however, is an abstract, rigid system which has lost its original connections to picture-writing. In order to overcome this problem, writing must always be introduced before reading, and the alphabet presented by being pictorial in character, and artistically related to the world, such as a fish which is transformed into an "f", or mountains into an "m" [145]. Reading must then proceed naturally out of the artistic activity of writing[146].

The outer world must be presented as living in all its facets, with direct appeal to the child's feelings. This is achieved through anthropomorphism, so that the plants, trees and clouds are all living beings that can converse with him. This fills the child's outlook on nature with imagination[147].

> "People have a horror nowadays of Anthropomorphism, as it is called.
> But the child who has not experienced anthropomorphism in its relation
> to the world will be lacking in humanity in later years. And the teacher
> must be willing to enter into his environment with his full spirit and soul
> so that the child can go along with him on the strength of this living
> experience." [148]

Education must also bring the beauty of nature to the child at the right time, so that the wonder that fills him around the ninth year is fulfilled and not dulled[149].

No behaviour of any sort should be instilled into the child through drill[150]. However, repetition has an important role at this stage if what is repeated does not demand the grasp of meaning. It must be an artistic activity that brings the child artistic or abstract material, the meaning of which will only be understood later on in life. It must be given to the child in the form of rhyme, rhythm, beat, melody or the harmony of colours. As long as the child is not required to grasp its meaning, which must remain hidden as a symbolic or unexplained content, such repetitive activities strengthen the child's feeling and will. The repetition enables him to remember, but the intellect is not prematurely aroused[151].

When the child awakens intellectually to the meaning of such material in later life he experiences it as a profound feeling of free and independent activity, which is of great importance to the period of adolescence[152].

As the child sees the world more objectively there should be a gradual, not a sudden transition in education[153]. Stories which evoke the child's imagination must gradually contain simple descriptions. Such description, for example of animals, must not be immediately objective. It must relate directly to man so that the child learns to feel that he is an essential part of the whole world of nature around him, not in an abstract but in a wholly living and real sense. If this is achieved it will provide a firm, unfaltering basis in the child's feeling and will for the introduction of moral concepts later on[154].

Similarly, the mineral kingdom should only be introduced once the child has found his place in the world — in terms of his feelings — towards the plant and animal kingdoms. Then the mineral kingdom is approached through the plant kingdom, which is most closely related to it. Dealing with the mineral world in the abstract, analytical way of modern science "spoils the child's inner mobility of soul" [155].

Physics, chemistry, history and geography must all begin with man and then be related outwards towards causal conceptions. What cannot be presented in this way must be postponed until later on[156].

Towards the end of this stage the child's interest in the outer world should be encouraged by introducing him in an elementary way to industry. For example in the first Waldorf School, Steiner wanted the children to know something about cigarette manufacturing in the Waldorf-Astoria factory, and also other factories. This should begin to draw on everything that the children have learned in other subjects in school[157].

All these activities come to fulfilment after puberty, so that what happens before puberty and what happens afterwards ought to be seen as mutually interdependent in education.

4.4   FROM PUBERTY TO ADULTHOOD

The onset of puberty comes between twelve and sixteen years of age[158]. However, usually around the age of fourteen, the Astral envelope, which has protected the Astral Body up to now, is discarded, and the Astral Body is "born" [159]. The birth of the Astral Body has a profound influence on the child's sense experience of the world (see 4.2.2). At puberty,

"The relation of the sexes is not the whole thing; the exaggerated importance given to it is just a consequence of our materialistic turn of mind. In reality, all connections with the outer world which begin to make their appearance at puberty are fundamentally of the same nature. We should really speak, therefore, not of sexual, but of earthly maturity. And under earthly maturity we have to include the maturity of the senses, the maturity of the breathing and another such sub-division will also be sexual maturity .... The human being ... acquires the faculty of being sensitive and not indifferent to his environment". [160]

This "earthly maturity" results from the release of the Astral Body which then takes hold of the Metabolic and Limb System, of which the sexual organs are a continuation[161]. The Will, which is an expression of the Astral Body, becomes independent of the whole organism[162] and bound up with the Metabolic and Limb System[163].

79

Once again at puberty the Ego stirs[164] and the child becomes aware of himself, this time not as one who is still tied to adult authority but as an individual developing his independence[165] of Thought, Feeling and Will[166].

During this stage the child comes into possession of his own mind[167], a process that only reaches fulfilment around the eighteenth year[168].

Whereas between the change of teeth and puberty the child had a two-fold nature of body and soul (Etheric), and soul (Astral) and spirit (Ego) (see 4.3), after puberty these two sides come into a direct relationship with one another. The physical and Etheric Body constitute man's objective nature, the means by which he relates consciously to the world. The Astral and Ego constitute his subjective nature, which awakens as if from a dream at puberty, and has to begin to relate itself to objective experience. This results in marked changes and developments in the character of the child.

> "The astral body is trying to relate itself in the right way to the experiences that are being undergone by the physical system, and thereby the whole surrounding world. This search for a right relationship between subjective and objective, gives rise to a kind of struggle in the human being, which accounts for the contradiction that children of this age often present." [169]

The Ego remains concealed and mostly inactive in the human being until after the age of about twenty. However, in this respect there is a natural difference between boys and girls. Whereas in boys the Ego remains inactive, it is drawn into the newly released Astral Body of girls. As a result of this, boys become more introverted and shy, and girls more extroverted and eager to express their characters. The liberation of the Ego after the age of about twenty is then more of a struggle for girls than for boys[170].

4.4.1   Developments in Thinking

After the birth of the Astral Body and the subsequent concentration of the Will within the Metabolic and Limb System, the faculty of judgement is mature, and the child begins to develop the ability to draw conclusions and make decisions for himself[171] (see 3.3.1.3). Before this age we may think that he is capable of these soul activities, and the child may even use the appropriate words but he is unable to do them. The child gradually becomes ready to exercise independence of mind and Will, and he experiences "a feeling of personality" [172]. His intellect awakens[173].

Steiner analysed the logical process into the threefold activity of forming a concept, forming a judgement of that concept, and then forming a conclusion about it. These soul activities have already been related to the body as follows: conceptualisation is a function of the Head System, judgement of the Rhythmic System, and conclusion of the Limb System (see 3.3.1.2 and 3.3.1.3). These processes must be studied carefully if the educator is to understand the way in which the development of the intellect ought to proceed.

Logically one would suppose that upon perceiving something, for example a lion, one would form a concept of it, then a judgement, and finally a conclusion. However, Steiner pointed out that in reality one does precisely the reverse. Upon perceiving the lion one first takes the most immediate and conscious step of forming a conclusion about it. It is the formation of the conclusion (lion!) that brings the perception into full consciousness. Having formed this conclusion one then forms a judgement about it (lion – animal ...) and then finally one integrates it with one's former knowledge and develops a concept of it[174].

Because before puberty the Astral Body has not taken hold of the Limb System which enables the forming of conscious conclusions, up until puberty the child's mind remains in a dreamlike state. Its concepts and judgements exist as pictorial images permeated by feelings (see 4.3.2).

When the forming of conclusions develops with the birth of the Astral within the Limb System, the logical process becomes complete, enabling what formerly existed as images to become conscious, logical thinking. This is the "intellect", which is capable of transforming pictorial images into concepts that are independent of images, or of thinking abstractly[175].

Verbalising concepts is not a process of conceptualising, but the reverse. In speaking, concepts are drawn into the form of conclusions[176], arising from the unconscious into the conscious mind[177].

When the teacher is able to grasp this process he will understand the way to educate the intellect correctly. If one attempts (as is done in orthodox education) to instil ready-formed concepts such as definitions into the child's mind, one is working against the natural process of conceptualising. A ready-formed concept contains its own judgement and conclusion, and acts on the child's mind as a rigid, deadening force, because the mind cannot work on it; cannot take it in as a perception and conclusion, transform it through the imagination and judgement and assimilate it into previous experience as a concept[178].

> "It is of very great importance to make it your constant and conscious aim not to destroy anything in the growing human being, but to teach and educate him in such a way that he continues to be full of life, and does not dry up and become hard and rigid. You must therefore distinguish carefully between mobile concepts which you give the child and such concepts as need undergo no change." [179]

4.4.2 Educational Implications for Adolescence

Just as with the previous stages, the task of the educator during the child's adolescence is to prepare him for the next stage which begins approximately after the twentieth year, when he will attain full independence as an adult. This stage is of great importance to the whole of life because it is the time when the child's subjective nature is maturing[180].

4.4.2.1 Preparation

Proper development in this stage depends on correct education in the previous stages. The child's urge to imitate during the first stage must be fulfilled before the need to follow an authority can unfold. Now, after puberty, if his need for and questioning of authority has been met, the adolescent can develop his freedom[181]. But this process cannot be handled by instruction; the child will not respond to being told what he should be or do. It must be grounded in human life:

> "The only right course is that the authority of the teacher, by his words and deeds, gives the child a natural faith. The teacher, who is the real representative of the world as far as the child is concerned, does not prepare him through the control of the understanding or of the capacity to form judgements, but through his own living person he prepares him to evolve further in his contact with the world as a living person himself. Life can only evolve with life." [182]

Intellectual development depends on the foundations laid for it before puberty. All these foundations must be in the form of imagery pervaded by feeling (see 4.3.4) if the intellect is to develop properly after puberty.

> "It is essential that the secrets of Nature, the laws of life, be taught to the boy or girl, not in dry intellectual conceptions, but as far as possible in symbols. Parables of the spiritual connections of things should be brought before the soul of the child in such a manner that behind the parables he divines and feels, rather than grasps intellectually, the underlying law in all existence. 'All that is passing is but a parable', must be the maxim guiding all our education in this period. It is of vast importance for the child that he should receive the secrets of Nature in parables, before they are brought before his soul in the form of 'natural laws' and the like." [183]

If intellectual concepts are given to the child too early, his ability to conceptualise is gradually deadened, eventually affecting his feelings and will. Abstract moral instruction may be especially harmful. The teacher must not

> "... prematurely give the child intellectual conceptions of religion and morality. If we do so before the twelfth or fourteenth year, we are bringing children up to be sceptics — men and women who, instead of healthy insight, in later life develop scepticism in regard to the dogmas inculcated into them — to begin with, scepticism in thought (the least important), but then scepticism in feeling, which makes them defective in feeling. And finally there will be scepticism of will which brings moral error in its train." [184]

4.4.2.2 From Authority to Freedom

If the child has experienced a sound authority relationship before puberty, he will begin to develop independent judgements and conclusions quite naturally afterwards.

"At puberty, a further stage is reached. The child begins to feel that he can judge for himself. He still however needs to feel the support of authority behind him; but the authority must be chosen by himself, must commend itself to him as self evident." [185]

It is important for the child to experience the stage at which he outgrows authority. However he can only do this if earlier he has become accustomed to accepting authority. A feeling of independence can only arise in contrast to a feeling of dependence, so that in order for him to experience the attainment of freedom, authority must pervade the child's life before puberty[186].

This is the only way in which a genuine feeling of freedom can be carried into later life, enabling the individual to find his right place in the Social Life[187].

The natural tendency for boys to withdraw at this age is a particular expression of their developing freedom, just as, in a different way, girls want to be more extroverted. The teacher must show that he understands and accepts these private feelings, and in lessons he must differentiate between the sexes[188]. This differentiation, far from being a reason to separate boys and girls in school, is on the contrary, a reason to have them together to enable them to grow into life with a right understanding of one another[189].

4.4.2.3   The Development of the Intellect

The principle of freedom must pervade all education at this age, even forming the basis for the development of the intellect. The teacher ought not to impress concepts on children after puberty, but give them the means by which they themselves can develop concepts.

"We must strive to educate in such a way that the intellect, which awakens at puberty, can then find its nourishment in the child's own nature. If during his early school years he has stored up an inner treasury of riches through imitation, through his feeling for authority and from the pictorial character of his teaching, then at puberty these inner riches can be transmuted into intellectual activity. He will now always be faced with the task of thinking what before he has willed and felt. And we must take the very greatest care that this intellectual thinking does not appear too early. For a human being can only come to an experience of freedom if his intellectuality awakens within him of itself, not if it has been poured into him by his teachers. But it must not awaken in poverty of soul." [190]

Taught thus, the child is able to develop the ability to conceptualise in the right and natural way. The intellect is properly exercised and strengthened, instead of being dulled (see 4.4.1).

The teacher must therefore learn to transform his intellectual conceptions into artistic conceptions, inspired by Imagination, Intuition and Inspiration. Presented

83

with such imagery, the adolescent feels impelled to abstract intellectual concepts from it, and in so doing he will experience a feeling of the free activity of his spirit[191].

> "If the child is coming into the domain of logic at the age of puberty, we (in our turn) must develop imagery, imagination ... if we can give them pictures, so that they receive images of the world and the work and meaning of the world, pictures which we create for them, as in a high form of art — then they will be held by what we have to tell them." [192]

Through practising the tasks described in <u>Knowledge of the Higher Worlds</u>, the Soul of the teacher is enriched and given the substance needed to transmute knowledge into a more profound, artistic content, pervaded with feeling and integrated with life[193].

Therefore the <u>intellect</u> must develop out of what has previously been absorbed by <u>memory</u>.

> "Those things are afterwards best grasped in concepts which have first been learned simply from memory in this period of life (before puberty), even as the rules of language are best learned in a language one is already able to speak .... Proceeding in this way, we shall be acting with due regard to the nature of the growing child. We shall, however, be offending against his nature, if at the time when the development of the memory is the important thing we are making too great a call upon the intellect." [194]

Concepts in science ought to be developed from direct observation of the facts, by engaging the child's senses, and not from intellectual descriptions and definitions. When the direct method is used, the child's Limb System, his will and feelings are engaged, leading him into the world instead of isolating him in his intellect[195].

Only after the age of about eighteen can the adolescent achieve an altogether objective grasp of the world without the help of an adult, so that up to this time the teacher must guide the use of the child's sense life[196].

Education cannot avoid leading adolescents into certain theoretical activities or abstract concepts such as those of mechanics or mathematics. However, pupils must be shown the relation of such abstractions to life. The understanding of the practical application of such concepts leads what would otherwise exist merely as head-knowledge into the feelings and the will[197].

4.4.2.4 Moral Education during Adolescence

Moral development after puberty will proceed successfully if the child has been able to develop natural feelings of reverence for his educators during the stages of Imitation and Authority. Feelings of reverence and veneration strengthen the Etheric Body, with beneficial effects for the whole thought-life of the individual.

"It is not easy at first to believe that feelings such as those of reverence, respect and so on, have anything to do with cognition. This is because we are inclined to regard cognition as a faculty by itself, unrelated to other happenings in the soul. We forget that it is the <u>soul</u> which exercises the faculty of cognition, and feelings are for the soul what foodstuffs are for the body. If the body is given stones instead of bread, its activities will die away. So too with the soul. Veneration, respect, devotion, are nourishing foodstuffs which make the soul healthy and vigorous, especially in the act of cognition. Disrespect, antipathy, underestimation of what deserves recognition, exert a paralysing, withering effect on the faculty of cognition. For the spiritual investigator this fact is visible in the aura." [198]

Before puberty, morality must be brought to the child in the form of stories, which arouse strong feelings of sympathy for, and pleasure in what is good, and antipathy and displeasure for what is evil. When the child reaches puberty, the aesthetic moral images that he has been given will be transformed into true moral understanding of right and wrong. The teacher "should not rob the child of the satisfaction of awakening to morality of his own accord." [199]

When the child's imagination and feelings are stirred by the teacher, the child's Rhythmic System is affected, and the influences reach deeply into the body itself through the breathing and the blood[200]. Therefore everything within the teacher's being must be imbued with a health-giving religious attitude of thankfulness and reverence towards the cosmos that has given man life. The teacher must be able to find an inner joy through gratitude which will pass over into the child's soul through the images he gives.

"The final chapter of every philosophy, in its effect on human feeling at all events, should be gratitude towards the cosmic powers. This feeling is essential in a teacher and educator, and it should be instinctive in every person who has the nurture of the child entrusted to him. Therefore the first thing of importance to be striven for in spiritual knowledge is the acquiring of thankfulness that a child has been given into our keeping by the universe." [201]

The correct approach to sex education in adolescence is through the development of strong aesthetic feelings for what is noble and beautiful in nature. Such feelings will restrain the tendency for the adolescent to become sensual or erotic, which is caused by the body's subjugation of the soul. The soul must be strengthened to enable the child to differentiate himself, as a free being, from the influences of the body.

"When you lead children to feel the beauty and glory of sunrise and sunset, to be sensitive to the beauty of flowers and the majesty of thunder and lightning, when, in short, you develop in them the aesthetic sense, you are doing far more for them than if you were to give them the

85

sex-instruction which it has now become customary to give to children in their tenderest youth, and which is often carried to quite absurd lengths. A feeling for beauty, an aesthetic approach to the world, these are the things that hold back the erotic nature within its proper limits." [202]

The teacher must not try to force conventions of morality or religion onto the child in a canonical, dogmatic way, but rather he must respect the child's unfolding judgement so that the child can feel confidence in his developing sense of manhood[203].

The adolescent is strongly influenced by the concerns of his future[204], and education must strengthen him to face the future. The way to do this is through ideals which will serve to lead him into life with confidence.

"And just as man's physical body needs strong, well-shaped bones if it is not to stagger and stumble but walk straight, so in this age of life does the astral body, within the ego enclosed within it, need ideals. I mean this in all earnest. Ideals, concepts that partake of the character of will — these must now be introduced, like a firm scaffolding, into the astral body." [205]

Such ideals should not be abstract principles but images of heroic figures and their deeds[206].

The adolescent must be given a foundation for his Social and Economic Life to complement his Spiritual Life. The three areas of life are completely interdependent for the full development of the human being.

4.4.2.5 The Social and Economic Life

In one of Steiner's most sincere and moving lectures, he described two great spiritual impulses which he saw striving to emerge in modern man.

"We see emerging in the depths of the soul, although misjudged and misunderstood today by the majority of civilised humanity, two moral impulses of supreme importance .... If people want to put them into practice, they do not know as a rule what to do with them. Nonetheless they are arising: in the inner life of man the impulse of moral love, and outwardly, in the intercourse between human beings, the moral impulse of confidence." [207]

Love and confidence would give men the strength of will to accomplish their deeds in the future. Moral love would give each individual the desire for selfless service, and confidence would lead him towards his fellow man. A new Social Life would only begin when these impulses took hold in each individual.

Steiner argued that ethical individualism was one of the forces which would enable man's evolution to progress[208] so that education had to work to that end.

One of the most destructive influences in modern social life is the sense of uncertainty engendered in people by their ignorance of industrial life and mechanisation. Education must strive to prevent this by introducing adolescents to the elements of mechanics, the construction of machines, and to surveying and planning methods in modern life[209].

Confidence must be developed in children by introducing them to practical applications of the physics and chemistry they learn in school, and through elementary technical skills such as spinning, weaving and woodwork. Children must experience practical life in this way to develop confidence in themselves and their contributions to life[210]. Education must always remain in touch with contemporary life, and not be completely absorbed in the past or in abstract intellectualism.[211]

Practical activities transform intellectual knowledge so that "thinking is led away from the head and carried down into the inner mobility of the hand." [212]

Education must also consciously awaken a sense of selfless love for mankind in the adolescent, which will encourage him to reach out to others in his life.

> "Brotherliness, fraternity, in economic life as it has to be striven for in the future, <u>can only arise in human souls if education after the fifteenth year works consciously towards universal human love.</u> That is, if all concepts regarding the world and education itself are based on human love, love toward the outer world." [213]

Love and confidence will guard men from being harmed by meaningless activities in industrialism, and will prevent them from being drawn into the world of the machine which has even pervaded the Social Life[214].

These methods are the only means by which the chasm which has opened up between adults and youth can be closed. The youth have rejected the authority of adults because they cannot identify with the materialism and intellectualism which such authority seeks to impose. But in rejecting it they find they have nothing to replace it; they have no inner substance from which to work. The result is that they find themselves wandering, unable to see what has gone wrong, and unable to achieve anything of practical value[215]. They cannot relate to their fellow man:

> "Proper imitation develops freedom; Authority develops the rights life; Brotherliness, love, develops the economic life. But turned about it is also true. When love is not developed in the right way, freedom is lacking; and when imitation is not developed in the right way, animal instincts grow rampant." [216]

4.5   EDUCATION OF THE WHOLE CHILD

The following section shows how everything that is present within the Soul of the Child while he is at school can be educated. The Soul has a three-fold nature of Thinking, Feeling and Will, each of which has an intimate connection with the human body, and the teacher must know how they interact before he can educate the whole child.

Steiner considered that modern man had almost lost his intuitive understanding of the way in which the Will and Feeling were educated, leaving it increasingly to chance[217].

The Head System is the centre of Thinking, the Rhythmic System of Feeling, and the Limb System of Willing (see 3.3.1.1 to 3.3.1.3). Just as the three bodily systems have no rigid demarcations between them, so too Thinking, Feeling and Will also interpenetrate each other.

> "... we can only say that will activity is chiefly will activity and has an undercurrent of thought within it; and thought activity is chiefly thought activity and has an undercurrent of will. Thus, in considering the separate faculties of soul, it is impossible to place them side by side in a pedantic way, because one flows into the other." [218]

Thinking, Feeling and Will come into being through the interaction of the downward flowing forces of the Etheric and the upward flowing Astral forces. It is this interaction which is of interest to education (see 4.3).

The Etheric forces descend through the Head System into the body, and have an inner character of "antipathy". The Astral forces ascend through the Limb System and have a "sympathetic" character[219]. Both forces give rise to different kinds of pictorial activity. The Astral pictures are living and coming into being (*"Fantasie"*, like an inspired sketch, vital and capable of evolution and growth[220]). The Etheric pictures are static, dead reproductions of past life (*"Vorstellung"*, like a photograph taken of a finished building)[221].

The antipathetic force of the Etheric apprehends the sympathetic force of the Astral, which carries living sense-experience in vital pictorial images upwards into the Head System. The Etheric transforms these living images into fixed, static pictures which have conceptual form[222].

The interaction of the sympathetic and antipathetic forces has several important consequences. Memory and the development of personality depend on the antipathetic force to separate man from the world[223]. It is the antipathetic force which prompts us to reject our instinctual life and develop moral ideals in opposition to it[224]. All abstract concepts depend on antipathetic forces to exist[225].

Both forces are essential to thinking, but if thought is excessively antipathetic it has a hardening, decaying influence on the whole of man's being, even on the body itself. The antipathetic process of transforming all living experience into fixed concepts must be countered by the strengthening of the sympathetic forces of the Astral Body which exist in living images. Education must therefore strive to bring children "as many imaginations as possible." [226]

The sympathetic force has a Will nature; the antipathetic force has a cognitive nature[227], and where they interact Feeling arises. The meeting of the sympathetic and antipathetic forces takes place in the Rhythmic, or Chest System, where the Astral animates the Etheric, giving rise to the basic two-fold nature (sympathy-antipathy) of Feeling.

> "In the soul as a whole you cannot keep thought and will strictly apart, and

88

still less can you keep the thought and will elements apart in feeling. In feeling, the will and thought elements are very strongly intermingled." [228]

Sense experiences are held by the sympathetic Will as living images which are carried towards the Head or Nervous System. When they encounter the antipathetic Etheric forces, Feelings arise. Then they are transformed into cognition as concepts and memories[229].

This is directly related to the "logical process" of concept, judgement and conclusion which was used to show the developmental sequence of logical cognition (see 4.4.1).

The implication for education is that everything given to the child through his Will flows into Feeling and thence into Thinking. This is a living influence which vitalises Feeling and Thinking. Conversely, if education deals with rigid, dead concepts, the Will and Feelings receive no sustenance and remain unconscious or semi-conscious. As such they are unable to arouse the imagination with anything but physical, animal urges. Education must therefore work on the Limb and Rhythmic Systems, which will then flow into Thinking and awaken the Head System with healthy influences[230]. In this way the Etheric and Astral forces can be brought into harmony with one another[231].

The following section will show how education can work from the Will into Feeling and Thinking through the central principle of Art.

4.5.1 Thinking

Steiner perceived that Thinking had changed in the course of history. From the Atlantean into the Egypto-Chaldean ages, Thinking still contained strong Will influences which brought man direct consciousness of the way in which the spiritual cosmos worked within his Soul and body. During the Greco-Latin age the sympathetic forces were increasingly overcome by antipathetic, cognitive forces, capable of logic, memory and conscious conceptualisation. In the modern age the antipathetic forces in Thinking have become so strong that they overwhelm the sympathetic, and man has lost almost every trace of awareness of the spiritual, moral impulses which once sustained his Thinking[232].

> "We may say, it is still barely possible, if men exert their intelligence and do not bear especially wild instincts in themselves, to look toward the light of what is good. But human intelligence will more and more develop the inclination to plan evil, to bring error into knowledge, and insert evil into man's moral life." [233]

What modern man experiences as "thinking-cognition" is only the antipathetic force within the Head System. He is hardly aware of the sympathetic forces. Yet, if these sympathetic forces were somehow shut off from the Head System unconsciousness would result, because living sensations and imaginings would no longer exist to be apprehended by the Head System. Thus the Head System is only the reflector of Thinking, not its originator[234].

Memory arises because of a complex process of imagination within the sympathetic Feeling and Will forces, which are grasped by the Head System as "a complex of mental pictures." [235] (see 4.5.2)

As the child grows up, the antipathetic forces of cognition grow stronger, especially once the Etheric is liberated. If children are urged to use this kind of cognition with fixed concepts, their thinking becomes increasingly devoid of the sympathetic, living nature of sensation and imagination, and their awareness becomes increasingly bounded by fixed concepts. The intellect becomes "hardened" and unaware of the way it receives information about the world from the depths of its being. It comes to believe itself to be isolated from the world[236].

The "hardening" of cognition ultimately has an effect on the physical body, predisposing man to diseases such as sclerosis[237].

It is essential to note that in this analysis of "thinking-cognition", Steiner is not making a case for education to be based on fantasy divorced from reality. Precisely the opposite is intended. Thinking here is a process set in motion by sensations from the world itself, and the sympathetic imagining process conveys perceptions in a living stream towards the Head System. These are grounded in reality, even though imagining and fantasy may follow their own course. The danger is not in leading the child into the real world through sense-experience. Such activity is life-giving. Harm is done by introducing abstract concepts about such direct sense-experience, or worse still, abstract concepts unrelated to the real world.

> "... I would earnestly beg you to make it a rule not to let anything come into your teaching and education that is not in some way connected with life.

> The same rule applies when you ask the children to describe something themselves. You should always call their attention to it if they stray from reality. The intellect never penetrates as deeply into reality as fantasy does. Fantasy can go astray, it is true, but it is rooted in reality, whereas the intellect remains always on the surface. That is why it is so infinitely important for the teacher himself to be in touch with reality as he stands in his class." [238]

Even legends, fairy tales and myths must be chosen not because they are an escape from life, but because they express truth in the living forms of imaginative pictures. Thereby they enable the child to enter into the world with sympathetic imagination which will later be transformed into concepts and then subjected to judgement[239]. (see 4.4.1)

Steiner's use of the terms "fantasy" and "imagination" have a deeper meaning than intellectual picturing. He referred to the kind of thinking that the teacher works with as *Gemüt* for which there is no exact English equivalent, except that of the medieval sense of "mind" which comes from the heart and feelings[240].

4.5.2 Feeling

Feeling is bound up with the Etheric Body in the Rhythmic System, and though it receives impulses from the Astral Body, Feeling must be helped to develop separately from the Will between the change of teeth and puberty. As Feeling develops, it becomes free to unite with thinking-cognition after puberty. Cognition which becomes permeated by Feeling has the quality of authority. Unless the Feeling of the child is strengthened independently of his Will, it remains almost unconscious and vaguely associated with Will impulses[241].

Feeling is educated through parables and pictures, especially stories conveying pictures of great historical figures. It is also educated by studying the secrets and beauties of nature, and by cultivating a sense of beauty and artistic feeling. The child's sense of rhythm must be awakened through music and he must develop a feeling for moulding and sculpture, line forms, design and architectural forms. A feeling for musical and colour harmonies must also be developed. Such education is possible whatever the economic circumstances of a community.

"However simple life has to be under certain circumstances, the objection can never hold that the circumstances do not allow of anything being done in this direction. Much can be done with the simplest means, if only the teacher himself has the right artistic feeling. Joy and happiness in living, a love of all existence, a power and energy for work — such are among the life-long results of a right cultivation of the feeling for beauty and for art. The relationship of man to man, how noble, how beautiful it becomes under this influence!" [242]

Artistic activities (not the abstract study of Art) have a profound educative influence on the inner being of the child, bringing harmony and strength into the Feelings and cultivating them.

"Music is nothing else but rhythm carried over into the rhythmic system of the human being himself. The inner man himself becomes a violin. His whole rhythmic system reproduces what the violin has played, what has sounded from the piano. And as in the case of music, so it is also, in a finer, more delicate way, in the case of plastic art and of painting. Colour harmonies and colour melodies also are reproduced and revived as inner rhythmic processes in the inner man. If our instruction is to be truly educational we must know that throughout this period everything that the child is taught must be conveyed in artistic form." [243]

The element of judgement in logical thinking is closely related to Feeling, so that the education of the Feelings is essential for the proper development of the intellect[244]. If the child's feelings are educated correctly (sympathy for the good and beautiful, and antipathy for the evil and ugly), they will provide a strong, moral foundation for his sense of judgement in later life[245]. Such feeling should never have the character of sentiment, especially during the period of the onset of puberty, because this would arouse an aversion in the child towards the life of Feeling[246].

When the teacher brings feeling (imaginative feeling from his own being) into his subject matter, the child's memory of what is taught will be greatly enhanced. If he appeals only to reason and intellect, children will soon forget what is taught[247]. Memory is not (as is imagined by modern psychology) the retrieval of a concept from the unconscious into the conscious mind. Memory is a complex process occurring in the Etheric Body[248] together with feeling, and it takes place in a similar way to perception. However, instead of the process being turned outwards as in perception, it turns inwards and "redevelops" the concept anew. When concepts are pervaded with feeling, this process of redevelopment or memory is strengthened.

> "The life of feeling, with its joys and its pains, its pleasures and discomforts, its tensions and its relaxations, is the bearer of what is permanent in the conceptual life. The concept or idea is transformed into impulses of feeling; and it is these stirrings or emotions of feeling which we perceive and which then lead to memory." [249]

Associations of feelings with concepts should not be pedantically planned. The child's feeling must just be aroused, either by the subject itself or by relating it to an association in life. Even concepts in mathematics or physics can be associated with feelings by the imaginative teacher[250].

Artistic concepts such as parables, pictures in stories, colour or musical harmonies and rhythms, and sculptural form, are taken in and stored by the child's feelings.

> "It is no mere figure of speech to say that man can understand with his feelings, his sentiment, his inner disposition, as well as with his intellect." [251]

After puberty, the material formerly absorbed as artistic concepts must be helped into more abstract form. The material must be recapitulated to enable what was apprehended by feelings and images to rise into logical thinking. The best way for this to happen is for the teacher to remain with his class for as long as possible. Continuity of the teacher-pupil relationship strengthens the feeling-life both in terms of the authority relationship and the development of thinking. The policy in most schools is to change the teacher each year. This undermines whatever has been built up between the child and the teacher during the course of the year.

> "Whatever the circumstances, the education of the heart forces suffers if the children have a new teacher each year who cannot follow up what has been instilled into their souls in previous years. It is a part of teaching method that the teacher moves up through the school with his pupils. Only if this is done can one work with the rhythms of life." [252]

The following section describes the education of the Will, whose influences reach deeply into the life of Feeling.

4.5.3 Willing

For the education of the Will before puberty, the teacher must realise that he is
dealing with a child whose needs are altogether different from those of an adult.
What is brought into consciousness in an adult (within his own being or in his
relationships with others) exists as unconscious Will impulses or semi-conscious
Feelings in the child. Therefore children must never be made to have the same
sort of education, or relationships with their teachers or peers, that adults have[253].

The Will of the child cannot be educated by telling the child what he should
or should not Will.

> "But the will is indeed 'asleep' and therefore you cannot give a child a
> direct training in the use of his will. For to try and make a child use
> his will, would be like admonishing him to be very good in his sleep, in
> order to bring this goodness into his life when he wakes again in the
> morning." [254]

The Will is constantly striving upwards as a sympathetic impulse. It is a
force of potential which is prevented from coming into its own in the human being
by the antipathetic, Etheric forces. However, after the death of the physical body,
these antipathetic influences diminish, and the Will becomes the Spirit-Soul reality,
consisting of Ego and Astral Body[255]. It is therefore a part of the human being
which is of the utmost importance for education, but of which modern man has
lost almost all his understanding.

Steiner traces the development of Will from its most primitive to its most
elevated form, analysing it into instinct, impulse, desire, motive, wish, intention
and resolution, and relating these to the overall structure of Soul and Spirit in
man[256]. However, for present purposes this is unnecessarily detailed. The educator
has to know that, until the age of about twenty, the Will is bound up with man's
body within the limbs and metabolism (the legs, arms, hands, muscles, blood and
breathing)[257].

Whereas in the adult "the will relates itself to the outside world in that it
realises itself in external actions" [258] in the child the Will is bound up with the very
means of action, the limbs. It is therefore through action itself that the Will is
cultivated; but it is <u>not</u> done through a single action, nor through the haphazard
or random actions of everyday life. The Will is educated when the child performs
actions which he does not consciously grasp the meaning of, but which nevertheless
have inner meaning and which are repeated systematically and consciously each
day. Such an activity is the Lord's Prayer, or the repetition of a task.

> "It is not the right thing to begin by exhorting the child and giving him
> rules of conduct: you must lead him to do something which you think
> will awaken his feeling for what is right, and get him to do it repeatedly.
> The more it becomes an unconscious habit, the better it is for the devel-
> opment of feeling; the more conscious the child is of doing the action

repeatedly, out of devotion, because it ought to be done, because it must be done, the more you are raising the deed to a real impulse of will. A more unconscious repetition cultivates feeling: fully conscious repetition cultivates the true will impulse, for it enhances the power of resolution, of determination." [259]

Such repetition is scorned as being dull and irrelevant in modern education because it is judged from an intellectual standpoint. However unless it is done, man's Will and consequently his Feelings become ever weaker[260].

All of this must take place under the authority of the teacher in such a way that the child <u>feels</u> that what the teacher directs is good and right. When the child does what his teacher directs him to do, his Will is strengthened[261].

What is important for the education of the Will is not merely that the Will be exercised, but that such exercise should draw consciousness, in the form of Feeling and Thinking, into it. The Etheric forces must be drawn into relation with the Astral. Thinking and Feeling must be vitalised by the Will, and the Will must be cultivated by Feeling and Thinking[262]. This makes man into a moral being. Ancient Greek culture recognised it in their activities of dance and wrestling, but the modern age demands more of education than was necessary for Greece[263].

Art provides the overall principle for the education of the Will. On the one hand, Art demands practice by repetition in which Thinking and Feeling may be drawn into activity. On the other hand, the Will brings fresh joy each time an artistic activity is done[264].

Will impulses carry sense impressions into the Rhythmic and Head Systems, but man is not aware of this. He first becomes dimly aware of sensation when it reaches his Feelings. The child's attention must be constantly called to what he is taking in through his senses, and the teacher must cultivate both his Feeling about what he senses (beautiful–ugly, and so on)[264] and his imagination about his perceptions (for example, the symbol of the plant within the seed)[265]. Thus the child may be guided to transform his sense-life into rich and varied experience which has strong educative influences on the Will.

"... man should be so educated that one sense should be developed with the same care as another, for then the connections between the senses, between the perceptions, will be sought quite consciously and systematically." [266]

Any activity that the teacher directs must have inner meaning which the child can feel but not yet understand. The movements taught in modern gymnastics may be the result of complex scientific research about how to develop the body, but they are meaningless and have no value for the Soul and Spirit[267]. Sport does not educate the Will, since the movements therein are derived from the body, not from the activity of the Soul as in artistic expression. Movements in sport lack, and are actually contrary to, inner meaning. They therefore encourage the animal, instinctual urges in the Will instead of qualities of Soul. Radical as this may sound it is essential that teachers should come to realise what happens to children when education is based only on rational, intellectual theory instead of a true understanding of man[268]. Sport had to be seen in its true perspective[269].

"As far as the body is concerned, nothing is more essential than that the teacher himself must be an artist through and through. The more joy the teacher can experience in beautiful forms, in music, the more he longs to pass from abstract words into the rhythms of poetry; the more of the plastic-musical there is in him, the better will he be able to arrange such games and exercises as offer the child an opportunity for artistic expression. But alas! Our civilisation to-day would like the spirit to be easy of access, and people do not feel inclined to strive too strenuously for spiritual ideals." [270]

The education of the Will through artistic activity arouses a need in the child for expression of the Will through play and games. This must be allowed to take place. Physical training should therefore follow artistic activity, and the right balance has a beneficial effect on the child's sleep[271].

Writing which is developed artistically, drawing the letters from natural forms, calls on the Will to engage itself in the skills of drawing and painting, and the formation of pictures with colour[272]. handicraft lessons[273] and sculptural exercises[274] strengthen the Will and lead it into feelings for design and practicality. The use of the voice in singing and the playing of musical instruments have powerful educative influences on the Will[275]. The telling of stories in such a way as to arouse the child's feelings and imagination evokes the sympathetic forces of the Will[276]. Eurythmy is an artistic activity, developed within the Anthroposophical Society, in which sound in language is expressed as gesture. This educates the whole man but particularly the Will, and it is practised in an elementary way with children[277].

Art, which strengthens the sympathetic Will forces, stimulates a balancing impulse of antipathetic thought in the child. Thinking takes hold of the sympathetic impulses and transforms them into picture memories and concepts. However, working from the sympathetic forces the teacher can ensure that the child's thinking is vitalised, and not hardened as happens when children are given intellectual concepts[278].

When the Will is educated artistically by teachers who are themselves artists, the youth will turn to such adults and accept their authority quite naturally. Such a relationship between the adult and child will enable the youth to grow strong in Will, Feeling and Thinking, and ready to take their place in the world without revolting against adults.

"What is to be learnt must be learnt. But it will be learnt when there is as natural an urge towards those who are older as the infant has towards its mother's breast, or as the small child feels when, by imitating, he learns to speak. This urge will be stimulated when the young find the artistic coming from the older generation, when truth first appears in the garb of beauty." [279]

4.6   EDUCATION TOWARDS INDIVIDUALITY: THE TEMPERAMENTS

Although, in common with Steiner, numerous modern thinkers hold that education should not merely "stuff" the child but allow his individuality to emerge, Steiner considered that little is known about the way individuality forms through the developmental sequence from Imitation to Authority and thence to Independence[280]. Moreover, modern educators have little understanding of what individuality really is in the human being, and therefore they do not know how to educate so as to develop the individuality of the child[281].

Steiner draws attention to the "great gap between what is called human nature in general and what confronts us in each human individual" [282]. The educator has to recognise this distinction and approach every child with entirely new feeling[283]. Children must not be made to fit a model, but enabled to develop their own individualities[284]. However, this is not simply a matter for passivity on the part of the teacher. He must learn to enter deeply into the individuality of each child, and the way in which this can be done is through a living knowledge of the four "temperaments" [285].

Changes in temperament occur slowly during the course of life, mainly as a result of man's experiences of Religion and Art[286]. The educator's task is to accept the karmic nature of the child's temperament, not to deny or oppose it, but to work with what he finds in the child[287]. Differences of temperament are not faults but qualities which the teacher must help to fulfil appropriately[288].

Temperament arises through the interaction of the four members of man: the physical, Etheric and Astral Bodies, and the Ego. The combinations of relative strengths that each member has within an individual may be infinite, but normally one member dominates the others and this gives the individual his temperament. However, temperaments are not sharply defined, but are tendencies[289].

Education must bring about "the harmonizing of these four principles" [290]. The teacher must know how to identify and tone down any tendency that becomes excessive[291]. Identification requires a study of "the whole external bearing and general habits of the child" [292], which would reveal whether the child had a Melancholic, Phlegmatic, Sanguine or Choleric temperament. These will now be very briefly described.

In the Melancholic temperament the influence of the physical body dominates that of the others. The Spirit and Soul cannot master the physical body, which becomes an obstacle for them. This causes feelings of pain, gloom, sorrow and inner grief. Certain thoughts tend to endure in the mind[293].

> "This mood is caused by nothing else than that the physical body sets up opposition to the inner ease of the etheric body, to the mobility of the astral body, and to the ego's certainty of its goal." [294]

The temperament is reflected in the Melancholic's body. His head droops, he glances downwards and has sad eyes. He walks firmly but with a slight drag[295].

The Etheric Body dominates in the Phlegmatic temperament. The Etheric is the "life-body" and brings on feelings of well-being and inner comfort, so that the Phlegmatic "feels little urgency to direct his inner being towards the outside world"[296]. His body tends to become corpulent and he has a dragging gait with an immobile, indifferent expression on his face[297].

The Astral Body dominates in the Sanguine temperament. The Astral Body is flowing and mobile and this is reflected in the Sanguine's constant moving of attention from one subject to another and his inability to sustain an enduring interest. He has a "fickle disposition"[298] and "a merry glance; inner joy and gaiety shine in it"[299]. He has mobile, volatile and fluid gestures, with a slender, supple body and an elastic, springing gait. The Sanguine child has a hopping, dancing walk[300].

In the Choleric temperament the Ego dominates. The Choleric always wants to assert his Ego and is aggressive and strong willed[301]. His eyes have a "strongly kindled inner light". He has a firm tread and, if the Ego so dominates as to hold back the growth forces of the other bodies, is short of stature[302].

The Phlegmatic and Sanguine temperaments often occur together in the same person, but the Phlegmatic and Choleric temperaments clash[303]. Some mental illnesses result from abnormal development of the temperaments[304].

The individual's temperament must be seen in the context of his age because each age of life has a dominant temperament.

"... all children are primarily sanguine even if they are also phlegmatic or choleric in certain things. All adolescents, boys and girls are really cholerics, and if it is not so at this time of life it shows an unhealthy development. In mature life a man is melancholic and in old age phlegmatic."[305]

Steiner's teachings with regard to the education of the temperaments are too detailed and extensive to include in this general account[306]. The most important principle for bringing the temperaments into harmony is not, as rational argument would have it, to expose the child to opposing influences in order to "balance" his temperament. One cannot "heal" a one-sided temperament by its opposite; one must rather deal indirectly with it by reflecting its own nature back to it. This effects gradual but deep harmonizing influences within the individual.

"Further, in an education such as this, we must have patience; the effect is not seen from one day to the next, but it takes years. And the way it works is that when the child is given from outside what he has within himself he arouses in himself healing powers of resistance. If we bring him something quite alien — if we bring comic things to a serious child — he will remain indifferent to comic things. But if we confront him outwardly with his sorrow and trouble and care he perceives from this outward meeting what he has in himself. And this calls out the inner action, the opposite. And we heal pedagogically by following in modern form the ancient golden rule: Not only can like be known by like, like can be treated and healed by like."[307]

This principle must also be used (subtly and unobtrusively) for the arrangement of seating in class. Children of like temperaments must be seated together to tone one another down. Each group must be carefully placed so that Cholerics and Phlegmatics are opposite one another and Sanguines and Melancholics between. The teacher's response to, and handling of the temperaments must become a natural and intuitive ability to turn to the appropriate group that he wishes to influence[308]. The teacher must learn to handle the temperaments sensitively and artistically[309].

The arrangement of the class according to temperaments assists the teacher "to keep a class in order". He must understand the way in which Cholerics try to dominate and in so doing subdue one another, or how Melancholics cheer one another up when they are together[310].

The teacher must pay close attention to his own temperament, and this ought to be an important part of teacher training. The teacher must learn how to control his temperament, which is deeply rooted in his own individuality[311]. Lack of harmony in the temperament of the teacher will have harmful effects on children[312]. For example, in the case of a Choleric teacher,

"A child who lives in constant terror of what may come to him as expressions of fury or anger from a choleric person, experiences something in his soul which immediately penetrates the breathing, the circulation of the blood and even the digestive activities. This is of great significance; in the age of childhood it is impossible to speak of bodily education alone, because soul education is also education of the body, and the whole soul element is metamorphosed into body — it becomes body." [313]

Through an understanding of the temperaments the teacher can approach the child's individuality much more intimately, knowledgeably and practically than would otherwise be the case[314].

The harmonizing of the child's temperament is fundamental for the fulfilment of his purpose in life, and without such harmony he could not achieve "freedom", which is "the task of self-development for every individual" [315]. The following section examines Steiner's concept of freedom, a theme that flows though all his work.

4.7   EDUCATION TOWARDS FREEDOM

When Steiner's book *Die Philosophie der Freiheit* (The Philosophy of Freedom) (1894) was published in English, he specified that the title be translated as The Philosophy of Spiritual Activity, and that the reader be asked to make this change throughout the book[316]. Closer attention must therefore be given to the idea of *Freiheit,* which constitutes the central goal of Steiner's teachings on education.

To Steiner, there are many factors that militate against *Freiheit* or Spiritual activity. One's race, tribe, nation, family and sex constitute a natural whole from which one originates, and one's state, legal and religious codes etc., provide a whole into which one fits.

"This being so, is any individuality left at all? Can we regard man as a whole in himself, in view of the fact that he grows out of a whole and fits as a member into a whole?" [317]

Steiner argued that whereas nation, race, sex and so on were subject to scientific study in which men could be reduced to specimens of a genus, such laws could not determine the unique character of the single individual. Individual intuition, whereby each man developed his conceptual life in connection with his percepts, was beyond scientific prediction[318].

The personal element of individuality exists in man as "the ... ideal*". It is capable of expression independently of instincts, passions and feelings which constitute the "non ideal". Such freedom can and must exist at a higher level than laws which dictate our actions for the general good: it can encompass such laws yet remain free if it is motivated not by duty but by pure love[319].

"To live in love of action and to let live in understanding of the other's volition, this is the fundamental maxim of the free man. He knows no other 'ought' than that with which his will intuitively puts itself in harmony. How he shall will in any given case, that will be determined for him by the range of his ideas." [320]

Freiheit is therefore an attainment the individual must strive for, not which is determined or conferred by an external agent. "The ideal" part of man must be strengthened by the use of the Will and the range of the individual's ideas. *Freiheit*, or Spiritual activity, then becomes the expression of a unique, individual moral impulse.

"Concrete ideas are formed by us on the basis of our concepts by means of the imagination. Hence what the free spirit needs in order to realise his concepts, in order to assert himself in the world, is moral imagination. This is the source of the free spirit's action. Only those men, therefore, who are endowed with moral imagination are, properly speaking, morally productive. Those who merely preach morality, i.e., those who merely excogitate moral rules without being able to condense them into concrete ideas, are morally unproductive." [321]

This attainment, "freedom and independence of the spiritual life", is the goal of education[322]. But Spiritual activity is developed according to spiritual laws, just as natural laws govern the physical world. The child must pass through the correct experiences of imitation in order to "unfold a free spiritual activity under the influence of natural authority". After puberty the teacher must help the child's Spiritual activity to unfold by appealing to his moral judgement. The child

---

*The use of the term "The Ideal" is closely related or identical to his later term "The I" or Ego.

experiences this as an awakening of morality from within if he is allowed to use his own imagination, intuition and reason to transform what he has absorbed as images in childhood into conscious moral understanding[323].

After the age of about twenty, "when man's ego comes into full recognition", true Spiritual activity can be developed on the basis of mature moral judgement. If the laws of development have been fulfilled the new adult will be ready to enter social life in which "man seeks, and finds, his fellow man" as a free individual[324].

For the teacher to be able to educate a child towards freedom, the teacher himself must be free. Not only must the teacher develop his own Spiritual activity, but the school itself must allow every teacher his freedom. Steiner claims that his teachings are not ideological constructions about education; they are descriptions of the laws of child development which do not constrain the teacher except in so far as they inform him of the universal facts of life with which education has to contend. Teaching itself must be a free act if the teacher is to make contact with the children and if he is to teach as an individual:

> "You will find the same subject taught in the most varied ways in the different parallel classes. Why? Well, because it is not a matter of indifference whether the teacher who has to take a lesson has one temperament or another. The lesson can only be harmonious when there is the right contact between the teacher and the whole class. Hence every teacher must give his lesson in his own way. And just as life appears in manifold variety so can a teaching founded in life take the most varied forms." [325]

Chapters 3 and 4 have been concerned with establishing an accurate and representative account of Steiner's holistic educational thought in which he fulfilled the prediction he made more than a decade before the first Waldorf School was conceived.

> "We shall not set up demands nor programmes, but simply describe the child-nature. From the nature of the growing and evolving human being, the proper point of view for education will, as it were, spontaneously result." [326]

Chapter 4 has shown how Steiner's description of child development relates to his model of man, and has direct implications for education.

It is now clear that these models are not reducible. Body, Soul and Spirit develop their characteristics only because they are fully interrelated within man, and each developmental stage evolves out of the last, including the life before birth. The latitudinal model of man must be integrated with the longitudinal model of development for the right perspective of education to emerge. These models exist within the context of man's Social, Economic and Spiritual life, as well as the broad cosmic purposes of life.

In the next chapter the aims of education will be abstracted from Steiner's thought. However, the section on principles will show how Steiner considered it imperative that education should not be reduced by abstraction to a mere list of principles, because what is necessary for education is an integrated understanding of the holism of life itself, rather than something that can be disintegrated into a series of rules for educational practice. Such rules contradict the very foundation of education, which is the wholly interrelated nature of man.

Therefore the study of Steiner's educational thought requires a direct progression from his model of child development into his methods for education, without abstraction into principles, which would distort the system. There are indeed principles within the system, but they must remain in the form in which they have been presented in Chapter 4 — directly related to the model of child development — and not divorced or abstracted from it.

Much has already been done in this regard, but Chapter 5 will outline the most important indications given by Steiner for methods to be used in particular subjects of the curriculum. These methods are not abstract rules of practice, but are drawn directly from his view of the child's nature, and the links will be indicated.

5

THE AIMS,
PRINCIPLES AND
METHODS OF
EDUCATION

In this chapter it will be shown that Steiner aims to provide an education based on a Spiritual Scientific understanding of man that will give the child a firm foundation for the whole of his life. To do this,

> "It is not just that the artistic element must be cultivated; the actual teaching of every lesson must be drawn from the artistic realm. Every method must be immersed in the artistic element. Educating and teaching must become a real art." [1]

For Steiner, no truly artistic education can be founded on a list of abstract principles; it must be a human matter between teacher and child. All the teacher's training and practice must bring the Imagination, Feelings and Will into real, living expression in himself, and thence into his practice of education. This will create an education which draws on the Feelings and Will to unite with Thinking in the growing child, so that in adult life he will be an integrated being whose Thinking, Feeling and Will are correctly balanced and in harmony.

Steiner gives general suggestions for the ways in which each subject can be taught artistically, and the most important ideas that he gives will be outlined. However, the details of the curricula for Waldorf Schools have been omitted because they are clear in their present form and would be too extensive to record here (see 2.2.2 for the curricula that have been published).

Once again, the aim of this chapter is to present an objective description of Steiner's thought, without criticism or comparison with other educational thought.

5.1   AIMS

Steiner points out that unless one understands the whole man, one will only be able to educate a part of him, and the remainder will become subject to animal urges. Illustrating the point with references to the turmoil in Russia at the time, he says,

> "The fundamental flaw hitherto has always been that people have stood in the world with their head nature only, merely trailing the rest of their being along behind. The consequence is that these other parts of man's being are now guided by their animal urges, indulging in untamed emotions — such as we are just experiencing in what is spreading so curiously from the Eastern part of Europe. Such a phenomenon has arisen because the being of man has not been fostered in its totality." [2]

Steiner holds that a knowledge of the whole man cannot be obtained in any way other than through Spiritual Science. When the findings of Spiritual Science are applied it will be found that, far from contradicting the findings of natural science, Spiritual Science will reveal the way that they can be put into practice in a most tangible and compelling form[2].

> "A really concrete knowledge of man with the power of seeing right into man himself, is the only possible basis for a true art of education ...
>
> The education of man today so often lags behind the talents and tendencies which his destiny has implanted in him. We must keep pace with these powers to such an extent that the human being in our care can win his way through to all that his destiny will allow — to the fullest clarity of thought, the most loving deepening of his feeling, and the greatest possible energy and ability of will." [4]

Education should not only be able to develop the whole man, it should also be able to bring man's being together as a harmonious, integrated whole[5]. This is not merely an educational goal; it is the purpose of life itself — to bring what is spiritual to fulfilment in the physical world.

> "In the human being, the interplay of thought and will does not come about of itself. In the animal, the process is natural; in the human being it must become a moral process. And because here on earth man has the opportunity of bringing about this union of his thinking with his willing, therefore it is that he can become a moral being. The whole character of man in so far as it proceeds from the inner being depends upon the true harmony being established, between thinking and willing, by human activity." [6]

Such an all-encompassing task for education should begin with an understanding of the way the child grows up, and of his needs in the different stages of his life. When the developmental sequence is grasped it will be seen how true education proceeds quite naturally out of it.

"Such lectures as these will only have achieved their object when they have become superfluous, namely, when there shall no longer be any necessity to treat this as a special theme, when we shall once again possess a philosophy, a knowledge of the world in which education is implicit so that a teacher having this knowledge is also possessed of the art of education, and can exercise it spontaneously, instinctively. Our need to talk so much about education shows how little impulse for education is contained in the rest of our knowledge." [7]

Education should be achieved through the human relationship between the teacher and the child[8], and what the teacher gives to the child through Imitation and Authority is of far more value than the intellectual content of the curriculum[9]. Therefore the teacher's knowledge of the growing child should not distance him from the child so that he believes his job is to transfer information to the intellect of the child. The teacher's knowledge should draw him deeply within an educational relationship as a being with whom the child comes into his own through Imitation and Authority[10].

"Pedagogics that makes the teacher clever is not of the right kind; the right kind of pedagogics makes the teacher inwardly alive and fills him with a life-blood of the soul which pours itself actively into his physical life-blood. And if there is anything by which we can recognise a true teacher or educator, it is that his pedagogical art has not made him a pedant." [11]

Education should not aim to raise man above his body into an intellectual or mystical idealism divorced from life. On the contrary, it should enable the Soul and Spirit of the child to enter the physical world in such a way as to fulfil their life-purpose with the body. Seen otherwise, education becomes impractical and inimical to life.

"For the task of man is to make the Spirit, which without him would not be on earth, into a living content of this world. The Christ himself came down to earth. He did not take men away to an earthly life in the heavens." [12]

A full knowledge of the child reveals that he is not, at first, an intellectual being, but one who lives within fantasy, imagination, Feelings and Will. Therefore what is brought to the child through education should exist in a form suitable to his nature; not formal concepts but imaginative pictures, rhythms and activities. In short, teaching "must be warmed through and fired by the artistic element." [13]

"From his seventh to his fourteenth or fifteenth year he seeks — not through theoretical concepts but through the living-together with human beings — what does not lend itself to be grasped in concepts but is manifested in the teacher; and it resists conceptual form. Concepts have form, that is to say, external limits. But human individuality in the sense described has no external limits, only intensity, quality; it is experienced as quality, as intensity, very particularly in the period of life referred to. It is experienced, however, through no other atmosphere than that of art." [14]

The atmosphere of art which should pervade education must be no dilettante affair. It should arise directly out of the living Will and Feeling of the educator who represents the world for the child.

"It is not just that the artistic element must be cultivated; the actual teaching of every lesson must be drawn from the artistic realm. Every method must be immersed in the artistic element. Educating and teaching must become a real art. Subject matter must not be more than the underlying basis." [15]

An artistic approach to education is essentially individual, a relationship between teacher and pupil, and the teacher cannot achieve the right relationship with a child until he becomes aware of the child's true nature; that he is not merely a physical organism but an expression of a spiritual being emanating from a pure, spiritual realm to unite with a physical line of inheritance. This being brings with it the fruits of former times which must fulfil their destiny in the world. The teacher's role is not to impose knowledge which is alien to the child, but "from the daily revelation of this mysterious spirit-soul being he discovers what he has to do." In this sense, "the greatest teacher in the Waldorf School is the child himself." [16]

"... what concerns the teacher springs in reality from the innermost centre of the child's being, and what the teacher can do for the child works right into his inner nature also." [17]

With the right knowledge and by working artistically, each element of the child's being can be awakened[18] and strengthened[19] at the right time. Thus, "all we do for the child is to satisfy the demands of his own nature" [20]. The correct method of education does not mould the child into a preconceived pattern but awakens and strengthens what is within him and then sends him out into the world as a free individual[21].

An approach to education which draws its method out of the nature of the child and then prepares him for the social and economic life is not confined to national boundaries but is fundamentally relevant to many countries and nations[22]. However, it is particularly relevant to the modern world, which is contaminated with one-sided intellectualism and materialism[23]. Waldorf Education provides a method of healing this one-sidedness[24]. But it is not a series of isolated solutions to problems. It aims to answer to the nature of man, and man is more than the sum of his parts; both within himself and in the progression of his life, man is holistic[25]. Only such an education that aims to be founded in life, and not based on intellectual, rationalist or ideological theory, can respond to the real needs of man.

"It is part of the nature of the science of spirit that it can adapt itself to every situation in life, for it is its intention to work directly out of life. It does not seek to hunt after utopian ideas in any way, but to create what is latent in the human being out of the immediate practice of life, out of the conditions that actually exist." [26]

5.2   PRINCIPLES

Of all the parts of this book, the modern educationist might expect this one to render the most condensed account of Steiner's thought. However, Steiner was more than aware of the tendency to reduce educational theory to a list of abstract principles, and nearly every lecture contains an attempt to arrest impatient theorizing and to encourage a more integrated approach to education.

"For no education will develop from abstract principles or programmes — it will only develop from reality. And because man himself is soul and spirit, because he has a physical nature, a soul nature, and a spiritual nature, reality must again come into our life — for with the whole reality will the spirit also come into our life, and only such a spirit as this can sustain the educational art of the future." [27]

Steiner also rejected the tendency to oversimplify the whole matter of education, so that even laymen imagined that they knew all about it[28]. Modern man's understanding of education was like being able to spell without being able to read. This was caused by our demand for a conscious, analytical approach to education to replace the intuitive approach of past ages. Man must now make the conscious effort to reintegrate educational thought into an organic whole which is not merely theory or ideology, but based on life itself[29].

Theory and ideology alone lead to endless questions about education, but concrete life provides an end to such questions[30]. Man must stop trying to twist the facts of life to suit his own idiosyncrasies, but must learn to frame his arrangements in accordance with the demands of life[31].

Once this is done, educators will be guided not by principles, but by "the life-processes that are going on in children" [32]. These life processes (see chapters 3 and 4) are not isolated from one another but holistic and organically interrelated: Thinking can never be educated separately from Feeling and Will. The principles of Imitation, Authority and Freedom form an interrelated process which is distorted if the principles are separated. The stages of development and the concepts they involve are interwoven and are intended to be seen as life-processes, not abstract theories, and they embrace the whole being of the child. Steiner stressed "the immense importance of seeing our whole teaching work as a complete organism, so that gradually we come to recognise everything in it as part of a living whole." [33]

Steiner's concepts are to some degree unique both within themselves, and certainly in the relationships of each to the whole. It is this which makes it possible to relate aspects of his thought to the ideas of other thinkers, but not to find sustained parallels. Moreover, the concepts that Steiner uses to describe the Soul can only be truly understood by going beyond a superficial level of thought into the nature of thinking itself; they are understood only by developing the ability to experience one's inner being (See 2.2.3).

> "No dictionary, however, can give us that mobility, that able knowledge and knowing ableness, necessary for an understanding of the etheric body, because the etheric body does not proceed according to the laws of nature; it permeates the being in plastic activity." [34]

When a teacher gains such a living awareness he enters the classroom as an altogether different person:

> "The boy or girl, seeing the teacher come into the classroom must not have the feeling: 'He is teaching according to some theoretical principles because he does not grasp the subconscious.' They want a human relation with the teacher. And that is almost always destroyed when educational principles are introduced." [35]

Waldorf educational principles are therefore bound up with living itself, and can only be properly understood in practical life. All the teachings of Spiritual Science are nothing but means of entering into life itself, countering the tendency of modern man to become imprisoned within his intellect.

> "The only hope for us to meet these boys and girls with understanding lies in taking the utmost pains to imbue our own instinctive life — our feelings and inner perceptions — with spiritual science. It is imperative that we press forward in this way with our own self development. And that is what I mean when again and again you have heard me say: 'Anthroposophy is itself pedagogy.' That is, it becomes pedagogy so soon as we are given the opportunity to educate. All we have to do is call up from the depths of our soul what has been planted there by Anthroposophy." [36]

Therefore far more is done in a Waldorf School than is evident to the casual observer. Not only is there the inner world of the teacher-pupil relationship within an artistic context, but each activity comes into its own when it is organically integrated with the whole curriculum as it unfolds year by year[37]. The way in which the curriculum must unfold in response to the child's development was described in Chapter 4. References to the use of subjects to balance and harmonise the child's Thinking, Feeling and Will are made in 5.3.2. An analysis of the holism in the curricula for Waldorf Schools (see 2.2.2) has been omitted from the present study for reasons of length, and because Steiner was more concerned that teachers themselves should take responsibility for creating their curriculum (see 5.3.1.1) on the basis of the principle of holism (see 5.3.2 Subject Methods, and especially 5.3.2.8 Geography).

5.3 METHODS

5.3.1 The Teacher

The following sections on the role of the teacher in Waldorf Education cover only the main ideas given by Steiner. His teachings in this regard permeate all his lectures, so that an exhaustive account would be too long to include here.

5.3.1.1 Practice

This account collates many of the practical policies necessary for the application of Steiner's educational thought in schools, and it therefore includes divergent ideas (presentation, diet, lessons, and so on) which find their unity in the nature of the child.

The teacher's work has to do with the four members of the child's being, the physical body, the Soul Bodies and the Ego[38]. As these change and develop during the child's life at school, the teacher should ensure that they are properly met by the child's experiences in school (see Chapter 4)[39].

The teacher's knowledge of the child should not merely exist in his head as a list of principles[40] ; it should be felt, as it were, in his very blood[41] and enable him to "approach the innermost being of the child" [42].

The teacher should shape all his teaching from what he "reads" in the child's whole being[43]. His feeling for temperament should become second nature so that he turns spontaneously to the individual or group that he is influencing[44]. Everything the teacher gives his pupils should be in answer to what he perceives in them.

> "For, in fact, if the educator is a complete human being he receives as much from the child as he gives to the child. Whoever cannot learn from the child what he brings down from the spiritual world, cannot teach the child about the mysteries of earthly existence ...
>
> It was not for the sake of mere symbolism that Goethe sought everywhere for things that suggest a breathing, outbreathing, inbreathing ... Goethe saw the whole of life as a picture of receiving and giving." [45]

The teacher of young children may have to compensate for what the child has not been given at home in his earliest years, so that the teacher should understand what the child needs to absorb through natural imitation[46]. (See 4.2.2 and 4.2.3).

The teacher has to try to relate and harmonise the content of subjects that the child is taking[47]. He should not make rigid demarcations between, for example, Geography and History, but have the presence of mind to show how they flow into one another[48]. The teacher should also develop an understanding of how subjects have a balancing effect on the child, such as between the Thinking activities of History and the Will activities of Singing or Eurythmy[49]. Moreover, children with different temperaments need different activities in subjects such as gymnastics[50].

Knowledge of the ways in which diet can assist with the child's education is important[51]. For example, children who have little talent for writing and reading may be helped by taking them off too many fattening foods and changing them to more of a vegetarian diet, preventing overfeeding[52]. Children should not be allowed to develop too much fat[53]. The child's memory can be strengthened by the inclusion of more fruit and root crops in his diet[54]. Sugar intake can be modified to help balance the temperaments, melancholics benefiting from an increase and sanguines from a decrease[55]. The teacher must be able to co-operate closely with the parents over the child's diet[56]. He also needs a knowledge of medicine in order to judge the health of his pupils and to modify his teaching and balance it in accordance with the child's needs[57].

Although the Waldorf School teacher is constantly using therapeutic methods in education, it is of great benefit to have a medical doctor in the school who understands the methods being used and who can assist every teacher[58]. Regular review of the child's physical development will reveal whether the right balance is being struck between Thinking, memory, Feeling and Will activities[59]. A true knowledge of the child will enable the teacher to understand how the correct education of the Soul and Spirit brings health to the physical body, and how incorrect education sooner or later finds expression in the physical body in the form of discomfort or disease[60], or faulty physical growth[61]. Within limits, over-stimulation of the memory can cause the child to grow lank, whereas overstimulation of the imagination and fantasy retards growth. This is bound up with the interaction of the Etheric and Astral Bodies and their influence on the physical[62].

In Waldorf Schools the child's day is not divided up into numerous periods, so that "in their heads they tumble through each other like the stones of a kaleidoscope"[63]. Every morning there is a main lesson lasting approximately two hours, and this must be devoted to one subject (though not pedantically) which must run for three to five weeks[64]. This has enormously beneficial effects on the child's concentration[65], and although the child may forget what has been done earlier in the year, this is small sacrifice for what is gained in other ways, and is made up for by recapitulating what has been done at the end of the year[66]. The process of forgetting and remembering is, in fact, a very important part of education, and should be developed rather than resisted[67]. These sustained lessons are, of course, not only intellectual, but involve artistic activities (see 4.5), and they are followed by subjects like foreign languages which require daily practice[68].

For younger children, main lessons incorporate writing and reading, arithmetic, and music and drawing, which provide the balance of Thinking, Feeling and Will activities[69].

Lessons should not keep rigidly to one subject, but rather be guided by what arises in the course of lessons[70]. Showing connections between subjects is enormously beneficial for the child, helping not only his mental digestion of the material, but also his physical digestive processes[71]. A large number of children can be occupied in different ways at the same time to cater for the needs of individuals or small groups, once the teacher has prepared himself spiritually for this[72].

The teacher moves up with his class each year for eight years[73]. (The class is then attended to by subject specialists). This long association enables the teacher to recapitulate in later years what was learned in pictorial form, or committed to memory as verse in earlier years, enabling the child to transform such knowledge into a more intellectual content[74]. It also enables strong bonds to develop between teacher and pupil, which is the sign of a good pedagogical relationship[75].

The teacher's own knowledge must become permeated with Feeling and Will in order to bring his concepts imaginatively to life[76]. The teacher should not feel that he is dealing with abstract ideas, but rather that, in for example Geography and History, places and people are concrete and real, thereby enabling the child to absorb this feeling[77]. The child ought to constantly feel that he is being led into the real world, and not into knowledge that is divorced from life itself. (See 5.3.2).

"Your method must always be, not simply to occupy the child with examples which you have thought out for him, but to give him practical examples out of life itself. You must let everything live up to practical life. In this way you can always show how what you began with is brought into fruition by what followed ..." [78]

The content of lessons should be presented in the way perceptions are made in life, beginning with the whole and then moving to the parts. This principle is in agreement with the way concepts are formed (see 4.4.1 and 4.5), wherein the human impulse is to perceive the whole (conclusion) out of which it creates (judgement) the parts (concept). The child has no impulse to reverse this process; to create a whole out of the parts, which is demanded in modern education. The child's impulse is to divide up the wholes with which it is presented[79].

This principle is particularly important in Arithmetic[80], Mineralogy[81], study of animals[82] and of plants[83], and in Geography, enabling the teacher to achieve great economy in his teaching[84]. (See 5.3.2)

The teacher should not try to interest children by sensationalism, nor be so dry as to make children feel that all his teaching is only concerned with intellectual understanding. Instead, what is taught should be permeated with deep and sincere conviction and feeling, so that the child feels a sense of awe and respect for what his teacher has to say[85]. The teacher's words should have weight and at the same time wings[86].

With an artistic approach to educational method (see 4.5), all children, the slow as well as the quick and intelligent, can be educated together.

111

"When we teach pictorially and imaginatively, as I have described, the child takes as much of the instruction as it can bear. A relationship arises like eating and being satisfied. This means that we shall have some children further advanced than others, and this we must deal with, without relegating less advanced children to a class below. One may have a comparatively large class and yet a child will not eat more than it can bear — spiritually speaking — because its organism spontaneously rejects what it cannot bear. Thus we take account of life here, just as we draw our teaching from life." [87]

Children should never be encouraged to become egotistical by putting the quick ones in a separate class[88]. The teacher should, of course, make allowance for slow children, but should not be too quick to judge so-called gifted or less gifted children, since those who are quick to grasp things only really digest them later on[89]. Children ought to be kept with children of their own age in school, and not moved out of their developmental grouping, which is generally judged in terms of age. With very exceptional cases, where abnormal development occurs a child is moved into a "Helping Class" in which the child's faculties of Thinking, Feeling and Will can be helped to develop harmoniously before he is returned to his own class[90]. Putting a child up or down a class is much more harmful than contending with problems of ability[91].

In order to create artistic concepts such as parables, stories of great men and women, or characterisations of minerals, plant and animal life (see 5.3.2), the teacher must be able to enter deeply into the child's way of viewing the world, wherein the child cannot separate himself from the world and thinks of it as living, like himself (see 4.3.3.1).

The teacher can use anthropomorphism and make plants and animals speak[92]. In this way human morality is reflected through the animal kingdom without resorting to pedantic moral precepts[93]. Fables about the kingdoms of nature gradually pass into the facts about them[94], and after the age of nine or ten nature study is begun[95]. However, even fables must be rooted in reality in both literal and symbolic content[96]. Logic should never be directly taught to the child but brought to him through the teacher's whole general attitude[97].

Imaginative concepts communicated through anthropomorphism, fables and parables change in form as the child grows up, so that after puberty he will be able to review what he was given in childhood and abstract its intellectual content. His intellect will be enlivened by this activity which he performs himself, freely, rather than having it done for him by an adult.

"But in school we supply the children with concepts and cherish the notion that they should remain unchanged for the whole of the children's lives. The child is supposed to preserve them in memory; fifty years hence they are to be the same as they are today. Our school text-books ensure that the child remains a child. We should educate the child so that all his concepts are capable of growth, that his concepts and will impulses are really alive. This is not easy. But the artistic way of education succeeds in doing it. And the child has a different feeling when we offer him living concepts instead of dead ones, for unconsciously he knows that what is given grows with him, just as his arms grow with his body." [98]

Through all that the teacher does to foster the child's aesthetic judgement (see 4.3.4), a sure foundation is laid for the development of strong ideals in adolescence, which will give children the love and confidence to enter adult life[99].

What children learn in school must be brought consciously into expression through their hands, artistically[100], beginning at first with simply copying the artistic pictures from which the letters of the alphabet are abstracted[101].

In order to practice education as an art, the teacher must be free, "responsible only to the spiritual world, to which the science of spirit enables him to raise his vision." [102] The teacher himself must create the education that he gives his pupils, guided by his knowledge of child development as it reveals itself in the children. This imposes a great deal of responsibility on the teacher.

"A curriculum that from the start lays down the timetable and all sorts of other things completely eliminates the art of teaching. And this must not be. The teacher must be the driving and stimulating force in the whole educational system." [103]

The teacher should make his own teaching aids, using his own creativity. This does become more difficult after the children's ninth year[104].

An artistic approach to education should do away with textbooks containing abstract material which only begins to mean something to children after the age of nine or ten, and which they can only understand fully at the age of eighteen or nineteen[105].

When children see their teacher reading to them from a textbook, they unconsciously develop the conviction that they need not learn what the teacher conveys to them thus, because the teacher himself does not know it. This develops into an unconscious resistance to learning[106]. When the teacher gives lessons they should be filled with vitality and freshness, which the children will absorb[107]. Unless children are interested and involved in their lessons they become physically unhealthy[108].

Therefore, children should make up their own text books in lessons, and work out their own exercises and examples to do. Working this way gives them satisfaction and a challenge[109].

Homework should be restricted to reading over what has been done in class, and writing for homework should only be started after the age of twelve[110]. Therefore, as far as possible, learning should take place under the teacher's authority.

A vital principle is "the value and usefulness, in teaching, of the unknown or half-known". At the end of a lesson the teacher should say what will be learned the following day, something of which the children are ignorant. This works in their souls as an unfulfilled expectation which stimulates their curiosity in the next lesson[111].

Moreover, literature should never be read and then pedantically explained to children. It should be allowed to be apprehended by the feelings, enabling children to "instinctively understand" what a poem, for example, contains[112]. Much should be left unsaid in teaching, which will stimulate pupils to continue after the lesson to ponder over what has been given. Thus teachers will "sow seeds for the children's imagination", whereas over-complete and obvious explanations deaden the imagination[113]. What the child accepts in this way, on the basis of the teacher's authority, will be immensely beneficial for him, and will grow with him through life[114].

Children should be told that there is much which is hidden in life, both in the mysteries of nature and the inner moral qualities of men, and that each person has to awaken feelings within himself to discover what will otherwise remain concealed from him[115].

The teacher should work with the understanding that precedes intellectual comprehension, and which holds sway in the feelings, memory and imagination:

"The little child receives the structure of language into the living organism of his soul, and does not require the laws of language-formation in intellectual concepts for the process. Similarly the older boy and girl must learn for the cultivation of memory much that they are not to master with their intellectual understanding until later years." [116]

A golden rule in teaching is economy, so that the teacher should strip his lessons of everything that will not bear fruit in later life. This is especially important after puberty, and brings meaningfulness and interest into lessons, particularly foreign language lessons in which the child values the ability to use the language far more than an abstract knowledge of its grammar, which in any case is learned more quickly and easily once he can speak the language[117].

The higher classes of Waldorf Schools should prepare children who desire it for public examinations, in order for them to be able to meet the requirements of adult life[118]. However, examinations have no value in themselves, and cramming for exams has a destructive effect on the nervous system[119]. At any age, slower learning is healthier than cramming[120]. Examinations are therefore dispensed with inside the school.

"Ideally we should have no examinations at all. The school-leaving examination is a compromise with the authorities. 'Exam fever' before puberty can become the driving impulse of the whole physiological and psychological constitution of the child. The best thing would be to get rid of all examinations. The children would then become much more quick witted." [121]

Rather than emphasizing tests and examinations, the teacher should always strive to get his pupils to do things as perfectly as possible from the earliest lesson,

114

by example, copying and repetition of artistic activities[122].

The teacher gives the child a "report" at the end of each year. This does not give a mark ("I must own that I have never been able to acquire this art of expressing human faculties by such numbers." [123]), but a little biography, including censure, of the child's life at school during the past year. Then a short verse is given to guide the child for the next year. This verse must be learnt by heart, and it has a strong effect on the child's Feelings and Will. To write such a report the teacher should know the child intimately[124]. Children love these reports, which give both them and their parents a meaningful idea of what the child's school life is like[125].

5.3.1.2   The College of Teachers

Waldorf School teachers meet at least once a week, and this group is called the College of Teachers. It is the heart of the school. In the meetings each teacher must discuss the experiences he has had in his class in full detail. The other teachers can then make suggestions which might help him; but these suggestions must be made out of an objective and selfless love and knowledge of the child in question. These constant meetings make the school into an organism, and their purpose "is not so much the principles but the readiness of all teachers to live together in goodwill, and the abstention from any form of rivalry." [126]   These meetings enable real reports, and not merely marks, to be drawn up for every child[127].

The College of Teachers therefore becomes a training academy in which experience is pooled and which maintains each teacher's inner freshness and vitality[128]. Every teacher must be allowed his freedom and independence, and no attempt should be made to mould teachers into a preconceived form[129]. However, every teacher must be willing to give his co-operation without interference to every other, which will make the school and the children's education into a living whole, and not a haven for individual extremism[130].

"Fanaticism — which is so rife among men — is here ruled out. Fanaticism is the worst thing in the world, particularly in education — a fanaticism which makes a man press on in one direction and push ahead regardless of anything but his one aim, reduced to precise slogans." [131]

Although the College of Teachers has Anthroposophists in it, Anthroposophy (knowledge of the Soul Bodies, Spirit, Reincarnation and so on) is not taught. Only the fruits of Anthroposophy enter the school through the teacher's bearing and character[132].

All teachers are paid the same in a Waldorf School, whether they take a senior or junior class[133]. (In many modern Waldorf Schools, salary is calculated according to need: rent, dependants and circumstances.) No institutionalised seniority exists in the College of Teachers because although there is a chair and a committee, they are re-elected by the College each year, and it is an executive, not a hierarchical body).

5.3.1.3 Preparation and Training

For Steiner, "the question of education is principally a question of teachers" [134], and "within the whole complex of this subject the training of teachers is the most important auxiliary question" [135]. The following account covers the main points that Steiner made in this connection.

First of all it is essential for teachers to realise "how feeble our ideas have become in modern civilisation" [136] and how teacher training and educational philosophy have been intensely and lastingly permeated by materialism[137]. Teachers must examine themselves and realise how far they are products of the age, and how deeply they have been called on to submit themselves — through long and arduous training at school and university — to the intellectual materialism of the natural-scientific point of view. This has led them far from the, as yet, uncontaminated minds of young girls and boys[138].

Teachers must learn to return to childhood in soul and spirit, taking with them their learning and experience[139]. Teachers must rediscover what it is to be a child[140].

In order to do this, the first step is to conquer the vanity and sense of superiority with which intellectualism fills us[141], and then learn to bring our dead intellectual knowledge to life by permeating it with Feeling and Will.

> "The whole of our being must work in us as educators, not only the thinking man; the man of feeling and the man of will must also play their part." [142]

Before they are presented to children, the dead facts of modern scientific knowledge must be brought to life with living pictorial imagination which is connected and in accordance with real life. This can even be done with concepts in Physics once the teacher develops a strong imagination imbued with feeling[143].

When the teacher develops his imagination with the guidance of Spiritual Science, he discovers that he does not have to invent the images which symbolise knowledge, he has only to discover the images already made for him by nature: "God himself has painted the picture into nature." The child has brought this spiritual wisdom of living, imaginative perception with him directly from the spiritual world. And far from being inferior to the teacher, it is the child who can reveal the secrets of the spirit in the way he views the world[144]. When the teacher participates in the exercises outlined in Knowledge of the Higher Worlds, he finds he is able to move out of the isolation of his intellect and enter right into the life forces of, for example, plants. He "dives right into the external world" and sees how nature lives in pictorial imaginations, rather than in the abstract lists of chemicals so revered by modern science, yet so far from life. Thinking then merges with the living interflow and movement of Feeling.

> "One awakens as from a swoon. But now one no longer receives abstract thoughts, now one receives 'imaginations'. One gets pictures. And a materialistic view would not recognise these pictures as knowledge.

Knowledge, it is said, proceeds in abstract, logical concepts. Yes, but how if the world is not to be comprehended in the abstract concepts of logic? How if the world be a work of art: then we must apprehend it artistically, not logically." [145]

Teachers who are unable to achieve this level of imagination must use their sound judgement and observation to decide whether the imaginative forms of others (such as Steiner) are true[146]. Whatever the case, the artistic images presented to children must be given with absolute conviction and faith that such concepts are not mere intellectual constructions, but rooted in Creation itself. Unshakeable conviction is essential for images to pass from the teacher into the child's soul and spirit. Every vestige of intellectual vanity and scepticism for such images must be eliminated from the teacher's being when he teaches[147].

An example of such images which Steiner often used was the butterfly emerging from the chrysalis; an image given by nature to symbolise the immortality of the human soul[148].

The personal qualities and strengths of teachers in Waldorf Schools are much more important than any intellectual knowledge or technical skills they may have[149]. The teacher must cultivate "the highest ideals of humanity" especially when engaged with younger children[150].

The teacher's superficial personal identity recedes and he is freed from his physical self as he ponders on the cosmic significances of the inner rhythms of the human body and the descent of the child from the spiritual world to receive what can only be experienced in the physical world. This enables him to form a quite different relationship with his pupils than would otherwise be possible[151]. A religious quality of love and reverence for the child — even for the "ne'er-do-well" — enters the pedagogical relationship[152].

This consciousness is extended by cultivating the awareness that mankind is entering upon a new age, and is developing a level of freedom that has never before existed[153]. Teachers need to be open to new wisdom[154]. They should learn not so much to be engrossed in acquiring subject matter, "but rather how to cherish and cultivate within ourselves the spirit of an education which bears the future within it." [155]

The teacher should never allow himself to develop narrow, partisan views. He must rather strive to see the good in differing points of view, and preserve his own balance[156]. He should see the world as a totality[157] and be interested in the destiny of the whole of mankind[158].

"The great essential is for men and women to be wide-hearted, to be able to participate with their hearts and souls in culture and civilisation as a whole. This is what we try, through the principles of education, first to inculcate into the teachers — for in the Waldorf School the primary thing has been to educate them — and then through the teachers, into the pupils." [159]

The teacher has to find within himself the adaptability to respond appropriately to children's temperaments, whatever their form[160]. Furthermore, he ought always to be ready to adapt to developmental changes in his pupils, and never take their needs for granted[161].

The teacher who puts aside pedantry and modern educational theory which divorces him from children, will find that humour and liveliness will come into his teaching as a health-giving influence[162].

Above all, it is love that must fill the teacher's soul: love for the child, but also love for education itself, the teacher's knowledge and method. If the teacher has such love, which is objective in character, he will be able to give the child genuine freedom after puberty[163]. Love can be seen as a tangible influence in education.

"Watch yourselves and observe the difference — first, when you approach a child more or less indifferently, and then again when you approach him with real love. As soon as ever you approach him with love, and cease to believe that you can do more with technical dodges than you can with love, at once your educating becomes effective, becomes a thing of power. And this is more than ever true when you are having to do with abnormal children." [164]

The teacher should strive, "not for obscure, nebulous mysticism, but for the courageous, energetic permeation of (his) being with spirituality" which will ensure that when he speaks of the physical world he will not be led astray into materialism[165]. He must develop moral intuitions from his innermost self[166] and strive beyond "the empty phrase" to a real grasp of truth; beyond convention to a direct relationship to his fellow man; and beyond routine to consciousness of every single action[167].

The teacher will become aware of what it really means to think with his whole being when his Will and Feeling interpenetrate Thinking in full consciousness. Then he will be capable of real Imagination wherein external physical existence is quietened[168]. His thoughts themselves will become gestures which reach out and help to educate children, rather than being mere reflections of inward activity[169].

The development of the teacher's imaginative and intuitive consciousness enables him to awaken the child's Feelings, and all this is carried over into artistic activities which engage the child's Will (see 4.5.3). Therefore teacher training should be concerned with developing the teacher's artistic sensibilities, his feelings for form, sculpture, space, colour, music and language. Such artistic training would truly prepare teachers to educate children, far more than modern attempts to instil theories and methods into them which are quite alien to the child's living, artistic nature. Moreover, it is Art that will provide the proper foundation for rational, logical thinking, which is so prized yet so little understood by modern man (see 4.4.1).

"The understanding which will arise from inward comprehension of modelling and music will make men inwardly more rational, and then, believe me, their training will in fact be accelerated rather than delayed." [170]

5.3.1.4   Authority and Discipline

The following section deals with Steiner's indications as to the way in which the teacher ought to exercise his authority with children.

Attention has already been given to the role of authority in education (see 4.3,1, 4.3.3.1, 4.4.2.2, and 4.4.2.3). It has been explained that just as imitation is essential for the development of the child in the first stage of life, so authority is essential in the second. The teacher has to hold his authority in order to fulfil the innermost needs of the child. Only on the basis of an authority relationship can the adolescent feel an awakening freedom and power to judge for himself. It is by receiving the teacher's artistic concepts on the basis of authority and not of reason that the child can freely exercise his own powers of reason, which come into their own after puberty, and transmute imaginative concepts into abstract, intellectual form.

Authority must not be established by the use of reason[171] nor by drill[172] nor by force[173].

Between the change of teeth and puberty, the child should feel that he does not add or spell in a particular way because of reasons or rules, but because that is the way his teacher does it[174]. Children should be encouraged to turn to their teacher to ask questions. For example, after a story, children should be allowed a question time to satisfy themselves about the content of the story, and here the teacher is the authority. The teacher should satisfy the children's feelings about the story, but he should not reason out symbolism for them[175]. The teacher's stories and comparisons must be given with complete conviction (see 5.3.1.3) in order for the child to feel that the teacher is speaking from his whole soul, as an authority, and not merely from his intellect[176].

The teacher should make himself into a person worthy of authority, to whom children can turn and feel a natural reverence. He must be able to show children what he is capable of in his artistic mastery of the curriculum[177].

> "During the primary school age and far beyond it, for as long as education holds good, the whole teaching must be warmed through and fired by the artistic element. During the primary school years everything must be steeped in beauty, and in later years beauty must rule as the interpreter of truth." [178]

The child's Will should always be brought to expression in artistic activity. Through art the child's Thinking, Feeling and Will work together and he experiences the rightness of what the teacher is doing with him[179].

The teacher's influence on his pupils should arise out of an intimate, personal relationship with them, and he should never resort to sensationalism[180]. It is the teacher's most sincere and earnest feelings in all he says and does that educate most profoundly between the change of teeth and puberty.

"We shall rightly experience the good, so that we tread its path in later life, if we are not given a code of behaviour to follow, but have realised from the teacher's own warm-hearted words how much he loves a good deed and hates a bad one. His words can make us so warmly responsive to the good and so coldly averse to evil, that we turn naturally to the good because the teacher himself loves it. Then we grow up, not bound hand and foot by dogma, but filled with a spontaneous love for what is true, beautiful and good to the beloved teacher. If during the first period of school life we have learnt to adopt his standard of truth, beauty and goodness, a standard he has been able to express in artistic imagery, the impulse for these virtues becomes a second nature, for it is not the intellect that develops goodness. A man who has over and over again been told dogmatically to do this, or not to do that, has a cold, matter-of-fact feeling for what is good, whereas one who has learnt in childhood to feel sympathy with goodness and antipathy to evil, has drawn right into his whole rhythmic organism the capacity to respond to the good and to be repelled by what is evil." [181]

When authority breaks down in class, the teacher must realise that many of the orthodox methods of dealing with it are ineffective and may be harmful. Reprimands are of little help in changing habits and inclinations[182]. Reprovals are, of course, sometimes necessary, but it is much better to be able to hold children through the teacher's lesson than to have to resort to reprimands that concede the breakdown of authority[183].

The teacher should not encourage children's egotism by appealing to their ambition[184], nor should he ridicule children because this makes it difficult for them to find a right relationship with their class again[185]. Caning is best banished because of the physical and moral harm it causes, but at the same time the teacher must not forget that greater physical and moral harm can be done through wrong teaching[186]. The teacher must take into account the soul-nature of the child, and it is not so much what he does that matters ("One slap more or less is not of much consequence"), as much as how he does it[187]. Whatever the problem, it is always better to face it squarely, remembering that if it is repressed through extraneous discipline it will always reappear in various disguises in later life[188].

"All actual punishment I should consider superfluous and even harmful. The essential thing is to arouse a feeling for the objective damage that has been caused and the necessity of making it good. And if teaching time has been lost in dealing with this matter, then it must be made good after school hours, not as a punishment but simply to make up the time which has been lost." [189]

The teacher should look to himself first as the cause of a problem, either because

120

the children are bored, or else because he has no real relationship with them[190]. The teacher has to work on himself to develop a balanced, non judgemental attitude towards his pupils, always striving to understand rather than cast blame[191]. For example, a parent might believe that a young child is stealing money from a cupboard at home. However, the teacher must be able to see that it may be the force of imitation at work in the child, who has watched his parents taking money from the cupboard[192]. Imitation influences children profoundly, and it is for the teacher to ensure that evil influences are countered, using the right methods for the child's age. These methods include the teacher's actions in front of the child which must become permeated with a moral quality[193].

Much behaviour which is considered naughty is really a very healthy sign in young children, and shows the early, clumsy expression of the spirit[194]. Mistreatment of little children for such naughtiness often emerges in adolescence as an ungovernable nature, but this can be changed if it is properly met[195]. Problems may also be encountered with children who have attended other schools, where the teacher will have to "remould what has been spoilt in them". This becomes more difficult the older they are[196].

The teacher must learn to treat children according to temperament. The teacher's control of classroom seating asserts his authority, and when children of similar temperament are seated together they influence one another beneficially (see 4.6). Sometimes the teacher can use this principle directly:

"When a fault is not too serious it can certainly be very good for the teacher to do just what the pupils are doing, to say, for instance, when the pupils are grumbling: 'Oh yes, I can grumble too!' In this way the matter is treated, as it were, homeopathically. Homeopathic treatment is excellent for moral education." [197]

However, when treating more serious imbalances of temperament the teacher should never show the very faults that he is condemning in his pupils[198]. He should never respond to anger in his pupils by becoming angry himself and making threats such as, "If I see you getting angry once more, why then — then I shall throw the inkpot at your head!" [199]

In such instances he should portray such behaviour artistically in order to reflect it to his pupils, while remaining personally detached. This is done through stories in which the teacher can show the temperaments working within characters while he retains his own humour and complete self-control. For example, when he tells a story about a choleric character the choler in his pupils is calmed and subdued. This effect is also achieved by asking a choleric child to re-tell the story which requires a strong expression of his own temperament. When the teacher tells the story he must do so with full artistic sensibility, for only thus will it achieve its effect.

"But there must be nothing artificial in all this. If there is anything forced or inartistic in what the teacher gives the child it will have no result. The teacher must indeed have artist's blood in him so that what he enacts in front of the child shall have verisimilitude and can be accepted unquestioningly; otherwise it is a false thing in the teacher, and that must not be. The teacher's relation to the child must be absolutely true and genuine." [200]

This principle is a direct consequence of the child's developmental characteristics after the change of teeth when the Rhythmic System dominates and the child must be approached through his feelings and through pictures (see 4.3.2).

"The fact should not be overlooked that bad habits may be completely overcome by drawing attention to appropriate instances that shock or repel the child. Reprimands give at best but little help in the matter of habits and inclinations. If, however, we show the living picture of a man who has given way to a similar bad habit, and let the child see where such an inclination actually leads, this will work upon the young imagination and go a long way towards the uprooting of the habit. The fact must always be remembered: it is not abstract ideas that have an influence on the developing etheric body, but living pictures that are seen and comprehended, inwardly. The suggestion that has just been made certainly needs to be carried out with great tact, so that the effect may not be reversed and turn out the very opposite of what was intended. In the telling of stories everything depends upon the art of telling. Narration by word of mouth, cannot, therefore, simply be replaced by reading." [201]

Teachers can use the method of story-telling to arouse shame in children without pedantically telling them that they should be ashamed, and without drawing attention to a particular child[202]. Indeed, as a general rule it is wrong to take overt notice of negative behaviour. A teacher who does not achieve balance in his lessons, who tells story after story without giving time for questions, or without turning to other activities, will soon find his pupils misbehaving because of the tension so developed. The teacher must always have confidence, yet he must learn to respond readily and correctly to the inner needs of his pupils. A teacher who cannot develop the right authority relationship with his pupils must be replaced[203].

When the class misbehaves at the instigation of a few, the teacher should know his class well enough to pick out a few leaders who do not go along with the instigators. He should speak to these leaders and have them point out to the class that such misbehaviour makes teaching impossible, and that children ought to feel gratitude towards their teacher. This will restore authority. If a ringleader can be identified he should be compelled to denounce his conduct "to the utmost of his power" in front of the class. Working thus through the children has a powerful effect on the class' feelings[204].

Adolescent boys and girls need different treatment when they misbehave. The adolescent boy tries to imitate others in order to try to gain a relationship towards the world. However, his true Ego is still concealed at this age (see 4.4), and he therefore appears quite different from what he really is. Therefore the boy's behaviour should be thoroughly inquired into, but the boy should see that the teacher does not take it very seriously. The boy's natural tendency towards introversion is not aggravated and the teacher's authority will not be rejected if it is handled in this way. By contrast, the extroversion of a girl should be allowed expression and then simply ignored — not scornfully but with delicacy and grace — in order "to bring home to her the foolishness of her coquetry or her forwardness." [205]

This concludes Steiner's more general suggestions for teaching methods. The next section will outline his recommendations for the presentation of particular subjects. It will be seen that Steiner continues to restrict himself to developing only an overall orientation even when dealing with specific subjects, leaving the formulation of lessons and the curriculum to the creative energy of the teacher.

5.3.2 Subject Methods

The ways in which subjects should be presented can only be properly understood on the basis of an understanding of the true nature of the child's being[206] (See Chapters 3 and 4).

The following account covers Steiner's suggestions for presenting the various subjects. The order of their presentation bears no significance for their importance in the curriculum. Each subject is begun in some elementary form from the beginning, and is then gradually evolved with the child's development (see 4.2 to 4.4). Every subject has a part to play in the development of the child's Thinking, Feeling and Will[207].

Of particular importance is the principle that the teacher himself must creatively evolve Steiner's ideas, which are only broad suggestions and require development. The lesson content must be the teacher's own creation, and not merely copied from someone else[208]. Steiner only gives indications for a general orientation in lessons, never a complete plan. His only thorough plan is his description of human nature and child development, whose very essence is the impulse towards the development of creative expression[209].

5.3.2.1 Kindergarten

In kindergarten, the teacher should "do all kinds of things that the children can copy out of their own inner impulse of soul". For this, the teacher must prepare his whole being to be worthy of imitation[210].

Children can be exposed imitatively to foreign languages from a very early age, but otherwise "all other school subjects should as far as possible be postponed until after the change of teeth" [211].

5.3.2.2   Writing and Reading

It is "boundlessly important" that writing and reading should be correctly taught[212]. Modern schools attempt to teach children to read from their very earliest arrival in school, but little is done by way of writing[213]. This involves the child prematurely "in a process of development exclusively concerned with the head instead of the forces of his whole being" [214]. Right from the beginning the child's true nature of soul and spirit is harmed by forcing him to work more and more through his intellect alone, so that in later life his intellect becomes devoid of feelings and imagination, and can only work with rigid concepts as if it were an automaton. The child will have become alienated from his real being[215].

Letters themselves are abstract symbols which are alien to the nature of the child. The child feels towards them as the North American Indians felt when they first saw European script and thought it to be witchcraft[216]. Therefore, the teacher must introduce letters to the child in accordance with the child's mode of perception; through imaginative, living pictures[217].

Writing should first be introduced through art, which involves the whole being of the child pictorially and through his feelings.

> "What is a G, K, or U to a seven-year old? He really has not the slightest kinship with it.   It has taken the human being thousands of years to acquire this relationship.   The child must acquire an aesthetic relation to it.   Everything is exterminated in the child because the written characters are not human; and the child wants to remain human." [218]

The teacher's sacred task is to help the child to develop out of the imitative stage in the right way, without destroying the delicate forces of the soul.   The whole child must be drawn into learning.

> "Imitation must grow into a more external relationship to the outer world; it must develop into a beautiful picturing.   And at this stage there is scarcely as yet any need to differentiate between subjects of instruction that call for bodily activity on the part of the child, and subjects that are more related to the acquisition of knowledge." [219]

The teacher should begin to teach writing by helping the children to separate out the single sounds from the beginnings of whole words, such as the F from Fish, until the single sound can be breathed.   The child should learn to draw and paint the picture of the object chosen, in this case a fish, in such a way that the shape can gradually be transformed into the form of the capital letter which begins the word*.   Picture-writing arose like this in ancient times, and only gradually did the pictures come to represent sounds which were formed into words.   Children

---

* In German, nouns take a capital letter. The use of capitals is not appropriate in English, but is often used to retain Steiner's sequence and assist the pictorial presentation.

must experience exactly this transition over again with each letter. Later it can be shown how the sound of the letter also appears in the middle of words as the same sound or contributing to other sounds, and thus the small letters may be introduced. The teacher should take care to continue to write each letter so that it is seen to arise from the original picture. The activity of creating the letter forms will give the teacher's presentation an artistic freshness which the child will benefit from copying[220].

Vowels should be introduced differently. Whereas the consonants give form to words, vowels give them feeling. Therefore the pictures for vowels must evolve out of the inner feelings which are associated with vowel sounds[221]. These inner feelings can be expressed as a bodily gesture, such as the sound of A (ah), which is an expression of awe. When the body takes the form of 'A' with its arms and legs reaching downwards and apart, the body expresses outwardly what is felt inwardly when the sound is uttered*. Each vowel can be shown to arise in this way from the sound to the feeling and then to the gesture which suggests the form of the letter. These body gestures are the same as those used in Eurythmy (see 5.3.2.5)[222].

This is not a dry, mechanical process, but must be filled with fantasy for the child. Fairy tales and stories which relate to nature must be brought vividly and pictorially to the children, and the images for the letters should arise out of these so that they are imbued with imagination and feelings[223].

Handwriting and spelling should not be called "good" or "bad", but the child should always be encouraged to follow the teacher's example. Spelling should be taught through good, clear speech on the part of the teacher, so that to begin with the child is not conscious of it as a separate matter from writing** [224].

On this foundation, reading — first of all the reading of handwriting — develops naturally, without the need for drill.

"It is thus possible for us in the Waldorf School to teach writing by means of art. Then reading can be learned afterwards almost as a matter of course, without effort. It comes rather later than is customary, but it comes almost of itself." [225]

The teacher should choose reading books carefully, avoiding most of the modern material which is trivial, unimaginative or abstract. He should choose reading matter that will benefit the child's soul[226].

---

* The linking of sounds to inner feelings may seem strange to those who have not thought of it before. Development of an awareness of these things is not a simple matter, and requires careful study and practice.

** German is a more phonetic language than English, but to begin with English can also be treated in this way. However, like English, German has many dialects whose sounds bear little relation to the written language, so that careful preparation is necessary for the children to develop the standard dialect as a basis for spelling and educated speech. This is not to condemn their dialect but to add to it (see 5.3.2.3). Steiner, R. (1919) : Practical Advice to Teachers, pp 179-180, and see editor's note, p 180.

5.3.2.3 Home Language: Speech, Poetry, Grammar and Writing

The development of speech as a consciously practised activity is a central task for education, because man's Will and Spirit come to expression in speech.

> "Now we come to the ego. As the astral body in music, so the true nature of the ego-organisation can be studied in language. It may be assumed that everyone, even the doctors and teachers, accept the form of language of today as a finished product. If this is their standpoint they can never understand the inner configuration of language. This can only be understood if you regard language, not as the product of our modern mechanism, but as that in which the genius of language works in a living and spiritual way. You can do this if you set yourself to understand the way in which a word is formed. In words there lies untold wisdom, far beyond the grasp of man. All men's characteristics are expressed in the way they form their words, and the special peculiarities of any nation can be recognised in their language." [227]

Our feeling of being a personality and an ego is largely dependent on the faculty of speech, so that by developing speech correctly and by permeating it with consciousness, the personality of the child can be awakened without arousing egotism[228]. The "sense of speech" is one of the twelve senses of man that should be cultivated in education (see 3.3.2).

The earliest development of speech can be assisted by lovingly supporting the child's early attempts to walk (see 4.2.2). This is because speech involves the whole organism in early childhood. In the presence of children adult speech must be filled with truth and beauty, because the child takes in the adult's speech which reflects inner qualities or deformities of character and is absorbed into the whole organism of the child and reproduced imitatively[229].

The teacher should prepare his speech with great care.

> "I should recommend you to take special care to find your way into the various forms of the sounds and the forms of the syllables; see that you really grow into these forms so that you are conscious that you utter each sound, you lift each individual sound into consciousness." [230]

By discovering both the forms and the music of speech the teacher can develop an artistic feeling for words and language[231]. This feeling is carried over into recitation lessons in which children learn to recite poetry artistically, allowing the pure musical element of language to flow through their speech.

> "The content is suspended in the general melody and the creative poetic activity is then the forming of the language, not the content, the forming of the beat, the rhythm, the rhyme, in other words the musical element on which poetry is founded." [232]

126

Poetry should never be analysed with children, but treated purely artistically.

"This would be a means of thoroughly eliminating something really dreadful that is still very much prevalent in our schools: the abstract explanation of poems. This abstract explanation of poetry, verging almost on grammatical dissection, spells the death of everything that ought to work on the child. The interpreting of poems is something quite appalling." [233]

However, the child must have some understanding, especially of anything he has to learn by heart. It should never be merely a matter of rote drill, but the child's feeling or mood towards the content must be aroused[234]. Therefore, in order that the poem should have some meaning for the child, the subject matter of the poem should be covered in another lesson prior to the recitation lesson. The child should bring to recitation whatever background information will be necessary for him to glean the meaning of the poem aesthetically[235].

Dealing artistically with literature through recitation without analysis of meaning has a powerful educative influence on the Will. Inner harmonies and images develop the Will and Feelings, whereas by laying bare meaning, Will and Feeling are weakened[236] (See 4.5).

When recitation lessons are handled artistically, children develop a delight and yearning for poetry[237].

Children should develop the standard dialect in school, but it is not done by pedantic drill exercises. Instead, at the time when children love to hear stories told over and over again, the teacher can gradually bring them to the point where they can retell the stories themselves, from memory. They will soon learn to tell the stories imitating the dialect of the teacher, who can encourage them with occasional corrections. This can lead on gradually to the teacher encouraging the children to relate their own experiences to him in the standard dialect[238]. (See 5.3.2.2)

From the age of approximately nine years (see 4.3.3.2), grammar has an increasingly important part to play in education. The "horror" of abstract grammar lessons should not blind the teacher to the value of a proper presentation of grammar, which serves to lift language into consciousness. The parts of speech should be characterised simply and boldly, without recourse to too much abstraction. Nouns can be shown to separate us from other objects, and adjectives express our feelings towards the objects.

In verbs we unite ourselves with the being of another and in our souls we participate in his being and actions[239]. Consciousness of the functions of the parts of speech in language enables us to form quite a different attitude towards it, and to realise the genius at work in it[240]. Modern linguistic science, impressive as it is, divorces language from man and is unable to see how language weaves into the Feeling and Will of the human being[241].

Grammar lessons should be largely conversational and abstract grammar textbooks should be avoided. After the age of about twelve the most economical method of teaching children grammar is through exercises involving the transformation of parts of speech from one to another. For example children should be shown how a clause such as "The meadow is greening" can be transformed into a noun phrase such as "The green meadow", and the changing effect of the two can be studied[242]. Where rules are necessary they should be written into textbooks without the use of examples, so that fresh examples must be made up each time the child has to return to the rule. This enables the child to develop a feeling for the rule itself and not to fix his thoughts on a few examples. Examples should be mainly discussed, and not preserved in writing. A passage should never be laboriously analysed, and the teacher should not make up "fantastic sentences" for discussion, but simply develop what serves his purpose without being too far divorced from life. These methods are also applicable for the introduction of Grammar in Foreign Language lessons (see 5.3.2.4)[243].

Essays and compositions should not be demanded of children too early. Up to the age of nine or ten the child should only be asked to retell what has been told to him in the form of stories. After that he can gradually begin to relate what he feels and thinks about the images and thoughts he is given. However, it is only towards the twelfth year that the child begins to acquire the inner thought structure which is necessary to write essays out of his own free feelings and ideas (see 4.3.3.1 to 4.3.3.3). If the child is asked to express himself too early, "at a later age of life the child will be inwardly weak and ineffective" [244].

Up to puberty (fourteen or fifteen years) the child should be asked to recount his experiences, in which he should practise bringing his sense impressions and recollections into consciousness and accurately describing them without becoming lost in fantasy. This is a vital and much underestimated skill in modern life, where many people are barely able to recall what they have seen or heard from one moment to the next. Without such education people are unable to be truthful about their experiences. Letter writing, including business correspondence, can also be practised before puberty. Such disciplined writing will lay a firm foundation for the development of strong creative expression after puberty. This is the correct approach for writing in Foreign Languages as well[245].

5.3.2.4   Foreign Languages

The choice of which foreign languages should be taught in school should be made more on the basis of expediency than for aesthetic reasons. It is less important which languages are done than that they are done[246].

Up to the age of about nine years, foreign language lessons should involve learning only to speak the language. The child's imitative faculty which is still strong should be used, so that when the child hears his teacher speak he absorbs not only the words but the inner genius of the language, its grammar and subtle rhythms. These enter the child's whole being of body, soul and spirit and are then reproduced imitatively. Languages learned after this age begin to be held only in the soul and spirit, so that it is an important educational principle to introduce foreign languages as early as possible in the correct way[247].

After the age of about nine the beginnings of conscious awareness of grammar can be developed, as with the home language (see 5.3.2.3).

Translation from one language to another is mostly a laborious waste of time, and it is by the direct method of learning to speak the language itself that the child can enter right into the language[248]. Words should be connected directly with what they represent and the child should not have to think of the corresponding word in another language[249]. In the case of "dead" languages such as Greek and Latin, which children should certainly not have to speak, the translation method is correct. However, these languages must only be introduced after puberty when the child is ready to learn abstract grammatical structures[250].

From the age of thirteen or fourteen, foreign language lessons should involve the child in reading the language and expressing his own thoughts in it. The teacher should help the child to read with the right pronunciation, and then, rather than translating the passage, the pupil should be asked to give a free rendering of the passage in his own language. The opposite procedure should be practised by discussing a subject in the home language and then attempting to repeat it in the foreign language. The level of difficulty depends on the ability of the child. Grammar should be approached by taking whole sentences in which the parts of speech can be transformed to develop different grammatical structures (see 5.3.2.3)[251].

It is a great advantage to have one teacher for all the languages that a class is learning, so that he can compare the characteristics of one language with those of another. In this way great economy can be achieved in language study[252]. Children should also compare the sounds of different languages, and learn how each language serves the purpose of the culture to which it belongs[253].

5.3.2.5   Eurythmy* and Gymnastics

This section couples Eurythmy with Gymnastics in order to compare them. The link between Eurythmy and the previous three sections on reading, writing and language will be made clear.

Eurythmy is an art form which was developed and is taught within the Anthroposophical Society and Waldorf Schools. Only its basic principle will be outlined here. Fuller accounts and diagrams to suggest the movements may be found elsewhere[254].

Eurythmy involves the outward, physical expression of what happens inwardly when one hears language and music. It is "the making visible of listening" [255]. When sounds are heard or uttered, the inner being makes an invisible gesture which one can discover when one develops a feeling for sound. These gestures are not

---

* The h is omitted because in Greek an aspirated rho does not keep the aspirate in compounds.

mime or conventional dance; they are movements which express the Feelings and Will which are aroused by the pure sound of a piece of verse or expressive language. The thought element — the intellectual content or meaning — is removed, and for each sound there is a movement, so that each movement of the body flows into the next.

> "Just as there are different forms of the larynx and other organs for A (ah), I (ee)*, L, M, so are there also corresponding movements and forms of movement. These forms of movement are therefore those expressions of will which otherwise are provided in the expressions of thought and will of speech and song. The thought element, the abstract part of thought in speech is here removed and all that is to be expressed is transposed into movement. Hence eurythmy is an art of movement, in every sense of the word. Just as you can hear the A so can you see it, just as you can hear the I so can you see it." [256]

The eurythmist also wears colour veils which express the overall mood and character of the verse used[257].

Eurythmy was developed some years before Waldorf education, and Steiner felt that schools could use it in its original form, without any special adaptation for education, just as music and painting should not be any different in education from what they are in adult life. Art should be infused directly into human culture[258]. Modern man tended to look for the artistic in the trivial, but what was needed was the experience of living impulses of Will and Feeling, and out of this "free activity" man would discover what it was to become truly artistic[259].

The value of Eurythmy for education is that it cultivates the Will and Feelings. Bodily movement can be developed in two directions: the body can be made to do purposeless, senseless activities which follow the demands of the body alone, or else the outer movements of the body can gradually become purposeful and penetrated with meaning as an expression of sound. The first direction tends to be that of Gymnastics; the second that of Eurythmy[260].

In the child's first year of school, simple gymnastics should lead over into Eurythmy which, together with singing, playing a musical instrument, painting and drawing, promotes the development of the Will "to a very special degree"[261]. The whole Will and Ego of the child come to expression in language (see 5.3.2.3) so that Eurythmy, which expresses the sounds of language as physical gesture, leads the Ego into activity. When Eurythmy lessons form the basis for writing and reading (see 5.3.2.2) the child is given his unity: two subjects which are normally divorced — reading and physical activity — are brought together through art in the Waldorf School[262].

Eurythmy, together with other subjects which demand bodily activity such as writing, handwork or music, provide a balance for the more contemplative subjects

---

* The sounds here are the German pronunciations.

such as History or Geography in which the child is physically still[263]. Eurythmy and singing "spiritualise" the child. They suffuse his whole being with living Will, and by balancing this influence through contemplative subjects that require the stillness of Thinking, the spiritual impulse which has been aroused is apprehended and absorbed into Thinking (see 4.5). Therefore Eurythmy and singing prepare the child for the contemplative lessons that ought to follow[264].

Eurythmy lessons are also balanced by Gymnastics lessons. Eurythmy done in the afternoon will continue to work on in the child's sleep at night, and if the child does gymnastics the following day, the spiritual, Will impulses from Eurythmy flow into the physical body as a health-giving influence[265].

Gymnastics ought not to be practised as an activity which is alien to man. The human being should not be forced to fit and mimic activities and postures which have been thought up and then imposed on him as precise, rigid models. The human being himself must be brought into Gymnastics. The child should be led to consciously experience his bodily activity with interested attention, and to become aware of the subtle feelings and sensations that accompany in-breathing or out-breathing, movements of the limbs, running and so on. The child must learn to "feel and perceive himself; he can consciously participate in all that is going on in his bodily nature." And it is from the child's living experience of his body, when thinking and feeling are engaged with the body, that the right activities or postures (for running, breathing and so on) should proceed[266].

Gymnastics should also lead the child to develop a feeling for external space, not merely three dimensional space which is a geometric abstraction, but space in relation to the body, above and below, left and right, behind and in front[267]. Within this context, movements for the development of agility and physical skill can be devised using a knowledge of anatomy and physiology. The teacher should use demonstration to show children what to do to practise physical skills and to develop a feeling for space[268]. Gymnastics may be contrasted here with Eurythmy:

"What is happening when the forces of your being flow into the limbs? In the ordinary gymnastic exercises the human being lends himself to space; in eurythmy he carries out movements that express his being and are in accordance with the laws of his organism. To allow what is inner to express itself outwardly in movement: that is the essence of eurythmy. To fill the outer with the human being so that the human being unites itself with the outer world: that is the essence of gymnastics." [269]

Individual children may require special exercises in Gymnastics, not only for physical reasons but because by working with the body, the teacher can influence the child's soul. Therefore the class teacher should also take the Gymnastics lesson so that a unity can be achieved in the child's education[270].

Intricate exercises in co-ordination are of great value in education. For example, if the child is given two sets of movements in which he has to touch a certain part of his body with a particular finger, and if he is then told to alternate these movements quickly, the child's whole nervous system is stimulated. Such exercises lay a good foundation for the child's ability to connect and separate ideas and perceptions[271]. The great alertness required for these co-ordination movements also makes the child's pictorial, imaginative thinking mobile and skilful, and if done at around the age of eight years especially, they will benefit the child for the whole of his life[272].

5.3.2.6   Mathematics: Arithmetic   and   Geometry

Steiner discussed the introduction of Arithmetic and Geometry quite separately.

Arithmetic is an important subject for the development of the child and the use of calculating machines is inimical to education. Teachers ought not to abdicate their role to machines as if mathematical calculation had mere utilitarian value.

> "Today when we speak of the objective method of teaching, we keep the teaching quite apart from the personality of the teacher.   We drag in every possible kind of gadget, even those dreadful calculating machines, in order that teaching may be as impersonal as possible." [273]

Arithmetic should be taught in accordance with the inner nature of the child himself, and not imposed on the child as a predetermined logical and abstract structure.   The teacher must develop a sense for the reality of the child's nature, and not only for logic.

> "A sense for reality is sorely lacking in our day, and this is due to the fact (though this is not always admitted) that a thing is considered to be true when it can be observed and is logical.   But logic alone cannot create truth, for truth can only arise when a thing is not only logical but in accordance with reality." [274]

The reality of the child's nature is that he perceives the world as concrete, whole realities, and not as abstractions or as parts of realities.   Therefore, if the teaching of Arithmetic is to be in keeping with the child's nature it must in every case begin with a whole reality and then proceed to divide the whole into its parts[275].

Education strengthens and enlivens the child if it is in keeping with his nature, but destroys something in the child if it opposes it (see 4.4.1).   Accordingly, the teacher of Arithmetic should always begin by awakening in the child an awareness of the whole[276].

The first "whole" that the child should develop an understanding of is the number one.   This may be done by pointing out that the child himself is an indivisible unit, a "one".   The writing of numbers should then proceed in the style of Roman numerals to begin with, so that "two" can be shown by putting the hands together, "three" by a group of children standing together, "four" by the legs of an animal, "five" by the hand and thumb separated as a V, and "ten" by crossed hands, and so on.   In this way the idea for each number is derived from real, concrete life as in the case of writing (see 5.3.2.2).   Only after the child has developed a living picture of each number should the idea of the sequence of numbers be introduced, and then physical activity and rhythm can be brought into counting by having the children stamp when the final number of a sequence is counted (1,2,3,4 ... 1,2,3,4 ...). The rhythm and stamping for each sequence strengthens the idea of the whole[277].

The child should be made to count while he is moving because in this way what takes place in the inner being is also brought to expression in the outer.

" ... what lies at the root of Arithmetic is consciously willed movement, the sense of movement. When you bring the sense of movement into activity in this way you quicken a child's arithmetical powers. You bring something up out of the subconscious ...." [278]

When teaching addition the teacher should begin with a group of objects (balls or pebbles) and then divide the objects among several children. In this way the usual process of addition is reversed (10 = 2+5+3), and the child proceeds from the sum to the addenda. When the child experiences addition in this order he develops a quite different understanding of it from the usual method[279].

In subtraction the usual process is to begin with the minuend and subtrahend and to have to find the remainder. However, this is not the way we experience subtraction in reality. In life we perceive a discrepancy between two wholes, an original amount (the minuend: "I had ten apples") and a subsequent amount (the remainder: "There are three left"), and we then proceed to work out the subtrahend ("Seven have gone"). This is the order that the teacher should follow[280].

Multiplication and division should not be rigidly differentiated in the first school years. Multiplication should be taught by providing the product and then giving the child one multiplicand and asking him to find the other. This is much the same as division, but the emphasis in teaching division should be towards developing a concept of measurement; not of dividing the whole into parts but of finding how often a smaller unit fits into a larger one[281].

Problems in Arithmetic should begin with a realistic situation (21 apples and 3 children) and the child should have to find the abstract part (the number each child should get). Such problems strengthen the child's thinking[282].

Moving from the whole to the parts as an educational principle has profoundly beneficial effects on the child's Thinking, but the benefits extend beyond the intellect into the child's whole soul, and therefore it has moral consequences as well. If a child's inner, natural need to find concrete, whole experience in the world is frustrated by constantly forcing him to fit together abstract parts into meaningful wholes, then he develops an inner acquisitiveness, a craving for wholeness. Conversely, when the child's need for wholeness is fulfilled and he is able to work towards abstraction of his own Will and ability, then he develops consideration and moderation.

"At first sight there seems to be no logical connection between the treatment of numbers and moral ideas, so little indeed that one who will only regard things from the intellectual point of view, may well laugh at the idea of any connection. It may seem to him absurd. We can also well understand that people may laugh at the idea of proceeding in addition from the sum instead of from the parts. But when one sees the true connections in life one knows that things which are logically most remote are often in reality exceedingly near." [283]

Taught in the right way the child will be much more susceptible to moral examples and sympathetic to what is good.

Once the child has been given a few examples of multiplication he can proceed to learn the tables by heart, an exercise which is important for the development of the memory in the early years at school[284]. The tables are restructured in accordance with the principle of moving from the whole to the parts (12 = 3x4) and they are said rhythmically[285]. (See 4.3.4 for the importance of using rhythm with the child between the change of teeth and puberty).

As far as possible, Arithmetic should only make the change from concrete problems to abstract numbers when the child is between his ninth and tenth years (see 4.3.3.2). This transition is greatly assisted by the old, English system of using units of dozens, scores, shillings, pence, feet and inches because these have a real, concrete meaning for the child. The human being can develop a right and healthy feeling for such units. The decimal system is based on an abstract concept of number and there is no terminology for referring to large numbers, such as a hundred, as ten tens. When a child can speak of ten dozen he can develop a real feeling for the number as a concrete reality. The size of such units is of no significance, it is their value as manageable, meaningful ideas that has educational importance[286].

Geometry has a profound origin in man's spiritual being. The Geometrical forms (cube, octahedron, dodecahedron, etc.) are not merely inventions of the intellect but part of the laws of the cosmos.

"These bodies are not invented, they are reality, but unconscious reality. In these and other geometrical solids lies a remarkable harmony with the subconscious knowledge which man has. This is due to the fact that our bone system has an essential knowledge; but your consciousness does not reach down into the bone system. The consciousness of it dies, and it is only reflected back in the geometrical images which man carries out in figures. Man is an intrinsic part of the universe. In evolving geometry he is copying something that he himself does in the cosmos." [287]

The conscious mind assumes that the sense of sight encompasses both colour and form, but in reality this is not so. If the sense of sight could be isolated from the other senses it would register only colour. Form is perceived in conjunction with the sense of movement which operates unconsciously as a Will-sense, and then reflects its activity into consciousness so that we imagine that we perceive colour and form with one and the same sense (see 3.3.1.3 and 3.3.2).

"Thus you call forth the form from your whole body by appealing to the sense of movement which extends throughout your body. This matches what I have already explained to you: the human being actually executes geometrical forms in the cosmos and then raises them into knowledge." [288]

Therefore Geometry lessons must involve the child in movement of his Limb System (see 3.3.1.3), using varied and inventive exercises in which a rod may be used to complete geometric forms with the body[289]. In this way the basic geometric forms (triangle, square, line, circle) can be introduced through drawing lessons. The transition to Geometry should begin only after the ninth year when the child should begin "the search for the relationships between forms" [290].

This "search" is destroyed when we give the child ready-made, abstract constructions of geometric forms. Instead we should begin by awakening and strengthening his sense of symmetry. This is done by drawing half of a form (such as that of a pear, etc.) on the board, adding a line down the middle, and then asking the child to complete the form. This awakens "an inner, active urge in the child to complete something as yet unfinished" [291].

"At first he will be extremely clumsy, but gradually through balancing out the forms he will develop in himself observation which is permeated with thought and thinking which is permeated with imaginative observation. His thinking will be all imagery." [292]

From a two sided symmetry and the conception of how an object is reflected, the child can proceed to more complex forms and a sense for inner and outer symmetry, contrasting enclosed forms with their complementary open, divergent forms. Steiner gives examples of such forms which are curving, artistically pleasing designs calling for the extension of one's sense of composition and harmony. The teacher should be aware that during sleep the child's Etheric Body continues to work towards perfection of forms which are given to the child as incomplete. If the teacher allows Geometry to work on in the child overnight, "great vitality can be generated in the being of the child" [293].

The teacher should never impose trivial and obvious "object lessons" on children. However, object lessons have their place, for example when they are used to demonstrate the Pythagorean Theorem. It can be shown concretely with diagrams instead of abstractly, that in a right angled isosceles or scalene triangle, the square on the hypotenuse is equal to the sum of the squares on the other two sides. Children can see the demonstration of the theorem rather than having only the abstract rule, and each time they want to remember it they can re-create it imaginatively. If the diagrams used are supported with the use of colour, the impression will be strengthened for the child. Geometry should always be based on concrete thoughts, and proceed from the simple and real to the complex. In this way teaching will prove to be much more economical than if the teacher were to try to get children to work with abstractions[294].

Geometry should be linked to Mineralogy (the forms of crystals) and thence to Physics, and also to Geography through the drawing of maps[295].

5.3.2.7 Science

Steiner took great pains to make teachers aware that modern abstraction in science is a powerful and dangerous influence in education so that they would realise the importance of adopting his method of transforming scientific concepts into an imaginative form that children can relate to. The following account reflects this concern before going on to describe the kinds of concepts that Steiner considered appropriate for education.

For Steiner, a great tragedy of the modern age is that children can no longer look to adults for knowledge and authority. Knowledge has become objectified and externalised from man (even physically, in the form of books) under the pervasive influence of natural science. Man has stripped knowledge of everything that is human. Modern scientific concepts are devoid of imagination and feeling or anything that assists man to relate personally to his world. They have become so abstracted from real life that the human being can only apprehend them with his intellect; no bridge can be forged between them and the rest of man's being of Feeling and Will. Steiner personifies natural science to create an image of the problem:

"But human beings do not really fit in with this objective creature who is strutting about in their midst, for true and genuine manhood has no kinship with this cold, objective, bolstered-up creature. True, as time has gone on, libraries and research institutes have been established. But the young, especially, are not looking for libraries or research institutes. They are looking in libraries for — it is almost beyond one to say the word – they are looking for human beings — and they find, well, they find librarians!" [296]

When reading books on modern science we must realise "how we are forced to plunge into an intellectual iciness". Such knowledge is useless and harmful in education because it destroys the true nature of cognition in man (see 4.4.1). Scientific knowledge must be humanised by the teacher before he gives it to children[297].

"Education must have soul, and as scientist one cannot have soul. We can have soul only through what we are artistically. We can have soul if we give science an artistic form through the way it is presented, but not through the content of science as it is understood today." [298]

By means of his own inspiration developed through Spiritual Science, the teacher must transform the dead, abstract concepts (definitions, laws, lists of elements etc.) in scientific textbooks into realistic, pictorial ideas which the child can relate to with his Thinking, Feeling and Will (see 4.5). Such artistic conceptions are not the rigid forms of thought so popular in modern education, which consist of facts and definitions that can be drilled into children and tested formally. Artistic conceptions are amenable to the imagination and they evolve as the child grows up; they respond to his inner nature which develops gradually through fantasy and imagination into more objective intellectual cognition.

"The teacher who in the twelfth year calls for the definitions that were used in earlier life is like a cobbler who wants to put the shoes of the child of three on to the child of ten. He can only get his toes into the shoes, for they no longer reach around the heels. A great deal of the spiritual and psychic nature remains outside of and beyond the education and instruction. What is necessary is that through the medium of what is flexible and artistic we give the child in picture form perceptions, ideas, and feelings, which are capable of metamorphosis, which can grow together with the soul simply because the soul itself is growing." [299]

An education which fails to cultivate man's Feelings and Will leaves these under the sway of his animal instincts, the results of which are more than evident in modern life (see 5.1).

Science lessons should call on the child to go beyond the information revealed to him by his physical senses alone. For example, he should learn to imagine the whole, new plant invisible yet present within the seed. "He must, in feeling, divine the secrets of existence". Stories and parables can be so created that they transform scientific information into living, pictorial narration which absorbs the child's whole being and precludes "what desolation is wrought in the soul and body by an instruction that rests on external sense-perception alone" [300].

In his stories, the teacher enables mountains, plants and animals to reveal their characteristics anthropomorphically, so that the child develops a flexible, imaginative and beautiful foundation for his knowledge of the world. Up to the age of nine (see 4.3.3.1 and 4.3.3.2) the child should only be taught to think of nature anthropomorphically. After nine, the transition from narration to a more objective study of the world must remain free from abstraction. For example, when a plant is studied it must be presented in its full, natural reality, so that the child can come to feel how the seed unfolds into the plant and the earth substances penetrate the root while the sun draws out the blossoms. The child must develop a feeling for the whole before he proceeds to study its parts[301].

The teacher should draw a clear distinction, both for himself and his pupils, between the activity of going out into nature and examining plants and rocks in their real surroundings, and what is done in the classroom where a specimen is divorced from nature for the purpose of closer study.

"The kind of feeling we should seek to arouse in the children is: Unfortunately we have to dissect nature when we bring it into the classroom. But the children should nevertheless feel this as a necessity, for the destruction of what is natural is also necessary in the building up of the human being." [302]

During the child's ninth year and up to his twelfth (see 4.3.3.2) the first simple phenomena of physics can be shown to the child. These should be presented as objective phenomena without demonstrating them at work in man's physical body – for example, the refraction of light can be demonstrated with the use of lenses, but it should not yet be related to the human eye. This is because although the child's Thinking has become capable of objective perception, it is only at the age of about twelve that it finds its inner relation to the physical world (see 4.3.3.3)[303].

Instead, the nine year old child's understanding of man should begin with a study of the forms of the body using drawing and modelling. The head is like a ball, perched on the trunk of the body which is like the segment of a larger sphere, and the limbs seem to be appendages inserted into the trunk from the outside. Such images will arouse a feeling for the body which will be strengthened when the forms are moulded in clay. Then the child should develop a feeling for the way his whole body works together as a constellation of organs. The eyes, ears, nose and mouth take in information and sustenance which unite with the organs for breathing and digestion and all are served by the legs which move the body, and the hands that reach out to the world[304]. (see also 5.3.2.10.2, Sculpture)

The child should always be led to the feeling that even in the forms of his body he has an essential unity with all the kingdoms of nature. For example, he should feel that the earth is a living being which brings forth plants through its inner laws, just as the human head brings forth hair through its own respective laws[305].

Moreover, the animal world can be presented to the child in such a way that he feels himself to be intimately united with it. If the child is merely given the names of animals (lion, camel, etc.) he can find no orientation towards them; they appear to be a random collection of phenomena. However, if the teacher uses his imagination he can unfold the characteristics of the animal kingdom in such a way as to give the child a vivid and vital conception of the interrelationships between animals and man:

> "How are we to regard the animals? Now, anyone who can contemplate the animals with imaginative vision, instead of with the abstract intellect, will find each animal to be a portion of the human being. In one animal the development of the legs will predominate — whereas in man they are at the service of the whole organism. In another animal the sense organs, or one particular sense organ, is developed in an extreme manner. One animal will be specially adapted for snouting and routing (snuffling), another creature is specially gifted for seeing, when aloft in the air. And when we take the whole animal kingdom together we find that what outwardly constitutes the abstract divisions of the animal kingdom is comprised in its totality in man. All the animals taken together, synthetically, give one the human being. Each capacity or group of faculties in the human being is expressed in a one-sided form in some animal species." [306]

There is no need to explain this to the child, but through the picture that the teacher develops of each animal, the child will come to feel the uniting influence of this principle[307].

138

For example, the natural history of the cuttlefish should be described in such a way that the child develops an artistic picture of how all its sense organs are contained within the body, and respond sensitively to impressions from the outside world. The whole body of the cuttlefish is therefore like the head in the human being, incorporating all the sense organs. By contrast, the higher animals (mouse, cow, horse, etc.) have sense organs in the head which, together with the limbs, protrudes from the body in such a way as to feed and protect the trunk. Man's greatest perfection lies in the differentiation between the legs and hands, which predisposes him to walk upright. The lower animals are therefore most like human heads moving around freely, whereas the higher animals are most developed in the trunk, and man in his limbs. This ordering has an important moral consequence. When the child sees man's body in this light he is led away from the egotistical belief that the human head and its intellect (which is sterile when divorced from the rest of man's being, see 4.5) is such a superior organ in nature. Instead, the feeling is awakened that it is through the work of his hands (his Will, see 4.5.3) that man can attain his greatest perfection[308].

Furthermore, the moral value of a "consciousness of the synthesis of all nature in man" is of the greatest importance for the modern age. It awakens Feelings and Will in man which enable him to find his place within the natural order of things as a whole human being, whose highest expression is to be found in the work of his hands.

> "You can instil this most particularly important moral element into the children's souls if you endeavour to shape the natural history lessons in a manner that will give them no clue that you want to teach them a moral lesson. But you will not be able to instil even a trace of anything moral into them if you teach natural history as something separate from man, if you describe the cuttlefish by itself, the mouse, lamb or horse by itself and even man by himself; this would be nothing but an explanation of verbal definitions. For you can only explain man by building him up out of all the other organisms and functions in nature. Schiller admired in Goethe the way his conception of nature led him to build up man in a naïve manner out of all the separate parts of nature; he expressed this admiration in the beautiful letter he wrote to Goethe at the beginning of the seventeen-nineties." [309]

Everything that the teacher takes from scientific textbooks must be illuminated, brought into vivid pictorial form, and integrated into a holistic conception of the living world before it is communicated to the child[310]. Scientific classification isolates and disintegrates knowledge and has arisen because natural scientists, far from being the realistic and practical thinkers that they deem themselves to be, have lost their understanding of the real, living, whole world, and have become the most theoretical of people. For example, Botany renders the world chaotic for the child. He can find no relationship between Botany and what he experiences as reality[311].

By the eleventh or twelfth year of life the child is ready to study mineralogy. He can now conceive of rock as an objective, lifeless reality (see 4.3.3.3). However, mineralogy must unfold as a concrete reality, and proceed from the whole to the parts.   It should be introduced by showing the construction of the earth and mountains, and then proceed to "try to unfold the whole mineral world out of a lump of rock". Quartz, mica, feldspar and so on should not be shown as isolated samples but mixed within a lump of granite[312].

From about the twelfth year the child is ready to study causality in physics (see 4.3.3.3), but in this the teacher should not stray too far from life, nor deal with trivia.   For example, the principle of the lever should not be introduced by abstract definitions, but by having the child work with a pair of scales as if he were weighing out goods in a shop, so that he develops a feeling for equilibrium and gravity.   Similarly, convection may be studied by observing the influence of a stove in a room; how the ceiling becomes warmer than the floor.

Electricity should be shown by means of a concrete demonstration, and vividly but realistically described[313].

Working in this way from reality the child will not tire, whereas by working with abstractions in which the Feelings and Rhythmic System have no part, the child soon tires and his memory for the material is weak (see 4.5.2)[314].

The teacher must develop his own feelings for natural and scientific phenomena so that he can arouse the feelings of the child.   He should always renew his first sense of wonder for such things as the mechanism used for telegraphy[315].   The idea of a vacuum, a space devoid of air, should have something of a feel of horror about it, and the teacher should read Goethe's treatise on granite to develop a mood and relationship towards "that primeval father, the sacred granite of remote antiquity".   This is how the teacher can bring life into his lessons; not sensationalism, but the real life of Feeling, so fostering the growth of the child's inner life, instead of burdening him with abstract, isolated and dead ideas[316].

Science lessons should achieve the harmonious education of the whole child, using the child's periods of sleep in the process of learning.   A concrete experiment in class or the study of a phenomenon in nature arouses the child's Will impulses (see 4.5).   These must then be balanced by going over the experiment again from memory.   The act of remembering calls on the child to use his Feeling and Thinking (see 4.5.2).   When the child goes to sleep that night, the images of what he has witnessed and recalled in memory flow through his Limb and Rhythmic Systems and form in his Head System.   These must be brought to fruition the following day by asking him to consider and reflect on them, so drawing them into full consciousness of Thought.   If this is not done and the teacher merely continues with more experiments, the images and ideas remain at a semi-conscious level and become confused and scattered among new incoming observations[317].

Science lessons should support what is done in Geography[318], and after puberty they should consciously aim to lead the child into practical life through activities like spinning and weaving, technical chemistry and the application of these things in factories.   The child should learn about and have experience of the world of technology, particularly those mechanical inventions that will be part of his life when he leaves school (from domestic appliances to trains and so on[*]). He should not feel alienated from the inventions of man, but should be able to find his place in social life. Up until puberty the child should learn about everything that relates man to nature; thereafter he begins to open out to the world, and education should prepare him to enter social and economic life in the right way[319].

5.3.2.8 Geography

For Steiner, Geography should encompass much more than it normally does in schools, so that within it, "the achievements of all the other lessons should meet and flow together in all sorts of ways."

> "Geography really can become a great channel into which everything flows and from which a great deal can also be derived." [320]

Geography should become so integrated with other subjects that much of it should be covered outside the Geography lesson, and many other subjects should be discussed in Geography.

> "It is indeed a good thing if you can use the Geography lessons to bring a unity to all the other subjects. Perhaps the worst thing that can happen to Geography is for it to be regimented into a strictly demarcated time-table, which is something we anyway do not want." [321]

For example, Geometry can be integrated with life by showing its use in geographical mapping. Geography can portray Physics, Chemistry and the natural histories of plants, animals and man in their real contexts within the world. In History the child should study the ways in which different peoples have developed their characteristics (languages, economic, social and cultural customs) in the context of their geographical settings[322].

While the child is between the ages of nine and twelve, Geography should concentrate on the child's own country, developing "the theme of the economic links between man and his natural environment." It would be too pedantic to begin with the local neighbourhood and then spread out gradually from there. Instead, the teacher should use the local neighbourhood to help find his bearings in relation to different landscapes. Then he can proceed to build up on the chalkboard a bold picture of the major mountain ranges and rivers of the country, showing representative lumps of rock from the main geological structures, and plants which grow at various altitudes. In this way the child gains a vivid picture of the whole country before moving to the parts, in which the teacher should give the child a picture of

---

* This suggests that Steiner would encourage schools to introduce children to computers even though he rejected the use of calculators in Mathematics (see 5.3.2.6); the point being that mechanical devices should be used to develop, and not replace, thinking and understanding in education.

the physical characteristics of particular areas and the way the people of each area live. The positioning of towns at river confluences and ore deposits can be described, as can the soil requirements of different crops, so that the child awakens to "some idea of the economic links that exist between the natural formation of the land and the conditions of human life." [323]

The drawing of maps is an important artistic activity, developing the child's pictorial conception of the whole of his country and gradually coming to see its various parts. Landscapes are transformed into maps, showing mountains, hills, rivers, forests, orchards, crops, pastures and villages, and using colour to enliven them[324].

Everything that the teacher develops into a picture for the child's imagination should as far as possible be drawn into real, concrete experience for the child, beginning by taking the child back to earlier ages.

> "And if you could even make little ploughs and let them cultivate the school garden, if they could be allowed to cut with small sickles or mow with small scythes, this would establish a good contact with life. For more important than dexterity is the soul contact made between the life of the child and the life of the world. It is a fact that a child who has cut grass with a sickle or mown it with a scythe, a child who has drawn a furrow with a little plough, will turn into a different person from one who has not done these things. Quite simply the soul element is changed. Abstract lessons in manual skills are not really a substitute for this." [325]

Before the child turns twelve, Geography should give him a preliminary feeling for distance and space. The teacher should begin from a drawing of the child's own region and extend it to the sea shore, tracing this and introducing the idea of the vastness of the oceans, colouring them as sheets of blue. The child should then be made aware of the existence of other continents. This provides an important foundation for what the child is to learn after his twelfth year[326].

The child's feelings for man's relationship with his natural surroundings and also his sense of physical distance or proximity have important moral consequences. Such conceptions afford a basis for the child's perception of his place in the world and for his feelings for living alongside other people.

> "Such things play no little part in the moral training of the children, and the lack of attention to Geography is partly responsible for the terrible decline in recent years of the brotherly love that should prevail among men. A connection of this kind may escape observation altogether, but it is there, and it plays its part. For there is a certain subconscious intelligence — or unintelligence — operating in the events that we see happening around us." [327]

The pictorial approach gives a firm foundation for geographical concepts. Between the ages of twelve and fifteen the teacher can proceed more systematically, giving the child an idea of the continents and oceans of the world, but in less detail than was used earlier for the child's own country. With a picture of the economic life of man and a general view of the world, the child is ready to study "the cultural environment made by the people who inhabit the different continents". However, this must be integrated with History lessons which should prepare the child for understanding and comparing the links between natural environment and culture by introducing the characteristics of different peoples. Combining Geography and History in this way is extremely beneficial for the child when he is between twelve and fifteen years old. At this age such activities as studying and imitating Japanese styles of painting, or making and using the ploughs and hoes used by primitive peoples, can be done in Geography[328].

The teacher should use as many sketches, pictures, travel books and colourful descriptions as possible to enliven Geography lessons[329] and he should attempt to make the subject matter of lessons as realistic as possible for the child.

> "When you describe an industry he should feel you are working there yourself, and similarly when you describe a mine and so on. Make it as lively as possible! The more life there is in your descriptions the better the children will work with you." [330]

5.3.2.9   History

Until the child's twelfth year, History should consist only of biographical stories narrated by the teacher. These stories should be strongly pictorial, and should arouse antipathy or sympathy for the historical characters and their deeds (see 4.5.2)[331].

History should be steeped in narration that stirs the child's imagination[332]. These stories have an important role in moral education:

> "In the history lesson especially, the teacher should lead his teaching in the direction thus indicated. When telling stories of all kinds to little children before the change of teeth, our aim cannot be more than to awaken delight and vivacity and a happy enjoyment of the story. But after the change of teeth, we have in addition something else to bear in mind in choosing our material for stories; and that is, that we are placing before the boy or girl pictures of life that will arouse a spirit of emulation in the soul.

> The fact should not be overlooked that bad habits may be completely overcome by drawing attention to appropriate instances that shock or repel the child. Reprimands give at best but little help in the matter of habits and inclinations. If, however, we show the living picture of a man who has given way to a similar bad habit, and let the child see where such an inclination actually leads, this will work upon the young imagination and go a long way towards the uprooting of the habit." [333]

At about the age of ten the child should be helped to develop a sense of time, but this should be done in a concrete, human way. The child should be stood in a line of children, the first child representing the children in the class, the second their fathers, the third their grandfathers, and so on. This enables the child to gain a concrete idea of how each century comprises three or four generations. A line of sixty generations leads the child back to the time of Christ[334]. The child must develop a feeling for the remoteness of historical figures, particularly those of his own country, so that he does not develop a false patriotism. He must have a realistic attitude towards the world, because "lack of objectivity is an outstanding evil of our age", leading to self-centred and morose attitudes[335].

A study of causality in History before the age of twelve will damage the child's imagination, particularly if it is done under coercion. However, after this age it is important that the child should develop a sense for historical coherence; the great historical connections by which civilisations have evolved from ancient times. Thus, History will be particularly concerned with the development of the cultural life of mankind and must be integrated with the rest of the curriculum[336], particularly with Geography[337].

After the age of twelve the child is ready to study causality (see 4.3.3.3) and the underlying forces or impulses at work in history should be introduced. For example, if the Crusades are studied the child should develop a feeling for the motives of the men who initiated them, and how the expeditions gradually stagnated, failing to achieve their aims. The teacher should make everything imaginatively alive for the child, so that History teaching "must always contain a subjective element."

> "It is easy enough to say that people should not bring opinions and subjective ideas into history. You may make this rule but it cannot be adhered to. Take any part of history in any country of the world; you will either have to arrange the facts in groups yourself, or else, in the case of less recent history, you will find them already thus assembled by others." [338]

The teacher's responsibility is rather to develop mature judgements, not to rid his teaching of judgement, and then he will teach well. He must develop a judgement by which he is able to overcome the narrow, partisan views of a particular nationality or religious or political creed, rising above these and creating a realistic and meaningful account (see 5.3.1.3).

> "Now it is just such points of view arising from nation or creed that must be overcome by teachers of the future. On this account we must earnestly strive that teachers shall be broad-minded, that they shall reach the point of having a broad-minded philosophy of life. Such an attitude of mind will give you a free, wide view of historical facts, and a skilful grouping of these facts will enable you to convey to your pupils the secrets of human evolution." [339]

The child should never develop the feeling that history is something to be contained in books. He must feel that it is alive and that man stands within its stream. This can only be achieved if the teacher is so prepared for his History

144

lessons that he has transformed all his intellectual knowledge into imaginative stories and pictorial descriptions and has no need to read from books. History must flow artistically from the teacher so that the child feels a personal relationship with historical figures, and his Will is aroused by imagining and re-creating the modes of life of former historical epochs (see 4.5).

"... everything we say must enter the domains of Feeling and Will in the child. He must himself be able to live within the events, to form himself within them by the way they rouse his own sympathies and antipathies. His life of feeling and will must be stimulated.

This will show you that just into the teaching of History the element of art must everywhere enter. The element of art comes into play when — as I often describe it — a true economy can be exercised in teaching. This economy can be exercised if the teacher has thoroughly mastered his subject-matter before he goes into the classroom, if it is no longer necessary for him to ponder over anything because, if rightly prepared, it is there plastically before his soul. He must be so well prepared that the only thing still to be done is the artistic moulding of his lesson." [340]

This means that it is essential for teachers to be given ample time to prepare their material. This requires careful organisation within the school[341].

5.3.2.10 Art

The following section begins with a summary of the pervasive role of Art in its widest sense within Waldorf Education (see also 4.5), and a description of Steiner's distinction between the pictorial and the musical arts. Then Steiner's principles for the treatment of painting, sculpture and music as separate subjects will be described. The other specifically artistic subjects, Poetry and Eurythmy, have already been introduced (see 5.3.2.3 and 5.3.2.5).

Through Art the teacher is able to reach and educate the Soul and Spirit[342], so that all education must be permeated with an artistic element from the beginning.

"For it is of very great importance that you not only make all your teaching artistic, but that you also begin teaching the more specifically artistic subjects, Painting, Modelling and Music, as soon as the child comes to school, and that you see to it that he really comes to possess all these things as an inward treasure." [343]

Art works particularly strongly on the Will of man which quickens and flows into his whole being of Feeling and Thinking. Conversely, an education which only engages man's Thinking through abstract, rigid or unimaginative concepts restricts its influence to the Head System (see 4.5). Therefore Art must begin from the child's first entry into school, and should include drawing, painting, sculpture, singing and using a musical instrument. The child should develop an artistic sense that enters into everything he does[344].

145

"Human life calls for more than education in the realm of meaning, it calls for education in what the will experiences in its sleeping condition: rhythm, beat, melody, the harmony of colours, repetition, any kind of activity not calling for a grasp of meaning." [345]

Art plays a central and vital role in human development, being especially influential in the Ego's transmuting of the Etheric Body (see 3.2.2.3) [346].

"When through the outer form, colour or sound of a work of art man penetrates with thought and feeling to the spiritual sources that underlie it, the impulses the Ego thus receives do in effect reach the etheric body. Thinking this through to its conclusion, we may gain some idea of the immense significance of art in human evolution." [347]

For Steiner, modern intellectualism had achieved astonishing heights and science had made innumerable extraordinary discoveries and inventions. However, all such material progress only led man to know more about the material world. Gradually his soul life was withering away. Man was no longer able to experience the inner life of the Etheric Body because "the stimulus to acquire the faculty for perceiving this subordinate supersensible member of man's nature can arise only out of artistic experience of the soul. Art must become the life blood of the soul" [348]. If education was to answer the needs of modern man it would have to proceed in such a way as to awaken and strengthen the child's Feeling and Will for Art: for rhythm, melody, harmony and beauty, and hence for truth.

"If one really looks into life today one will find that the period between the age of imitation and the age at which the human being can receive knowledge in the form of truth must be filled if humanity is not to pine away. This must be done by giving the human being with artistic beauty what he needs for head, heart and will. The seven-foldness of grammar, dialectic, rhetoric, arithmetic, geometry, astronomy and music, grew out of an older cultural order; it was of the nature of art. Today too we need art but, according to the demands of the consciousness soul, it must not be specialised in the way of the Seven Liberal Arts. During the primary school age and far beyond it, for as long as education holds good, the whole teaching must be warmed through and fired by the artistic element. During the primary school years everything must be steeped in beauty, and in later years beauty must rule as the interpreter of truth." [349]

Art should permeate all lessons (through narration, Eurythmy, speech, music, singing, rhythmic activities, painting and modelling, wherever these are appropriate) but specific lessons for artistic subjects should be arranged[350]. Such artistic subjects prepare the child for the more contemplative subjects such as History so that the timetable should take this into account[351].

There are two streams in Art which are "polar opposites": the sculptural and pictorial, and the musical and poetic. The sculptural, pictorial stream derives from

146

the fact that "there is in the totality of harmonious human nature a sculptural, pictorial element towards which man's will tends to be oriented." (see 4.5, *Fantasie* and *Vorstellung*.)[352]   In Sculpture and Painting man exercises this element by imitating the world which is experienced through his senses[353].   However, Music and Poetry (when freed from the modern tendency to crowd out the purely musical element with prose content or meaning[354]) springs from deep within the Will. Instead of taking on pictorial form, the more one enters pure musical harmony and rhythm, the more one penetrates the impulse of creation itself.

> "In the sculptural, pictorial realm we look at beauty, we live it, whereas in the musical realm we become beauty .... The highest imitation of a cosmic celestial order is an imitation of the world in sculpture or painting. But in music man himself is the creator.   He creates something that does not come from what is already there but lays the foundation and firm ground for what is to arise in the future.   Of course a certain musicality can be created by simply imitating in music the sighing of the waves or the singing of the nightingale.   But all real music and real poetry is a new creation." [355]

These two polarities, the pictorial and musical, are capable of a higher synthesis through Eurythmy when this has been fully developed to encompass the full expression of music through the sculptural medium of the body[356].

The two streams of art, when practised correctly, will "harmonise human nature through and through", and this would be a great achievement for education[357].

5.3.2.10.1   Drawing And Painting

For Steiner, teaching children to draw with lines is only really justified in subjects such as Geometry, or when studying perspective.   To draw a horizon, for example, by means of a line is an abstraction and untrue in terms of nature itself.   In reality the horizon results from the meeting of two adjacent but separate colours, the blue of the sky and the green of the land.   Therefore the teacher should "gradually come to appreciate that the forms of nature really arise out of the colours and that therefore drawing is a process of abstraction" [358].

What is usually taught in drawing should be replaced by painting with colours, or shading areas of dark and light.   In this way the child's feeling for colour, light and shade is developed without being spoiled by the abstract conception of line drawing[359].

The teacher should study Goethe's theory of colours, paying particular attention to the way he "always permeates each individual colour with a nuance of feeling" such as the challenging nature of red, the stillness and absorption of blue, and the shining expansiveness of yellow[360].

Early on in the child's first year of school[361] the teacher can begin to awaken his feeling for the harmony of colours.   This should progress very slowly and simply, and the teacher should begin by having children pair blobs of primary colour, such as yellow and blue, on one side of a piece of paper, and then pair one of the primary colours with a secondary colour, such as yellow and green, on the other side. He should warn the pupils that they will not immediately understand what he is about to say to them, but that they will in time, and should then tell them that the first combination is "more beautiful" than the second.

> "This will sink deeply into the child's soul. It will be necessary to return to it with him several times in repetition, but he will also puzzle away at it himself; he will not be entirely indifferent to it but will learn to understand quite well from simple, naïve examples how to feel the difference between something beautiful and something less beautiful." [362]

Children should not use the ordinary paint boxes with colour blocks, but jars of dissolved colour from which they can lay washes of colour side by side, or surround one colour with another on the paper*. The creation of form should be secondary to the experience of colour, and should arise not from drawing but from the relationship between colours.

> "... enormous progress can be made when children get a direct relation to colour in this way, and learn to paint from the living nature of colour itself, not by trying to copy something in a naturalistic way. Then colour mass and colour form come seemingly of their own accord upon the paper. Thus to begin with, both at the Waldorf School and at Dornach, what the children paint is their experience of colour. It is a matter of putting one colour beside another, or of enclosing one colour within other colours. In this way the child enters right into colours, and little by little, of his own accord he comes to produce form from out of the colour." [363]

Gradually the child begins to develop a feeling for colour harmonies and colour melodies[364]. He feels a connection with the world through colour; it is no longer something merely seen, but something felt as well[365]. The dry reality of everyday life is met in quite a different way by someone who has learnt the living experience of the language of colour[366].

5.3.2.10.2   Sculpture and Modelling

The child's sculptural imagination should be encouraged from early childhood by giving him simple rag dolls to play with instead of rigid, plastic forms (see 4.2.3):

> "If the child has before him a folded napkin, he has to fill in from his imagination all that is needed to make it real and human. This work of the imagination moulds and builds the forms of the brain. The brain unfolds as the muscles of the hand unfold when they do the work for which they are fitted." [367]

---

* Usually the paper is dampened so that the colours spread evenly and do not produce hard lines or sharply defined forms.

Steiner counts "the awakening of the feeling for architectural forms, for moulding and sculpture..." to be of great value in education[368]. In painting the child learns to allow form to arise from a feeling for colour, but in sculpture the child observes the forms of nature and transmutes his observations into modelling exercises. This has a "wonderfully vitalizing effect on the child's physical sight and on the inner quality of soul in his sight". Simple modelling exercises should begin as early as possible.

"... if the child is to learn to observe aright, it is a very good thing for him to begin, as early as possible, to occupy himself with modelling, to guide what he has seen from his head and eyes into the movements of fingers and hand." [369]

However, more conscious modelling of forms and figures should only begin from the ninth or tenth year, and "in a primitive way", so that the child learns to notice and observe things in his environment[370].

Children should also learn to carve toys, which have moving parts requiring manipulation. This brings a strong limb, and therefore Will element (see 4.5.3) into both their construction and use[371].

The teacher should also try "to create a genuine feeling for that dynamic element that finds expression in architecture". The teacher has to take account of whether his pupils are ready for this but, as with the lessons on colour harmony (see 5.3.2.10.1), children do not need to have an immediate understanding before what they are told by an accepted authority (see 4.3.1) is able to work powerfully within their souls. The fact that they have not fully understood creates an expectation and inner activity which ponders and puzzles over what has not been understood. This exercises the soul in the same way as a parable, and is a good principle for all subjects[372].

All teachers should have a strong feeling for form developed through sculpture (see 3.2.2.1), and this should not be merely an ability to slavishly copy outer forms. The teacher should discover an inner feeling for form, an ability to sense how forms of the body emerge from inner principles which have spiritual and cosmic origins. Steiner considered that the Greek sculptors worked from such intuitions, which was why they achieved such incomprehensible genius in their sculpture.

"When the Greeks created their *Venus de Milo* (which is the despair of modern sculptors) then they took what streamed out of the cosmos, and although this could only reveal itself imperfectly in any earthly work, they strove to express it in the human form they were creating as far as they were able to do so. The point is that if you really set out to mould the form of man according to nature you cannot possibly do it by slavishly following a model, which is the method of studios today. You must be able to turn to the great cosmic sculptor who forms man out of the 'feeling for space' which man himself can also acquire." [373]

In a much more modest way than the Greeks, but with the same principle, the teacher should encourage children in science lessons to model the organs and forms of the body, not merely imitating a model but feeling intuitively the forms within man[374]. He can also encourage their sense of design in handicrafts, so that the child learns to suit designs to the forms of things that are made. Such an artistic exercise "penetrates right into his limbs. This is a teaching that works far more strongly into the physical organism than any work in the abstract." [375]

5.3.2.10.3 Music

All children should at least be present for every musical activity. An element of musical talent, no matter how deeply buried, can be found in every child and will develop with loving encouragement[376].

From the beginning of school life children should develop "the musical element" in two distinct ways. They should express it from within through song and also listen to tones from outside themselves by learning to produce notes through a musical instrument[377]. These two activities, singing and listening to the music they play, balance one another in the human being and should be alternated in lessons. Singing brings the musical element into the Head System, while listening brings it into the Rhythmic and Limb Systems[378].

A piano is not the right instrument to use in education because it requires too much memorisation. Instead, an instrument which can be blown will teach the child the most about music* [379].

From the beginning the child should learn in an elementary way to listen to the relationships between notes[380], and, as with colour (see 5.3.2.10.1) to distinguish between concordant (beautiful) and discordant (less beautiful) notes[381]. The child should never do this through theory, which would "bemuse" him, but through a direct experience of singing, playing and listening to musical notes[382].

The child who is slow to grasp these aspects of music can be made aware of the difference between notes and rhythms by caricaturing the differences, but these exaggerations should nevertheless be artistically presented[383].

As with sculpture and colour, the teacher should develop an inner understanding of music which will enable him to understand man's life of Feeling far more deeply and meaningfully than any abstract study of man could achieve[384].

Music and Eurythmy release the Spirit (Will) of the child, and should precede subjects requiring stillness and contemplation (such as History) which balance them and hold the spiritual impulses that have been released[385]. Music and Eurythmy lessons should be given in the afternoon to prepare the child to receive his main lesson the following morning (see 5.3.1)[386].

---

* The instrument usually used in Waldorf Schools is the Recorder, which is a fipple flute with eight finger holes.

5.3.2.11 Handicrafts and Technical Subjects

Handwork lessons such as knitting or woodwork are not merely activities to develop the dexterity of the hands. Whatever cultivates the physical part of man also cultivates his soul, so that by leading dexterity into the child's hands, education has the effect of cultivating his mind as well (see 4.4.1). The child's ability to think logically is best educated indirectly by means of handicrafts, and not by direct exercises in logic which only weaken a child's thinking and consequently have a debilitating effect on his body[387].

When the child makes things that are useful and meaningful this often has a more truly spiritual significance for his education than when he does subjects which are thought to be more directly spiritual[388].

Handwork lessons have an important contribution to make in preparing children for social life. One of the great failings of single-sex schools is that they develop a one-sidedness in the human being. Waldorf Schools aim to develop boys and girls to fit into modern society in which most of the old distinctions between sex-roles are eroding and the sexes must begin to understand one another. Therefore in handwork lessons young boys and girls should do crafts hitherto reserved for one sex only. This enables children to develop balanced attitudes towards both their own social and economic roles in life, and those of the opposite sex[389].

Handicrafts prepare each child to manage practical, everyday problems with ability and confidence. Children should always be encouraged to make things that are really useful, which will give them satisfaction and will stimulate their instincts for the practical side of life.

> "At the Waldorf School, the children do not merely 'have an idea' in their heads; they feel the idea, for it flows into their whole life of feeling. Their being of soul lives in the sense of the idea, which is not merely a concept but becomes a plastic form. The whole complex of ideas at last becomes human form and figure and in the last resort all this passes over into the will. The child learns to transform what he thinks into actual deed." [390]

The child should learn to exercise his feelings for creating appropriate designs for the objects he makes. He should not merely be set instructions and then have to carry them out mechanically[391]. He should also learn to think not only about the external appearance of a dress or chair that he makes, but also how it will feel to the person who uses it[392].

After Puberty, education should not merely impart "head knowledge" to the child, but should prepare him for practical life through "subjects that will bring him into touch with the external world" [393]. This principle leads to two problems for Waldorf Schools. Firstly, many compromises have to be made in the curriculum to meet the demands of modern customs. For example, Steiner would have liked to have had a shoemaker on the staff of the Waldorf School in order to teach children both the theory and practice of shoemaking. This was not permitted because of government regulations, and handicrafts were restricted to woodwork, bookbinding, dressmaking and such conventional crafts[394]. Secondly, Waldorf education is faced with the task of preparing children for the social and industrial mechanisation of modern economic life which offers nothing to arouse the human soul and spirit (see 1.2.7). Children have to be equipped with inner strength to create their own soul and spiritual lives, so that "senseless industrial willing has to be confronted with a meaningful willing-out-of-the-spirit" [395].

Older children may practise separate technical skills appropriate to their sex, but each sex should be present to watch the other's activities because of the social understanding that this promotes. What is learned theoretically in Physics and Chemistry should be transformed into a "theory of practice", so that boys should learn technical mechanics and machine construction as well as surveying and planning, and girls should study such things as the technical background, practice and products of spinning and weaving, and hygiene and first aid.

The aim is always that the adolescent should not enter an alien, unknown world; he should feel a part of it so that even factories are a meaningful part of his personal life. If such a feeling is awakened at puberty it will remain with the adolescent into later life. It is too late to try and awaken it in young adults of nineteen or twenty because by then they have developed such an objective view of the world that it can no longer become part of their subjective nature[396].

Adolescents should never be allowed to grow to ignore the technical inventions that surround them in life. When they see something they do not understand they should feel a sense of uneasiness and inquisitiveness. This is encouraged by teaching them — from their thirteenth to their sixteenth year — the elements of what happens in, for example, soap or spinning factories and so on. They should fill an exercise book with condensed descriptions of different branches of industry, so that their inquisitiveness about the workings of machines and manufacturing is constantly stimulated. Thus, "towards the end of the lower school we should employ all the different subjects in a comprehensive sense towards a social education of our pupils" [397].

Such an education will fit a child to enter life with a feeling of self possession. The child should have a wide, unspecialised preparation for life which will stand him in good stead when he comes to choose a career in adulthood.

> "Every single thing a child learns during the course of his schooling should in the end be presented so broadly that threads may everywhere be found linking it with practical human life. Very, very many things that are now unsocial in the world would be made social if we could at least touch upon an insight into matters that later need not have any direct bearing on our own work in life." [398]

5.3.2.12 Religion

Religious experience, like artistic feeling (see 5.3.2.10), has a strengthening effect on the Etheric Body. It is therefore of great importance in life, but particularly for the child after the change of teeth when the Etheric Body is newly released (see 4.3). The individual develops a healthy Will (Astral Body and Ego[399]) if the Etheric Body is firmly strengthened by feelings of gratitude and reverence towards the "Everlasting Powers".

> "How a man feels his place and part in the universal Whole – this will find expression in the unity of his life of will. If he does not feel himself linked by strong bonds to a Divine spiritual, his will and character must needs remain uncertain, divided and unsound." [400]

Therefore, a religious mood should pervade the teacher's actions as well as the subjects of the curriculum. Religion should not only be confined to a particular lesson (see 1.2.6). Even the mere fact that the teacher of Religion also teaches other subjects helps children to feel that religious experience is part of the whole of life and is not only a "subject" [401]. The Waldorf School aims to make religion live throughout the school with a Christian character, but without ever proselytizing or connecting religion with any sect or church movement[402].

Catholic and Protestant pastors are called in to give lessons on Religion to members of their churches. Under this arrangement children who are non-conformist would receive no religious instruction and so their teacher takes them for Religion. These lessons have nothing to do with Anthroposophy (Spiritual Science).

> "The Waldorf School is not a school for a philosophy of life, but a method of education .... If anyone thinks the Waldorf School is a school for Anthroposophy it shows he has no understanding either of Waldorf School pedagogy or of Anthroposophy." [403]

It would be completely out of keeping with Waldorf educational principles to present Anthroposophy to children in the form that it is studied by adults. Instead, a "free religious teaching" which has a deeply Christian character is offered, and children are only admitted with their parents' consent[404].

Even in Steiner's time these lessons became so popular that many children wanted to leave the lessons given by the pastors and attend their teachers' lessons[405].

Up to the age of nine, the child should be introduced to a "religious naturalism" wherein he is taught to feel "gratitude in the contemplation of everything in nature". The stories he is told should "lead the child to perceive the Divine in all things". This "Nature-religion" is the right preparation for the child to gradually progress after the age of nine to the Gospels, through which an understanding of the "Christ Mystery" can be unfolded in the higher classes[406].

> "He who would educate in the sense of true Christianity must realise that before the age of nine or ten it is not possible to convey to the child's soul an understanding of what the Mystery of Golgotha brought into the

world, or of all that is connected with the personality and divinity of Christ Jesus. The child is exposed to great dangers if we have failed to introduce the principle of universal divinity before this age, and by universal divinity I mean the divine Father-Principle. We must show the child how divinity is immanent in all nature, in all human evolution, how it lives and moves not only in the stones, but in the hearts of other men, in their every act. The child must be taught, by the natural authority of the teacher, to feel gratitude and love for this universal divinity. In this way, the basis for a right attitude to the Mystery of Golgotha just between the ninth and tenth years is laid down." [407]

An important part of lessons on Religion is the preparation for the celebration of great Christian festivals, such as Christmas and Easter. The significance of these festivals is emphasised far more than is usual in other schools. The festivals are an expression of gratitude, which is the basis for an understanding of the universal Father-Principle[408].

"Gratitude is a definite moral experience in relation to our fellow men. Sentiments and notions which do not spring from gratitude will lead at most to abstract precepts as regards morality. But everything can come from gratitude. Thus, from gratitude we develop the capacity for love and the feeling for duty. And in this way morality leads on to religion." [409]

Thus, religious instruction does not consist of moral precepts or dogma, but of pictures, feelings and actions (festival dramas, etc.) which are evoked by stories and parables, drawn first from nature and then increasingly from the Gospels[410]. This will educate the whole child.

"In no sense do we work towards a blind, rationalistic Christianity, but towards a true understanding of the Christ Impulse in the evolution of mankind. Our one and only aim is to give the human being something that he still needs, even if all his other teaching has endowed him with the qualities of full manhood. Even if this be so, even if full manhood has been unfolded through all the other teaching, a religious deepening is still necessary if the human being, in an all-round way, is to find a place in the world befitting his inborn spiritual nature." [411]

Although the child will have heard many of the Old Testament stories in earlier lessons, a sequential study of the Old Testament is only started when the child is twelve or thirteen[412].

On Sundays, a service with a ritual "similar in many respects to the Mass" is held for children who do not belong to a Church. The service is always adapted to the age of the child, and a separate service for adults and those who have left the school is also held[413].

It is essential for children to have the right mood in lessons on religion. This is achieved by the teacher himself cultivating a natural mood of reverence and piety[414], and by believing implicitly in the images he gives his pupils[415] (see 5.3.1.3). However, this will be in vain if the child is not prepared beforehand. Religion lessons should always be preceded by a lesson which is factual and requires discipline, such as a lesson on the business letter. This will create "the mood that is calling for its antithesis" and the children will readily respond to the mood of the teacher in the Religion lesson that follows[416].

5.3.2.13 Economics and Accountancy

Economics enters education early in the child's school life, but not as a separate subject. It is an important part of Geography (see 5.3.2.8) and exercises like the business letter come into Writing (see 5.3.2.3).

The right time for more formal lessons is between the age of twelve and fifteen. At this age the teacher can balance with the child's awakening judgement his instinctive interest in profits, wealth, ownership of property and trade. The child of twelve does not have selfish feelings towards ideas such as interest rates. However if the child does not encounter these concepts until he is older, by then he will only be able to think egotistically of his own self interest. Elementary economic concepts should therefore be introduced at the right time[417].

Actual bookkeeping is less emotive and based more on reason, so that it should be started later on[418].

Rudolf Steiner in 1915, aged 54.

6

STEINER'S
EDUCATIONAL
TEACHINGS IN
PRACTICE

In the five years that this book took to research the author visited Waldorf Schools in South Africa and Great Britain. These include Michael Mount Waldorf School in Johannesburg; Michael Hall in Forest Row, Sussex; Bristol Waldorf School; Wynstones School, Gloucester; Michael House near Shipley, Derbyshire; and the Rudolf Steiner School of Edinburgh. He also visited Emerson College in Forest Row, Sussex, which is a centre for adults to study and practise Steiner's teachings, drawing students from throughout the world. Teacher training is one of the services that Emerson College offers.

During these visits the author met many Waldorf School teachers, and was invited to attend dozens of their lessons. From these a small sample has been selected in order to give an indication of the way individual teachers practise some of Steiner's most central principles. This chapter is important because these experiences showed that no theoretical study of Steiner's teachings, however penetrating, can hope to realise the intense vitality of a class of children working with a teacher who is adhering to Steiner's principles. The author's background of both Remedial and Class teaching in government as well as independent schools made him aware of the great differences — in almost every respect — between orthodox teaching methods and those employed in Waldorf Schools. Even when more orthodox methods parallel Steiner's teachings in certain respects it became evident to him that the combined rhythms of working artistically from Will to Feeling to Thinking through the Limb, the Rhythmic and the Head systems respectively (see 6.4) create a sense of satisfaction and fulfilment among Waldorf School pupils that is far beyond the scope of other methods.

Obviously, the examples given could not show all of Steiner's thought in practice. This is rather the task of secondary research projects for which this book hopes to provide a theoretical context.

This chapter begins with a general description of the institutions visited and then goes on to describe some lessons. However, these <u>cannot</u> be taken as model examples of Waldorf Education because every teacher and every school must develop an individuality of his or its own in order to be in accordance with Steiner's educational principles (see 4.7). The aim of this chapter is not to evaluate modern practice of Steiner's thought (which would be a major research project) but to illuminate the thought itself.

6.1   THE SCHOOLS

Each Waldorf School is independent of others, but is affiliated to a regional — often a national — federation of Waldorf Schools which meets each year. From time to time these regional federations hold international conferences. Wherever possible the various federations share their knowledge, abilities and material wealth. Waldorf Schools in England and South Africa have a constant financial struggle because, in order to cater for as wide a cross section of the community as possible, they keep their fees as low as they can. Teachers in the schools visited received salaries of between a third and three quarters of those paid to government school teachers[*]. The schools aspire towards the West German policy whereby the government grants an equal amount of money for the education of every child whether they go to state or independent schools.

Most schools were founded by means of a trust fund contributed by teachers and patrons. This was used to buy old buildings such as large country houses, old schools or business premises. One school collected enough for prefabricated classrooms and then gradually built permanent premises. The schools were started wherever a demand was perceived, however large or small. Some began with only three or four pupils and now number up to a thousand with a staff of fifty teachers. The success of such schools has depended entirely on the dedication and capability of the teachers who have convinced the public of the value of Waldorf Schools[1].

Each College of Teachers (see 5.3.1.2) appoints a Council of Management to administer the school. Councils operate as non-profit making companies registered as charities. They usually have about a dozen members, half of whom are parents or interested members of the public, and half are teachers from the school. Teachers are included because it is considered essential that administrative decisions, especially those concerning finance, are not made on materialistic grounds alone but

---

[*] The money available for salaries is usually shared out equally with a small increase for teachers who have the most experience, and extra is given to those who have dependants to care for. Some schools cannot afford to pay teachers who take leave, and small pension schemes are offered.

for the good of the whole school. The Council may appoint sub-committees for different projects.

The College of Teachers makes the policy decisions and refers administrative matters to the Council for consideration.

The Chairperson of the College of Teachers is appointed each year by the full College. This is done by open discussion which continues until agreement is reached as to whether the nominees' qualifications and circumstances fit him or her for the job. No vote is taken; discussion continues until unanimity is reached. This method applies to all decisions by the College and aims to prevent divisions developing among the teachers. Appointments and dismissals of teachers are decided by the whole College on the recommendations of the Chairperson or of a sub-committee.

Parent-Teacher Associations are considered important and are usually actively involved with working groups, lectures and fund raising activities. Parents are encouraged to visit the classroom either during or after school, and teachers try to visit the family of each of their pupils. Parents are invited to the four seasonal festivals of Easter, Midsummer, Michaelmas and Christmas (see 5.3.2.12) to watch their children perform the festival dramas and to see exhibitions of the term's work. Class teachers may call meetings for parents of their pupils to arrange outings to farms, theatres, concerts, museums or even to other towns or countries. These meetings may also be held to answer parents' questions about Waldorf Education or to work out problems.

Wealthy parents pay full fees as with other independent schools. Various arrangements exist to ensure that parents who are not wealthy but who wish to send their children to a Waldorf School are able to do so. These include bursaries, fee reductions and, in the case of Waldorf teachers, the waiving of fees.

Waldorf Schools do not have strong links with neighbouring orthodox schools. Such links only exist if they are considered desirable. Competitiveness in sport or at school is never encouraged, but each child is adjured to play and work to the best of his or her ability. Tours to other Waldorf Schools are undertaken by a class orchestra or drama group and the public are invited to festivals. This helps to ensure that the schools do not become too isolated or introspective.

Before parents register their children they are interviewed to discuss the basic policies of the school and their expectations and financial situation, etc. Bursaries are available for children whose parents cannot afford the full fees[*]. One school visited asked no set fee. Parents decided how much they could give the school in consultation with a teacher. This was considered the ideal way to run a school by every Waldorf teacher consulted, because they believed that education was part of the Spiritual life (see 1.2.4) and as such should be sustained by the "free gifts" of the community. However, teachers from the larger schools flatly rejected this plan

---

[*] Fees vary greatly between schools and are constantly changing to cope with inflation and the unique needs of each school. Fees rise steadily as the child progresses.

as a practical proposition for their own institutions. The school concerned was indeed struggling financially. The teachers received paltry salaries, yet in general these teachers seemed to be happier and more sincerely devoted to their work than many of their colleagues in wealthier schools.

Teachers were given freedom to formulate their own curriculum, but had to justify what they were doing to their College of Teachers. Most of them based their curriculum on the Stockmeyer or von Heydebrand published versions (see 2.2.2).

Waldorf Schools deal with public examinations in various ways. Children may choose to write the exams if they want to, and in order to provide for those who do, schools generally opt for one of two approaches. Either they carry their Waldorf curriculum right through to class twelve and run extra classes for public examinations in the afternoons, or else they stop the Waldorf curriculum a year before the public examination and change entirely to the orthodox requirements. Whichever method is chosen, it is considered to be an unfortunate compromise because public examinations are too one-sidedly demanding on the intellect. The Waldorf curriculum attempts to compensate for this by educating the whole child (see 4.5 and 5.3.1.1).

Misbehaviour is always dealt with in terms of the needs of the particular child (see 5.3.1.4). Detention systems exist in most schools to cope with time wasting or work not done. One teacher said he felt that modern teachers were shying away from authority, and questioned their right to impose their will over children. This was the reverse of what happened in the past when teachers directed and controlled their pupils to the extent that egotism crept in and they began to manipulate children with feelings of selfish gratification, becoming subtly corrupted by a sense of power. He rejected both approaches. The teacher who abdicated his or her authority forced children prematurely into making decisions and choices, and the authoritarian teachers affected children through the deformities of their behaviour. Authority should rather be based on humility and the desire to reveal the world to the child in a thoroughly moral way. Attitudes of reverence and devotion should be the link between the child, the teacher, and the curriculum. Children should find their lessons sufficiently satisfying not to want to cause trouble, but if a child could not be controlled he or she would have to be asked to leave the school.

The sports which the schools arrange vary. Most rejected team sports because of the competitiveness and frenzy they generate among players and spectators (for example in rugby and football). Most also rejected football because of the one-sided demand it makes on the feet and legs. They preferred sports such as tennis or hockey where the skill is in the arms and hands and the legs are used for conveyance. They felt that this was the right balance between the lower, middle and upper body for the development of children. However, one school allowed football to be played because it was so much a part of the social life of the community and they felt that to suppress it would cause their pupils to become alienated either from the school or from their peers in other schools. Some of the boys in the upper primary school named the lack of football and rugby as one of their strongest reasons for wanting to leave the Waldorf School and attend an orthodox secondary school.

None of the schools visited had prefect systems, but they did enlist voluntary help from the seniors to look after younger children.

Teachers at Waldorf Schools come from the most diverse backgrounds, and in the English speaking schools visited there were many people from Europe and the United States. Some were former orthodox teachers and university lecturers who had become disenchanted with the "narrow goals and methods" of orthodox education. There were former artists, journalists, housewives and businessmen, as well as those who had encountered Steiner's teachings while at university, or who had attended Waldorf Schools as pupils.

For example, one teacher had graduated with a Master's degree in the United States and had then lectured for a few years before using his hobby – carpentry – to work his way across Europe. In Switzerland he met his future wife who was teaching at a Waldorf School, but Steiner's teachings made little impression on him until he accompanied his wife to the main centres of Waldorf education in West Germany. There he saw whole communities — factories, businesses, medical centres, schools, religious and cultural activities — all run according to Steiner's teachings. The realisation dawned on him that Steiner had not merely thought up some "good ideas" which were taken in faith by a few zealous disciples, but that there was a major spiritual impulse behind it, containing insights initiated by one man but now developed much further and practised by hundreds of thousands of people across the world. He had worked at a Steiner School for the handicapped for a while, and was now teaching Woodwork, Art and History of Art.

Many Waldorf teachers considered it an advantage to have come to teaching with the experience of another profession behind them. None felt that orthodox teacher training had done or would do them any good in a Waldorf School. They placed great value on their practice of education as an artistic expression, and, whatever their subject, strove to develop their powers of narration and imaginative description, as well as their painting, music and production of class dramas, or activities to express the subject matter of lessons artistically (see 6.7).

Courses in the various aspects of Waldorf Education such as the Temperaments, Eurythmy, painting and music are constantly in progress at most schools, often run by teachers who have trained in Europe under the best practitioners in the world. Waldorf teachers are expected to refresh their knowledge by attending these courses, which also serve to provide a basic training for potential teachers. Therefore, most of the teachers were able to speak about Steiner's teachings quite confidently. Because of the efficiency of these in-service training courses, few Waldorf teachers study Steiner's lectures to any great extent. There were experienced Waldorf teachers who openly admitted to having read only a few of the lectures and perhaps one of the books of occult teachings, such as Theosophy. They were usually familiar with secondary sources, in particular those which give practical ideas for structuring the curriculum, such as Roy Wilkinson's booklets (see 2.2.2). Steiner's lectures were generally regarded as both complex and profound, requiring an extensive understanding of terminology and an experience of the Spiritual and Soul life before they could be properly understood.

The teachers interviewed varied from open to guarded in their replies, with some of the inexperienced and poorly read teachers exhibiting defiant scepticism of the author's qualifications for attempting such an analysis. Many of the more widely read people showed intense interest in the author's research, and some admitted to having nursed private ambitions to attempt such an analysis. Most were astonished at the ambitiousness of the project and a few asked emphatically that a copy be sent to their school when it was completed[*].

Some of the difficulties encountered in researching Waldorf Schools were revealed to me by the fate of a short questionnaire that was submitted for consideration in one school. This teacher energetically rejected it for several reasons, mostly centering around two features of the questionnaire. Firstly, some of the question responses were structured on a Likert (Agree–Disagree) scale in order to enable teachers to answer it quickly and concisely. This was seen as absolutely inappropriate for Waldorf teachers whose ideas were felt to be much too individualistic to be confined to "little boxes". Secondly, in the main section of the questionnaire statements sympathetic to and contradicting Steiner's thought were presented. Respondents were asked to rate their level of agreement or disagreement to each statement in order to reveal their understanding of the basic principles of Waldorf Education. This was indignantly rejected, mainly because the contradictory statements were interpreted as evidence of profound ignorance of Waldorf Education and an attempt "to take a prod at the movement to see what happens"!

Further details of this questionnaire have not been given because it was jettisoned on the grounds of these and other more minor faults, and it has had no influence on this book. It is mentioned in order to recommend qualitative research methods when studying Waldorf Schools.

Another reason for abandoning it was that, before being accepted by the school, the questionnaire would have had to have been examined and discussed by the College of Teachers, a factor which would have largely invalidated it.

Many of the most experienced teachers interviewed regarded Steiner's ideas as ideals to aspire towards. They did not see the teachings as rigid rules but as indications about the nature of the child that the modern world would not be aware of without the vision of someone like Steiner. One of these teachers, a very influential and most impressive man who had recently retired from a lifetime of working with Steiner's ideas in England and Europe, told me that he preferred not to intellectualise Steiner's ideas into a formal system. He said such systematizing was the German approach to Steiner, but the British were more content to keep it at the level of direct experience with the growing child. He saw education as the ability to use heart, head and hand harmoniously, and he felt that if he achieved that balance in a lesson then it was successful. Steiner's teachings made him aware of things that he would otherwise not notice in life, but they had to be borne out

---

[*] These points are not raised in order to exaggerate the significance of this project but to reveal the attitudes of Waldorf teachers towards Steiner's thought.

by his personal experience before he fully accepted and understood them.

Most teachers felt that the techniques of Waldorf Education would add up to very little without Anthroposophy (Spiritual Science) which gave it meaning and value. Spiritual Science was seen as far more than a method of finding out about life; it was the spiritual goal of life itself, capable of bringing the whole human being to fulfilment (see 3.1.3).

The following selection of lessons aims to reveal something of Steiner's thought in practice. They do not succeed in capturing the reality of a teacher at work with his pupils, nor can they replace first hand experience of a lesson. Nevertheless, they attempt to enhance the reader's understanding of Steiner's thought by contextualising it.

6.2 Kindergarten (4-6 years old) : Imitation (see 4.2 to 4.2.3)

There are 72 children in this nursery school, divided into four classes of 18, two for four to five year olds and two for five to six year olds. One of the teachers takes the author in first thing in the morning, and children are already playing energetically in a sand pit, building a crude brick house and climbing in trees and a "jungle gym". The teacher says that they encourage children to practise climbing because it develops control of every part of the body, and builds self confidence. Teachers do not admonish children to be careful while climbing, yet they have never had an accident. If stuck, children are guided down and never carried.

The teacher leads the way into a kitchen, and explains that they try to create the atmosphere of a farm in the nursery school. The teachers cook soups or bake bread when the weather is cold, or ice cakes and make butter when it is hot. Children watch and join in while the teachers are working (see 4.2.3 and 5.3.2.1). Outside, gardening is practised and the children water the flowers and vegetables. This is a humble attempt to replace the loss of home life in modern society.

A rhythm and pattern of events is established for each day and week to satisfy and develop the child's sense of security. By about nine o'clock the children have all arrived and they are summoned to the classrooms by a bell. The class forms a ring and is brought to complete silence by the teacher who says nothing, but stands with her arms crossed over her chest, hands flat against opposite shoulders. Each child takes this posture as he quietens down. A verse of gratitude for everything in life is said, and then the class welcomes each child in turn ("Good morning, Sarah!" etc.). This is followed by toilet routine.

By the time the children return the teacher has prepared a small meal — the products of the cooking and gardening — and a prayer of thanks is said before it is eaten.

After this they begin the activity of the day. There is painting on Monday; crayoning on Tuesday; handwork, sewing and modelling with bees' wax on Wednesday and Thursday; and Eurythmy on Friday. In Eurythmy the children act out stories, fairy tales and verses about nature, princesses, gnomes, butterflies and flowers. They may recite a poem with emphasised rhythm and drama, expressing the inner feelings (such as pride, sorrow or laziness) of the characters in the tale with the appropriate eurythmic postures. One fable for this age was that of a boy who was a dullard but one day caught and tamed a fiery horse and together they succeeded in winning a competition for the princess' hand. The dull boy and the fiery horse symbolised the dual nature of the Will which, when captured and balanced, was able to find its spiritual prize. Such a fable (unexplained of course) worked on the child's soul as a pictorial impression, unconsciously motivating the Feelings and Will to become more controlled (see 4.3.3.1 and 4.3.4).

Alternatively, Eurythmy may consist of performing archetypal movements as a whole class. Inward and outward spirals may be done, likening them to the shell of a snail.

Each activity is preceded by a song or verse which gives the children a feeling of contentment. After the main activity of the day the children help the teacher to clear up, and then they are told a story before being allowed out for "break-time".

Birthdays are made into a special occasion for each child, as are the seasonal festivals. During the author's visit they are celebrating the spring festival (Michaelmas) and practising the symbolic drama of Michael slaying the dragon and rescuing the beautiful maiden. Two children are chosen as Michael and the maiden, and glow with pride as they are adorned with their costumes. The rest of the class forms into a writhing, hissing dragon which weaves through the classroom as the whole class, led by the teacher, recite the legend in verse form.

The class has also prepared seed beds of cress to see the seed germinating with the rebirth of spring. This contrasts with the festival of St John held at mid winter, when the children bring bare branches to school, paint them and hang them with eggs that were blown for the Easter festival.

Christmas is the most important festival. The class prepares an Advent garden, Christmas cards are painted, and presents are made in the sewing lessons. The great transition from the Old to the New Testaments is symbolised through the decoration of the Christmas tree. To begin with it is hung with apples which are later eaten as a symbol of the Creation Story. The apples are then replaced on the tree by candles, to symbolise the advent of the Light of the World (see 5.3.2.12).

This kindergarten has been built with considerable help from parents, both in collecting the money for it, as well as in the planning and construction. It is a most attractive building, with elements of Steiner's styling on the Goetheanum, breaking monotonous rectangles and box-like rooms with arched ceilings panelled with jig-saws of wooden strips and decorated with an amber varnish. Each class has a sanctuary; a small recess for the construction of festival models and to contain indoor gardens and seed beds. Paintings are hung on the walls, mostly water colours painted in colour layers so that overlaid tones and hues create colourful compositions. A cut out design of Michael slaying the dragon is stuck to a window, allowing the sun to shine through the brilliant reds, yellows and blues of the composition. Toys are placed on shelves around each class. There are no plastic models, only chunky, handmade, wooden trailers, crude models of trains, and colourful patchwork rag dolls (see 4.2.3). The teacher tells me that if a toy is broken the teacher and child set about repairing it together, which is an important part of moral training. This practice is often not possible with modern plastic and metal toys.

There are no abstract educational toys such as the sets of triangles, squares and circles which have to be slotted into boards. Nor are there any story books. Everything is intended to bring the child into contact with life: with other human beings, with the earth, the seasons, and God through the child's participation in natural and artistic activities (see 4.5 *et seq.*).

6.3   Class One (6-7 years old) :
From Imitation to Authority   (see 4.3.1)

Monday morning. Class One has 32 lively children. Their teacher has been with them for eight months. He has a degree in fine art, some experience of teaching in a government school, and completed his training the year before at Emerson College.

He stands at the door of his classroom, waiting for the children to form into an orderly line. They know what is expected of them and so he gives no instructions, but watches them until they are ready. He allows them into the classroom one at a time, greeting them by name and shaking each one by hand. In return, each must look him in the eyes and greet him by name. He explains that most Waldorf teachers practise this greeting in some form in order for the teacher and child to recreate a direct, personal relationship with each other every day.

One boy at the back of the line — frail in stature and with a heavy mop of blond hair — is constantly restless, pulling, pushing and running out of line. The teacher watches him, saying nothing, but is especially insistent that this boy compose himself and meet his gaze before entering the classroom. Once all the children are inside and at their desks, the teacher stands in front of them, silently communicating his insistence that the children do as he is doing. The boy who was restless in line is still rushing back and forth, tugging at a girl's satchel and grabbing at a boy's pencil. Finally the teacher calls his name firmly and sharply and he too stands still, but his eyes continue to dart around the classroom.

Today is the day of the weekly assembly, and so after saying a short verse, the children file out to the hall. A teacher stands in front of the whole school and nothing is done until all are standing silently. The teacher begins the song for the day and the children join in. There are no flat notes; singing is so much a part of their lives.

It is the turn of the Class One teacher to tell the children a story, and so after the singing he steps forward, accompanied by audible delight from his class who are seated in the front of the hall at his feet. Quite suddenly he transforms himself from a sedate adult into an animated story teller. He has chosen a fable about a Jackal who awakens one morning and is horrified to see the emaciated form of his shadow cast by the sun. The Jackal decides he is so hungry that he could eat a whole camel, and disdainfully ignores a rabbit that he sees as he sets out to hunt. However, evening comes and he returns to his lair without seeing another living creature, and he thinks to himself how grateful he would be now if only he could find a little mouse to eat. The teacher completes the fable, stepping back to his place. No interpretation is given, and a profound silence fills the hall; the image is left to do its own work.

The main lesson lasts one and a half hours. Class One begins with songs and verses, the recorder is played (see 5.3.2.10.3), some counting is done accompanied by limb activities (see 5.3.2.6 and 6.4), a story is told, and then the children paint a picture, evolving the form of a letter of the alphabet (see 5.3.2.2). Before each activity the teacher insists on complete composure and often a verse is recited or a song is sung if the children's attention seems to be flagging or wandering.

Throughout the morning the restless boy continues to disrupt the class. Not only is he extraordinarily energetic but he is intelligent, often deliberately misbehaving and ignoring the teacher's presence. When the teacher sees that his personal example (imitation) will not stop the boy, he calls his name firmly. Often this is enough to direct the child's feet to his own desk, but when it fails the teacher walks quietly to his side, touches his shoulder and gently leads him back to his desk. The teacher betrays only the slightest evidence of the strain that this child's behaviour has imposed on him month after month. He shows no anger, only a firm and complete insistence and persistence that his will be obeyed (authority). At the end of the morning the child pushes to the front of the queue to leave the classroom, and the teacher sends him to the back. The boy is looking at the ground when he finally comes to shake hands with the teacher. There is no "telling-off"; no "preaching". The teacher only takes his chin and raises it gently until the child looks him in the eyes and greets him by name, and then he is free to scamper off.

The author expresses concern at the child's behaviour and the teacher sighs in assent. Asked about the persistently calm way in which he treats the child, he replies, "Today was a particularly difficult day because that child is left to his own devices at home and stays up late watching television. But you know, children of that age do not see you as an adult would see you — as a personality with big eyes and a long nose. They see you as 'a striving'. And it is your striving — your will that you express through all your behaviour that sinks into them. Rules or punishments mean very little at that age."

This young man's dedication realises two of Steiner's basic principles for educating young children: Imitation and Authority. He refuses to resort to suppressing the child's behaviour by instilling fear through punishment. Nor does he attempt to avoid the problem by labelling the child "hyperactive" and packing him off to a doctor for medication. He works constantly with the purely human relationship between adult and child, building the child's nature, and undoubtedly his own, with patience, good will, and unrelenting self denial.

6.4   Class Two (7-8 years old):
A Main Lesson in Arithmetic (see 5.3.2.6)

The following account shows the progression from Will to Feeling to Thinking activities in a main lesson on Arithmetic (see 4.5 *et seq.*). It includes a demonstration of working with temperaments in a class (see 4.6), and interspersing the subject of the lesson with a story and drawing, which is then used to develop the main lesson.

This Class Two has over thirty pupils. The teacher says that Waldorf Schools prefer big classes because of the balance of temperaments and abilities that they give. The class is brought to complete composure by the teacher who simply stands in front of them with her hands crossed over her chest, palms resting on opposite shoulders. This is the Eurythmic gesture of inner composure, and soon all the children are imitating her.

Led by the teacher, the class says a verse to prepare them for their school day and to give thanks for God's blessings in life. The children are then told to form a large circle, right around the walls of the class, and suddenly they begin to swing their arms and stamp forward, reciting the "even numbers" with great rhythmical emphasis, "2 ... 4 ... 6..." etc. The teacher identifies those who are not getting it right and has them do it together. Then the class says the "odd numbers" with equal rhythm and volubility. After this they do the sequences backwards, which they are not yet sure of. As they proceed they gradually slow down and become subdued, and the teacher says, "Oh, we are tired this morning, children. Well then, let's do it very, very slowly, like a fish swimming in a deep, quiet sea." They smile and set off, enjoying this change of temperament (see 4.6 — Phlegmatic).

As the children return to their desks, the teacher explains the importance of rhythm in learning something by heart (see 4.5.2) and that, through these rhythmical exercises, they will soon develop a strong mental facility for numbers. The teacher moves to the front of the class and uses Eurythmic movements to bring them to order: a raised arm with palm facing forwards for silence, and then arms folded across her chest for composure. The children copy her so that within seconds there is silence and a penetrating, tangible feeling of calm throughout the class.

The teacher calls the class to gather around for a story. She explains that they have just completed a series of stories on St Peter showing the Choleric temperament (dominance, leadership). They are now going on to stories of St Francis which will portray the Melancholic temperament (the burden of the physical body and sorrow for the world). However, in addition to the overall temperament of each story, the other temperaments are also drawn in to give balance.

The teacher describes to the children how poor St Francis was, and how he wept when he met someone poorer than himself. One day he was praying in preparation for a sermon. He was standing under a tree, and nearby was a donkey which began making a dreadful moaning noise (Phlegmatic), while in the tree dozens of birds gathered, singing with restless excitement (Sanguine). The teacher asks the children to show her how the birds were behaving, and they all burst into a delighted chorus of twittering, bouncing around and fluttering their hands.

"My dear sisters, the birds, and you, brother donkey," says St Francis sternly, "It is now my turn to speak. You have had your say... !" This story shows the Choleric dominating the Sanguine and Phlegmatic temperaments. The moral content conveyed pictorially by the symbols of Francis and the animals is that the Ego, or Self, must learn to control the undeveloped Soul faculties before it can find its expression in life, which is symbolised by the sermon.

The children then return to their desks and take out their drawing books. The teacher draws an illustration of the story on the board, using short, shading strokes without outlines. Francis is shown in blue (the colour of the Melancholic temperament) surrounded by an aura of yellow and red dashes (Choleric). The birds are shown in yellow (Sanguine) (see 5.3.2.10.1). The children are then left to copy the teacher's drawing, but they are allowed to do so freely, without pedantic constraints or criticisms that their drawings are not exact replicas. The natural influence of imitation is allowed to operate.

The teacher now explains to the author the progress of the lesson. She has first brought the children's Will into expression while doing the "odd and even numbers" by using strong rhythm and emphatic stamping and swinging of the legs and arms (see 4.5.3). Then she brought the fruits of this Will and Limb activity into Feeling through the story and drawing which aroused the temperaments and their imaginative, pictorial faculties (see 4.5.2). Now she is to complete the lesson by using what has been aroused as Will and Feeling in an activity that demands Thinking (see 4.5.1). This is to be done with "sums", always through the principle of beginning with whole numbers and working to their parts (see 5.3.2.6).

The teacher sends the children outside to collect 40 pebbles each. When they return she tells them there are 40 birds in St. Francis' tree, each represented by one of their pebbles. She asks them to work out how many groups of ten there are. When they have it she writes on the board $40 = 4 \times 10$ and the children copy it down. She then asks them how many there will be in each group if she divides 40 into four parts ($40 \div 4 = 10$). Now they add ($40 = 10 + 10 + 10 + 10$), and subtract ($40 - 10 = 30$), and the teacher leaves them with a problem ($40 = 17 + ?$). When they have the answer she tells them to make up some of their own sums in this way. There is a gradual increase in noise, but the teacher tells them that they must work silently or stay back at break. This enables the teacher to see their individual work as she walks around the class.

To end the lesson they practise the recorder, with the teacher standing in front of the class and showing her finger work clearly so that the children can imitate it. There are no pedantic exercises; they go straight into a melody. To an adult mind this seems a difficult way to learn, yet the children soon pick up the tune after a confused beginning. They then sing songs in German and French, and finally say a Grace before break when they eat sandwiches.

This lesson has been described in detail because it is the clearest and most methodical translation of Steiner's educational thought into practice that I have seen in a single lesson. Many teachers use the same rhythms of Will to Feeling to Thinking, but not quite as clearly arranged and integrated over a whole lesson.

Another arithmetic lesson (Class 4) involved the rhythmic saying of tables but with the order reversed and accompanied by clapping (8 is 1 x 8, 16 is 2 x 8 etc.). This class also practised numbers in sequences (8, 16, 24, 32 ...) or patterns, again with clapping (1, 5, 2, 4, 3 .... 1, 5, 2, 4, 3 ... etc.). They then went on to show the most remarkable facility with mental arithmetic, working at great speed. The teacher began with a single, realistic problem: Six farmers each brought six bulls to another farmer who had six; how many bulls were there altogether? She then went into a rapid development of exercises: Take the last answer divide it by two and add three. Take the last answer, add one and share it between five. Take this number, multiply by eight and divide in four ... etc. When the children were asked to give the answer at the end of it all, at least three quarters had managed to keep up and get it right.

Such exercises are often accompanied by clapping in complex combinations (two claps, five claps, three claps, four claps, and then repeated), or doing exercises to control the fingers or feet and legs (see 5.3.2.5 for the far reaching purpose of these). In each case no instruction is given. The teacher simply demonstrates the exercise and the children follow the example.

With older children teachers find it more difficult to integrate the rhythm of Will to Feeling to Thinking, but they nevertheless take care to attach arithmetic lessons to realistic situations. For example, a Class Nine (14 to 15 year olds) teacher begin his maths lesson simply by taking the class to the gym for a game of basketball as a Limb activity. He then proceeded to use the remaining hour of the main lesson to do combinations and permutations by studying "The Gambler and his dilemma: Probabilities". He went on to use logarithms to show that the more throws one takes with a disc or a coin, the closer one comes to achieving a given combination of numbers.

In a lesson on projective geometry, children in Class Ten developed complex and beautiful forms — a subject which requires a study in itself — but their pictorial activities were not integrated with Limb movements.

6.5   A Foreign Language Lesson with Class Two   (see 5.3.2.4)

The following lesson was an Afrikaans lesson to children from English speaking homes. Some of the children had already developed a working knowledge of Afrikaans, so that it was not a foreign language to them. However, the principles used in the lesson were the clearest demonstration of teaching a language witnessed in a Waldorf School.

This teacher is enormously popular. He takes the class after their main lesson and break, and by the time he reaches the door of the classroom he has several children already clinging to his arms, while others call out their welcomes. Nevertheless, he walks quietly to the front of the class, crosses his arms over his chest and waits for the children to quieten down.

Before long he is pointing to parts of the room, and then to items of clothing and parts of the body, asking children to name them in Afrikaans. Then he leads them in a boisterous recitation of a poem they have learnt, followed by a song. Both poem and song have strong rhythms and rhymes (see 5.3.2.3. and 4.5.3).

Again he waits for the children to quieten down before asking one child to relate in Afrikaans what the previous day's story was about. When the child falters he allows another child to take the description further, occasionally filling in and supplying or asking for an English word or phrase for central parts of the story so that the slower pupils can follow. He then tells the same story again, and it contains vocabulary used earlier together with a simple tale. Most of the pupils are engrossed in, and understand the story. However, the teacher is watching a boy at the back of the class whose mind is clearly on other things. He is corpulent and has a slack facial expression, which are the physical characteristics associated with the Phlegmatic temperament. Quite suddenly the teacher's emphasis in his story changes. He begins to describe the preparation and eating of food, emphasizing the pleasure of it all. In a moment the child's attention is caught. His glazed eyes take on a new shine. He swallows, moves in his chair and begins to listen to the story. Later the teacher explains that food is one of the loves of the Phlegmatic, and never fails to alert their attention if mentioned in a lesson.

The teacher then asks the children questions (see 4.5.1) about the story, and they have to try to answer in Afrikaans. Finally he tells the children to draw an illustration of the story in their books. He allows them to emphasise the part of the story they wish to, and the Phlegmatic child draws a string of sausages with great concentration. The teacher explains that the stillness and absorption of the drawing activity prepares the children for their next lesson.

6.6   Class Six (12-13 year olds) : Mineralogy (see 5.3.2.7)

This class also enters their classroom one at a time, shaking hands with their teacher. He has been with them nearly six years and they are clearly fond of him. He has something personal to say to many of them.

Once inside they recite a verse to prepare for the day's learning: "I do behold the world wherein the spirit dwells, wherein the stars do shine, wherein the rocks do dwell..." It is a verse used by several classes I have visited.

The teacher then moves into practising the spellings of the words used in Mineralogy (igneous, metamorphic, sedimentary, etc.). Firstly, he writes the words on the chalkboard. The children face the board and chant loudly and in unison: "Igneous, I,G,N,E,O,U,S, Igneous". The class stamps and claps rhythmically with each word and letter they say (see 4.5.2). Then the process is repeated, facing away from the board. Finally, the children write a test on the words, which is given to the author to mark while the class sings some songs: a melodious song of a nightingale (Melancholic); a lively song which the children enjoy (Sanguine); and then a quiet, slow one (Phlegmatic).

The marking reveals a small group of children who have barely one correct spelling between them, in contrast to the remainder of the class who have them all correct. The teacher explains that the small group has recently been sent to the school as a "last resort" to try to salvage their education. He says they were labelled "dyslexic" by their last school and given remedial lessons without effect. He is confident they will soon improve once they develop a rhythmical sense which will strengthen their memory (see 4.5.2). Even in the few weeks they have been there he has already noticed improvements in their work and attitudes.

The class now moves on to meanings of words, discussing lava, magma, and volcanoes. They go on to granite and discuss its three basic constituents: mica is often black and peels in its pure form. It gives granite its sparkle. Quartz is whitish and gives granite its light. Feldspar is opaque and varies in colour, giving granite its red, brown or green tints. Samples of rock are passed around to demonstrate these points.

The teacher then speaks of granite as if it has moral life. He describes it as an unselfish stone which accepts into itself other kinds of stones, like an unselfish person who absorbs the good qualities of other people into himself, thereby becoming useful in many ways.

Granite is then contrasted with lime. Granite is a stone formed by fire, whereas lime is formed by water. Unlike granite, lime seems to be a selfish stone in the way it greedily absorbs the moisture from one's palm when one holds it.

The teacher completes his short lecture (which the class has listened to with silent attentiveness) by commenting that the human body consists of many different minerals, and then he identifies places in the world where concentrated deposits of granite (Mt. Everest) and lime (Dover) are situated.

Later the teacher explains that there is no need to use sensationalism to absorb children in a lesson. What is necessary is that the children should *feel* a sense of identification with the subject matter. This is only possible if the teacher is able to build a bridge from them to the subject matter. In mineralogy this is done by attributing human qualities to minerals. It is also done by the use of verse and acting, as will be described at the end of this lesson.

The children take out the paintings they did in class the previous day. They are attempts to depict their impressions of granite crystals using yellow surrounded by blue, with the forms of the crystals developed through tone and colour-intensity within the yellow. The teacher holds up one which captures what he was hoping for, but when the children ask whose it is he says firmly, "It doesn't matter; that isn't important." Again, later he explains to me that egotism should never be encouraged in children. Egotism is quite different from self confidence, which develops from within through the child's experience of mastering various activities.

171

Therefore in a Waldorf School the teacher should develop the child's self confidence through good teaching rather than through praise.

The teacher then gives the class an exercise: to write a conversation between different kinds of rocks, with each claiming their different qualities (see 4.3.4 Anthropomorphism). The teacher comes over to answer some of my questions and soon there is a busy hum around the class. Suddenly a child calls out, "Sir, can we draw it?" — a question that astonishes with its conception that a conversation can be portrayed through drawing. The teacher replies to the child that he can try to draw it, but when another child asks how it can be done he tells him to write it. The teacher explains to the author that the first child has strong pictorial and colour senses, which the second child does not have. When the first child has finished we see that he has drawn two crystals of different rocks with rainbow-like streams of colour from one to the other, each colour representing a quality.

The teacher explains further that all kinds of creativity are encouraged in Waldorf Education because of the belief that a basic imaginative kind of thought can be metamorphosed in later life into any form of thinking activity. Artistic thinking is therefore a sound basis for whatever profession the child may choose in later life (see 4.5 to 4.5.3 and 4.4.1).

The author comments on the teacher's lack of text books in the class, and he replies that he uses none whatever. Everything he does is presented either concretely (for example the rocks themselves) or else through his own narration or description in which he can imbue the ideas with imagination and feeling. He leads the way to his storeroom and presents me with a beautifully illustrated booklet he made up called "My First Reader", explaining that before his class ever read the book they learned how to write and knew the fables in the book almost by heart. When presented with the book they were therefore able to read it immediately. He says that the "right time" was when the children were in class three (9 years old), much later than in most schools, yet none of them had any difficulty with reading or spelling and all read widely (see 5.3.2.2.).

As the children begin to complete their writing exercise, the noise in the class increases considerably. The teacher explains that this noise provides an important balance in a lesson. To begin with he kept the children under strong control during his lecture, the spelling and singing. Then he released them to work on their own, and they have now swung to the other extreme of a lack of control. This rhythm is necessary in a lesson for the development and release of tension, or concentration followed by relaxation. However, it is vital that the teacher should not have to shout at his class in order to bring it under control again. He must be able to bring them together through their own free respect for his authority. By way of demonstration he simply walks to the front of the class and begins an inconspicuous, rhythmical combination of clapping and clicking his fingers. In their own time the children put away their work, and one by one they join in, until the whole class is following the changing rhythms with complete concentration (see 3.3.1.2).

Then he tells them to go into their groups and practise their performance for the forthcoming festival. They are to present a drama demonstrating what they have learnt in mineralogy. The drama takes the form of mime which accompanies a verse. This verse is learned by heart and serves to remind them of the gradual development and characteristics of the rocks they have studied. Their mime consists of suggesting the forms and qualities of rocks: the flat, sandwiched layers of mica, or the strong angular forms of quartz crystals. The teacher has composed the verse and he encourages the children to emphasise the rhythm and rhyme. The whole class ends with the final verse —

> Our mother earth, alive and well,
> Can through her rocks and crystals tell
> The secrets of her inner being
> To every single human being.

6.7   Educating the Will

The process of educating from the level of Will through the Limb System and then into Feeling through the Rhythmic System and finally into Thinking through the Head System (see 4.5 *et seq.*) is carried out in diverse ways in Waldorf Education. The basic forms of expression – limb movements, singing, rhythmical activities, imagery and so on – are used by every teacher, but the ways in which they are organised depend on the teachers themselves.

The best impression of what is meant by the education of the Will through the Limb System can be gained by witnessing a lesson in Eurythmy (see 5.3.2.5). An exercise in which the author participated involved the "G" sound. A simple, pictorial and alliterative line was used: "Go, goose and gander through the golden gate!" We began by saying the line, and naturally we placed little emphasis on the "G" sound. More and more the Eurythmy teacher showed us how to involve ourselves in the sound, not only by expressing it with our tongues and mouths, but by using our whole bodies to express the words we used. On the word "Go" we had to make a forceful gesture, pushing away with our arms and hands, and each pronunciation of "G" had to be accompanied by an emphatic thrust of the heels of the hands, the heels of the feet, and with strong, heavy steps. We had to project the sound forcefully from our mouths. So intensive was this experience of a single consonant that it has remained a vivid experience ever since.

The Eurythmy teacher concerned said that for a Eurythmist, language must involve the whole body, so that a word is not only an action of the mouth, vocal chords and lungs, but is accompanied by the movement that the word summons up. Each sound in the word must be related to the movements that it subtly arouses in the body. In this way the Eurythmist tries to bring language into full consciousness and involve Will, Feeling and Thinking in every word that is uttered. By practising each consonant and vowel sound the Eurythmist can develop an understanding and conscious awareness of the profound spiritual significance of the spoken word for human life.

The purpose of Eurythmy — or indeed of any attempt to educate the Will — is not merely to develop physical skills. Steiner taught (see 4.5 to 4.5.3) that the education of the Will was the foundation for the education of the Feelings and Thinking. Whatever brought harmony, rhythm and order into physical activity (such as when a child learns to shade with short pencil strokes instead of merely scribbling) also brought harmony and order into Feeling and Thinking. To Steiner, the human being was a whole, but the laws that governed this whole had to be understood in order to educate correctly.

There seem to be many stages in the development of Eurythmy. These vary from bringing individual sounds into full vocal and physical expression (as in the lesson described above), or accompanying the saying of a verse with actions expressive of the content, to genuine Eurythmy in which the semantic and phonetic content of the spoken word is entirely sublimated within feeling and gesture. Instead of merely allowing speech to have intellectual, utilitarian value, Eurythmy attempts to bring the individual's speech to expression in the Feelings and Will. Because of the intimate relationship between language and thought, Eurythmy serves to integrate the individual's Thinking with his body and soul.

The most emphatic demonstration that the author witnessed of Steiner's belief that education should first be founded in the Will was a "remedial" lesson. The child involved was a girl of nine, daughter of a couple who were both senior teachers in a government school. In the course of her first year at an orthodox school she seemed to progress normally, but then suddenly her work began to deteriorate alarmingly. Her parents took her to a remedial clinic where she improved briefly and then deteriorated again. She became nervous and withdrawn, unable to carry out the simplest instructions or tasks, and was clumsy and disorientated. Her parents brought her to the Waldorf School as a "last resort", knowing nothing of its methods but acting on the advice of a friend.

At the Waldorf School the girl was put into the normal class (3) for her age, and was taken alternately by the Remedial and Eurythmy teachers for periods of six weeks each. To begin with these special sessions lasted no more than ten minutes, but at the time of my visit six months later she was able to manage half an hour.

The Eurythmy teacher explained that remedial education should never work through the child's intellect. Such efforts would only achieve weak and temporary improvements and would make the child more nervous, resulting in further deterioration. Instead, one should always begin with the body. By bringing harmony and rhythm into the limbs the right basis is laid for the development of Thinking. Mental exercises (reading or arithmetic, etc.) should always be the last aspect of the lesson.

The lesson began with the girl lying on her back, holding a red ball in her right hand, a blue ball in her left hand, and a yellow one between her feet. She had to raise one or other of the balls in response to tones that the teacher played on a xylophone. She then had to sit at a desk holding a red crayon in her right hand and a blue one in her left. She was told to draw a figure of eight with her right hand, allowing the left hand to follow it. Following this the teacher sang a song and the child had to accompany it by beating the rhythm with her fingers. Next she had to skip and then watch the teacher and clap the number of times the teacher had skipped. She had to throw a ball against the wall, allow it to bounce on the floor and then catch it, or clap and then catch it. The teacher explained that following verbal commands was important for developing intake of auditory information, and that, although many of these exercises may seem easy for a nine year old, this child had been unable to do any of them to begin with.

Then they did the letter "I". The teacher said, "I am Mrs ..." and the child had to respond by saying her own name: "I am ... " The teacher asked, "What do I look like when I say the word I?" And the child had to stand erect. The teacher drew the letter on the board and the child had to copy it. After this the teacher introduced the letter "S". She walked the shape on the mat, led the child along the shape, and told her to do it alone. Finally the child had to think of some words beginning with "S".

Back in the girl's own class, the children were doing more advanced rhythmical activities, singing and playing recorders in unison or overlapping, with three groups, one slightly behind the other. They also performed complex clapping routines in groups, with each group contributing a different variation. The girl from the remedial class was allowed to follow this as well as she could, and was never singled out for individual attention in front of the class. These children were far ahead of the girl in intellectual achievements as well, but her class teacher confirmed that she had improved considerably since arriving.

As the subject matter of lessons becomes more abstract in the senior classes, so the teacher has to draw on all his or her ingenuity as well as the class skills developed over the years in order to integrate theory with physical activity.

One Physiology lesson with a Class Seven (12-13 year olds) was on the heart. The diagram on the board showed a simplified representation of red and blue blood flowing from and to the heart and through the lungs. The teacher began the lesson by splitting the class in half, one of which represented the flow of the blood, and the other the flow of air into and out of the lungs. The two groups moved in circles but met and weaved in a figure of eight at one point which represented the lungs. Once the children were able to do this they had to introduce clapping and stamping, the circle representing the blood using a faster rhythm (four to one) than that representing the breathing rate. The ultimate effect was almost hypnotic with the intense concentration and rhythm involved.

The teacher went on to develop an image of the heart as being like the sun which gives us a daily rhythm. She then spoke about the purpose of the heart and drew a diagram on the board for the children to copy. When they had almost completed the drawing with colourful shading, some of the names of its parts were introduced (pulmonary arteries and veins and the superior and inferior vena cava, etc.) Next a piece of dictation was given in which the heart was described poetically, and finally the children each painted the forms of the human body, showing the flow of the blood to and from the heart.

There seemed to be considerable variation in the ability of teachers to integrate limb and rhythmic activities with the intellectual content of lessons. Most Waldorf teachers developed a pictorial approach to their subject matter, or related it directly to concrete reality, but there were some lessons in which the only limb activity was a game of basketball and no effort was made to integrate the activity with the subject matter of the lesson. It was only used to arouse the bodily processes and the forces of Will in preparation for the intellectual activity of the lesson (see 4.4.1).

This chapter aimed to give the reader a closer understanding of Steiner's educational thought by presenting it in practice. The next chapter will compare some aspects of Steiner's thought with that of other well known educational theorists. This is important in order to show some of the main points at which Waldorf education is linked to, or separated from, "main-stream" educational thinking. Such an orientation would have to be the subject of a much more extensive study, but some central points can be made which will enable us to reach some conclusions about Steiner's relevance to modern educational theory.

7

RUDOLF STEINER

A MODERN
PERSPECTIVE

The purpose of this work has been to collate an analysis of Rudolf Steiner's thought on education. However, it would be precipitate to close such a study without a perspective of Steiner within a broader context of educational thought. For this purpose some comparisons will be made between Steiner and some of the educational thought of the ancient Greeks, several "child-centred" theorists, and some twentieth century thinkers. Whereas many more comparisons can be made, those chosen aim to highlight fundamental aspects of Steiner's thought which seem most relevant to a modern perspective.

7.1   STEINER AND
ANCIENT GREEK THOUGHT

Many of Steiner's ideas have parallels elsewhere, but it was his integrated vision of child development and educational method that he claimed to be unique. This holism supports his contention that his educational thought was not eclectic, but was drawn out of a profound and complex understanding of the nature of man. However, strong parallels can certainly be found with ancient Greek education which Steiner referred to extensively in two series of lectures[1]. He maintained that the ancient Greeks had an intuitive understanding of education, much of which we have lost in modern times. The following quotation from Plato confirms how closely Steiner's ideas concur with the best of Greek education.

> "And when the boy has learned his letters and is beginning to understand
> what is written, as before he understood only what was spoken, they put

into his hands the works of great poets, which he reads at school; in these are contained many admonitions, and many tales, and praises, and encomia of ancient famous men, which he is required to learn by heart, in order that he may imitate or emulate them and desire to become like them. Then again the teachers of the lyre take similar care that their young disciple is temperate and gets into no mischief; and when they have taught him the use of the lyre, they introduce him to the poems of other excellent poets, who are the lyric poets; and these they set to music, and make their harmonies and rhythms quite familiar to the children's souls, in order that they may learn to be more gentle, and harmonious, and rhythmical, and so more fitted for speech and action; for the life of man in every part has need of harmony and rhythm. Then they send them to the master of gymnastic, in order that their bodies may better minister to the virtuous mind ..." [2]

This quotation refers to the use of stories which must be memorised as a basis for moral education (see 4.3.4), and to the use of music and gymnastics (education of the Limb System) to bring harmony and strength to the mind (see 4.3.4 and 4.5 *et seq.*).

Steiner was particularly interested in Plato. His examiner for his Ph.D. was Heinrich von Stein, author of Seven Books of Platonism which Steiner discusses in his autobiography[3].

Steiner argued that both Socrates and Plato were initiates of "The Mysteries", and that Plato's Dialogues were mystical teachings which only a student of occultism would recognise.

"For them, fire flashed forth from his words, for others, only thoughts." [4]

Steiner's descriptions of the archetypes (see 3.2.2.2) suggest that he considered Plato's teachings with regard to these to be based on spiritual perception. Plato's Myth of Er refers to Reincarnation: "... some souls rose out of the earth stained with the dust of travel, and others descended from heaven, pure and clean" [5]; as well as to Karma, "For every wrong he has done to anyone he must pay the penalty in return ... " [6] (See 4.1.1 and 4.1.2).

Steiner's contention that "We can awaken what is in the child, but we cannot implant a content into him" [7] finds a parallel with Plato's Cave Metaphor:

"... we must reject the conception of education professed by those who
say that they can put into the mind knowledge that was not there before
— rather as if they could put sight into blind eyes." [8]

This whole metaphor reveals the great difference between Plato's concept of knowledge and the more intellectual conception. Steiner, like Plato, sees "knowledge" as having profound spiritual import (see 3.1.3).

Plato's insistence on censorship[9] has a parallel in Steiner's use of fables, legends, and stories of heroic deeds for moral education (see 4.4.2.4). The transformation of aesthetic education into rational thought (see 4.4.2.3) is identical in both Plato and Steiner:

178

"For rhythm and harmony penetrate deeply into the mind and take a most powerful hold on it, and, if education is good, bring and impart grace and beauty, if it is bad, the reverse. And moreover the proper training we propose to give will make a man quick to perceive the shortcomings of works of art or nature, whose ugliness he will rightly dislike; anything beautiful he will welcome gladly, will make it his own and so grow in true goodness of character; anything ugly he will rightly condemn and dislike, even when he is still young and cannot understand the reason for so doing, while when reason comes he will recognise and welcome her as a familiar friend because of his upbringing." [10]

Steiner considers aesthetic education, in which the child is taught to love beauty and dislike ugliness, an important part of painting and music lessons (see 5.3.2.10.1 and 5.3.2.10.3).

Steiner's stages of development are closely related to Aristotle's: an early period when growth is mainly physical; then a period of appetites and passions; and finally the development of reason. Aristotle identifies three sides to education: gymnastics, to develop skill and physical grace; the inculcation of habits for the training of character in which music plays an important part; and, when the rational part of the soul appears, it will have a sound basis in a firm moral character[11] (see 4.2 to 4.5.3).

Like Aristotle, Steiner sees man as having an almost unlimited capacity for raising his consciousness to perceive the divine, but in human life he must live between the demands of himself and society, and between the polarities of work and leisure[12] (see 3.1 et seq., 1.2.4 and 4.4.2.5).

The concept of the Humours or Temperaments was widespread in ancient Greece, and its origins are lost in Hindu antiquity[13]. However, research into temperaments and "body types" has continued in the twentieth century. Kretschmer, Sheldon, Joensch, Jung, Worringer and Bullough have all attempted to develop this sort of conception of human nature[14].

Steiner's understanding of the temperaments is integrated with his perception of the interrelationships of the physical and Soul Bodies and the Ego, which sets him apart from other thinkers in this regard (see 4.6).

7.2   STEINER AND THE CHILD-CENTRED THEORISTS

Although Steiner falls firmly in the tradition of basing his principles for education on the nature of the child, many of his conclusions conflict with those of other "Child-Centred" theorists.

Rusk argues that, before Rousseau, John Locke (1632-1704) should be regarded as the father of the child-study movement: "Most of his followers do not know their master." [15]

Locke rejected the ancient Greek idea of "inborn knowledge" on the grounds that knowledge cannot antedate experience[16]. He also distinguished ideas and knowledge from faculties, abilities and powers which may be inherited[17]. It followed that the mind was initially a *tabula rasa* on which the educator could make whatever impressions he wished[18]. The influence of Locke's doctrine was to turn education from cultivating what was within the child through gymnastics, music and literature, towards implanting a content which would fill the empty page of the child's mind.

By contrast, Steiner has a holistic view of the individual, in which knowledge is an inseparable part not only of Thinking, Feeling and Will, but also of the incarnating Spirit (see 4.1.1 and 4.1.2). Like Plato, Steiner sees knowledge as being intimately bound up with imitation and Art in childhood (see 4.2.2 and 4.5 *et seq.*). Factual knowledge ought to be introduced to education only towards adolescence, before which knowledge should be presented in imaginative, pictorial form. For Steiner, many concepts such as purely abstract approaches to letters of the alphabet or numbers are not suited to a child's pictorial way of thinking before puberty (see 4.3.4, 5.3.2.2 and 5.3.2.6). Therefore, although Steiner believes that the teacher ought to convey a content to the child, the concepts should be in an artistic form which is accessible to the child's mode of consciousness.

Locke believed that education should attend to that " ... which will be of most frequent use to him (the child) in the world" [19]. This principle underlies all of Steiner's educational thought, but with the emphasis that early education through imitation and imagery should be allowed to develop into objective knowledge in its own time. Pedantic instruction destroyed the energies in the child's mind instead of stimulating and strengthening them.

Rousseau (1712-1778) recognised childhood as a period of maturation in which natural law should be allowed to fulfil itself, unobstructed by social goals and values. He stressed that children should learn from experience and nature[20].

"A child ... should remain in complete ignorance of those ideas which are beyond his grasp. My whole book is one continued argument in support of this fundamental principle of education." [21]

By contrast, for Steiner it is the mode of presentation and not so much the subject matter which should differ in the education of the child as compared to that of the adult. As long as the subject matter can be presented in artistic form, through the imagery of stories, songs or poems, whatever is needed in adult life should have its foundation in childhood. In early childhood, education is absorbed from Imitation; after the change of teeth, Imitation becomes internalised as picture-thinking in the form of imagination (see 4.3 *et seq.*), and whatever is absorbed through these means will become transformed after puberty into intellectual thinking, with its roots firmly set in the Feeling and Will of the child (see 4.4.2.2 to 4.4.2.4).

Kant (1724-1804) addressed himself to the problem of freedom in the development of morality. Kant's child ultimately finds freedom in obedience to law, the reasonableness of which he or she is able to see for him- or herself[22]. Steiner, on the other hand, sees freedom as an experience which the child feels when he or she is released from the influences of Imitation and Authority. Such an experience has a maturational basis with the release of the Astral Body at puberty, but it needs the support of a correct education in order to be fulfilled. Only from such an experience of freedom can the adolescent realise his independence to act according to his personal judgement (see 4.7). Steiner states his opposition to Kant as follows:

> "Kant's principle of morality: Act so that the principle of your action may be valid for all men — is the exact opposite of ours. His principle would mean death to all individual action. The norm for me can never be what all men would do, but rather what is right for me to do in each special case." [23]

For Steiner, full freedom is something attained through Spiritual Science wherein the initiate gradually becomes aware not only of his or her actions, but the reasons for them[24], even those which are normally completely unconscious[25]. Therefore he or she is able to act knowing why he or she is acting and with full choice. The adolescent achieves an experience of "freedom" by interpreting intellectually what he or she has absorbed in earlier years through Imitation and Authority.

Steiner's ideals for education accord with many of Pestalozzi's: the importance of love, of the home, the study of human nature, the harmonious development of the whole person, the principle of readiness, the importance of concrete experience and of the forces of nature in education, and the belief that education should draw out the potentials of the child[26]. However, the belief in the "innate goodness" of the child which Pestalozzi shares with Rousseau is much more complex in Steiner's thought because of the doctrines of Reincarnation and Karma (see 4.1.1 and 4.1.2) whereby the child is an incarnating individuality which has its own unique destiny to fulfil.

The relationship between Steiner's thought and that of J.G. Fichte (1762-1814) is deep[27] and complicated by Fichte's change from a cosmopolitan view of Europe to a nationalistic one after Prussia had fallen under the control of Napoleon. Steiner's thought on education is more developed than, and often opposes Fichte's, but it is strongly in sympathy with his idea that education must be based in morality, developing a love of the right, and only secondarily concerned with the intellect[28].

Fichte's famous German successors, Herbart (1776-1841) and Froebel (1782-1852) laid the groundwork for the educational principles of the late nineteenth and early twentieth centuries[29].

One of Herbart's central aims of education, which Steiner shares, is the development of morality and character. However, in their methods of achieving this aim they are diametrically opposed. Herbart's pedagogy begins in cognition. Once the child has the right concept of morality he or she will develop the right feeling, and then his or her moral will is expressed through action.

" *'Ignoti nulla cupida* — the circle of thought contains the store of that which can gradually amount by the steps of interest to desire, and then by means of action to volition .... If inner assurance and personal interests are wanting, if the store of thought be meagre, the ground lies open for the animal desires.' " [30]

Steiner's method is the opposite of this. Morality must begin in the Will and then develop into Feeling and finally into Thinking (see 4.3.4, 4.4.2.4 and 4.5 *et seq.*). Without this order in education the child's whole being is damaged (see 4.4), and indeed, the developmental sequence from Imitation of action (Will), to Feeling for Authority and freedom of Thinking after puberty is at the foundation of all Steiner's pedagogy (see 4.2.2, 4.3.1 and 4.4.2.2). Steiner sums up his attitude towards Herbart quite simply:

"A pedagogy like the Herbartian, which takes its start in a training of the faculty of thought and ideation, has the effect of ruining the child's body. This should be known by all who are engaged in education." [31]

Steiner praised Froebel's love of children and his recognition of the role of imitation in child development, but criticised him for permeating all educational activities with intellectualism (see 1.2.5). This is a criticism shared by Rusk who points out that the mystical qualities that Froebel's "gifts" may assume for an adult could not mean the same to a child[32].

Like Froebel, Steiner emphasises that the role of education is to bring the child's soul and spirit to unfold itself in the body. However, Steiner does not fall into the trap of the over simplistic "analogy of the gardener" [33].

Froebel recognised that, "Knowledge acquired in our own active experience is more living and fruitful than that conveyed only by words." [34] Activity is also an essential constituent of Steiner's concept of "Knowledge", the process whereby a child develops a concept (see 4.4.1), but Steiner's explanation of the role of activity in learning through the involvement of the Limb System (see 4.5.3) is quite different to Froebel's.

Steiner took cognisance of the necessity of preparing children for their lives in modern industrial society (see 4.4.2.5 and 5.3.2.11). This was a central concern in the education of the adolescent. His thought contains many pragmatic elements such as his willingness to compromise with social customs in preference to alienating education from its social context (see 4.5.3, sport, and 5.3.1.1, exams). The holism of his thought establishes the purpose and usefulness of each element of his education. For example the pictorial arts and music are not only for the education of the soul (see 3.2.2.1 to 3.2.2.3 for the description of the way in which form, music and language are part of the essential nature of the Soul Bodies and Ego), but they are also related to the physical body through the Rhythmic System (see 4.3.2 and 4.3.4). Steiner is therefore strongly pragmatic, but in a different way to a thinker like Dewey (1859-1952). Whereas Dewey looked for relevance in the social and economic usefulness of activities, Steiner was also concerned (especially in the case of younger children) with physical, spiritual and soul relevance: for Steiner, the relevance of an education presented artistically was that it developed the whole child (see 4.5 *et seq.*).

Dewey overcame the problem of a dualistic moral education, which imposed the will of an adult upon the possibly conflicting wishes of the child, by arranging education so that the child would discover morality from his or her own experience[35]. For Steiner, moral education before puberty is achieved through Imitation and Authority. This is not an imposition on the child because, for Steiner, these two principles are in keeping with the child's inner nature. Therefore Steiner's idea of Authority avoids the problem of dualism, while making moral education a fully human process. Steiner rejects the idea that morality can be drawn out of the child as if it were already somewhere within him (see 1.2.4, 4.2.2 and 4.3.1). Whereas Dewey believes that the child should develop morality from his experience in the world, Steiner sees experience also as the stimulus to bring what has been absorbed in childhood through Imitation and Authority into full awareness (see 4.4.2.4). Steiner emphasises that morality has to be nurtured from infancy, which is one of the strongest reasons that the child should go through his whole education before puberty with the same teacher (see 4.2.3 and 5.3.1.1).

Montessori (1870-1952) emphasised the value of games, toys and devices to enable children to discover things for themselves[36]. Steiner considered that such activities were inimical to education before puberty (see 4.3.1) because not only were they intellectually engineered devices and therefore foreign to the child's nature, but the child's need for Imitation and Authority would be denied by channeling education away from the human presence of the teacher, and directing it into various objects. Thus the child would reach puberty without the foundation he or she would need to develop his independence (see 4.3.1).

Of course, Steiner also disagrees with Montessori's rejection of the use of fantasy in education[37]. For Steiner, fantasy is the young child's mode of consciousness, which is deeply bound up with his Will and imagination. Through fantasy, artistic images are drawn into the child's being and serve as a foundation of symbolism for his or her moral life (see 4.3.4).

A.N. Whitehead (1861-1947) rejected the commonly held belief that children underwent a "uniform steady advance" in development. He saw life as being "essentially periodic".

> "The interior spiritual life of man is a web of many strands. They do not grow together by uniform extension ... the development of mentality exhibits itself as a rhythm involving an interweaving of cycles, the whole process being dominated by a greater cycle of the same general character as its minor eddies." [38]

Basing his ideas on Hegel's analysis, which separates child development into periods of Thesis, Antithesis and Synthesis[39], Whitehead identified three stages of development to which approximate ages could be given. The first, lasting until thirteen or fourteen, was the Romantic stage at which "knowledge is not dominated by systematic procedure". It is the stage of "immediate cognisance of fact" with only rare attempts to dissect and analyse knowledge[40]. The child is gradually "awakening to the apprehension of objects and the appreciation of their connexions" [41]. The stage "is dominated by wonder, and cursed be the dullard who destroys wonder" [42].

The stage of Romance is succeeded by that of Precision which lasts until approximately eighteen years[43]. The stage of Precision "is barren without a previous stage of romance". It is the stage of "exactness of formulation" and of "analysing the facts" [44], a process which is constantly dependent on a sustained sense of wonder.

"The organism will not absorb the fruits of the task unless its powers of apprehension are kept fresh by romance." [45]

Whitehead accuses the "aimless accumulation of precise knowledge" of being responsible for pupils' lack of intellectual zeal and "paralysis of thought" [46].

In the stage of Generalisation, which lasts from approximately eighteen to twenty two years, the youth "relapses into the discursive adventures of the romantic stage, with the advantage that his mind is now a disciplined regiment instead of a rabble" [47].

The task of education is not so much that of deciding what should be taught as how it should be taught:

"The problem of a curriculum is not so much the succession of subjects; for all subjects should in essence be begun with the dawn of mentality. The truly important order is the order of quality which the educational procedure should assume." [48]

It will be noticed that there are broad sympathies between Whitehead's period of Romance and the first stages up to puberty that Steiner identified, in which fantasy and imagination hold sway. Like Whitehead, Steiner emphasised the importance of the early years as a preparation for the stage after puberty (see 4.4.2.1), and Steiner also identified the age of eighteen as one of significant change (see 4.4.2.3).

Whitehead and Steiner share a concern over the way subject matter is presented to the child. Whitehead tends to analyse child development in terms of intellectual faculties, so that even when describing the infant he says, "It is a process of discovery, a process of becoming used to curious thoughts, of shaping questions, of seeking for answers, of devising new experiences, and noticing what happens as the result of new ventures." [49] However, when he turns to the curriculum itself, Whitehead, like Steiner, shows his recognition of the child's pictorial mode of thinking by prescribing "stories, histories, and poems illustrating the lives of other people and other civilisations" [50], and he relegates language analysis to the period between twelve and fifteen[51].

Steiner's analysis of man's psyche into Thinking, Feeling and Willing was by no means unique among his contemporaries. One of William James' educational maxims, stated in what Sir Percy Nunn called "the finest psychological sermon in any language" [52], reads as follows:

"Don't preach too much to your pupils or abound in good talk in the abstract. Lie in wait rather for the practical opportunities, be prompt to seize those as they pass, and thus at one operation get your pupils both to think, to feel, and to do. The strokes of behaviour are what give the new set to the character, and work the good habits into its organic tissue." [53]

Steiner carries this idea into all education, even in such things as teaching the multiplication tables (see 6.4) because it draws the Will into learning. Steiner identifies limb movement as containing the forces of the Will, and rhythmic movement as arousing the Feelings (see 4.5 *et seq.*) so that the process of learning should employ these bodily activities. This principle of James', including his recognition of the educational importance of imitation and emulation[54] (hearkening back to Aristotle) accord closely with Steiner's educational principles.

Nunn (1870-1944) analysed conation closely, defining it as a "conscious 'drive' towards a consciously pursued end" and differentiating it from mechanical activities for the attainment of the end. He argues that automatic, "hormic" activities (habitual or "conditioned" behaviour) are no longer part of conation because they are not conscious[55].

Steiner's concept of Will differs considerably from this. For Steiner, Will impulses originate within man's Spirit; from subtle, unconscious activities of the Astral Body and Ego, or else from instinctual processes. The way to educate the Will is not through the conscious intellect, or through adjuring the child to will something, but through the disciplining and cultivation of the Limb System with which the Will is bound up. When such education becomes habitual and therefore unconscious it does not cease to become Will, but on the contrary, it becomes part of the Will of the individual and therefore no longer needs to be consciously motivated. Moral habits should be developed in children from their earliest years without their knowing why such habits are "moral". After puberty they will begin to awaken to the value of this foundation of morality within themselves, and only on such a basis will they be able to develop strong, individual and conscious Will impulses (see 4.5.3).

On the question of freedom, Nunn follows Kant's line, affirming that "The higher values of freedom emerge only when it (the child) chooses worthy ends and in pursuing them submits itself to the control of well-inspired forms or methods" [56]. Moreover, Nunn does not differentiate, as Steiner does, between the role of freedom in the education of the young adult and that of the young child. His basic aim is identical to Steiner's:

"We shall stand throughout on the position that nothing good enters into the human world except in and through the free activities of individual men, and that educational practice must be shaped to accord with that truth." [57]

However, instead of basing adult freedom on child-adult relationships of authority and imitation, Nunn supports the line of thought that runs through almost all "progressive" education: that the role of the adult in the education of the child is peripheral insofar as the adult becomes not the source, but the "facilitator" of education.

For the young child, Nunn adopts Caldwell Cook's "Play-Way", and Montessori's discovery learning, which decentralise the value of imitation and authority[58]. Therefore, it is possible to contrast Steiner's thought with much of modern educational theory by showing how Steiner draws education into the sphere of interpersonal experience, placing emphasis on the importance of the teacher's morality, whereas Nunn and others begin with Rousseau's belief in learning from concrete experience without the direct intervention of adult values. Such a contrast is, of course, a reduction of complex bodies of thought with roots in both philosophy and psychology. Freud and Jung had strong influences on the Progressives, and Nunn's book also takes into account the ideas of McDougall and Bergson as well as many others.

The above discussion indicates the importance of seeing Steiner's educational thought as a holistic system. No simple comparisons are appropriate when dealing with such a system.

Most of the concepts of interest to "Child-Centred" theorists are prominent in Steiner's thought: readiness, growth, authority, freedom and so on. However, with regard to these concepts, Steiner finds no sustained parallels among other thinkers, although his ideas are not so different as to defy comparison. Indeed, many similarities may be found among important educational thinkers, including the more modern ones, and some of these will be described in the following section.

7.3   STEINER AND MORE
RECENT EDUCATIONAL THOUGHT

Because of its emphasis on child-study and on basing education on the nature of the child, Waldorf Education can lay claim to be "child-centred" in its approach. However, as has already been indicated, there are fundamental differences between Steiner's belief in Authority (see 4.3.1 and 4.4.2.2) and those child-centred theorists who look to the judgement of the child for a theory of educational relevance.

The existential belief that man is condemned to be free[59] has been followed in education by thinkers such as Carl Rogers, who is convinced that a constantly flexible, teacher-facilitated educational environment is the means to the child's development of creativity and emotional balance[60]. The claim for the value of freedom, discovery learning and individual choice in the curriculum has been widely popularised by John Holt[61], Neil Postman, and Charles Weingartner[62].

However, Steiner finds support among educationists such as R.F. Dearden, who upholds the argument for the value of adult authority by showing that claims for the value of a curriculum chosen by the child,

"... do not do full and explicit enough justice to the relatively much greater knowledge of the more educated and experienced adults who are a child's parents and teachers, especially when these have had a professional training and have reflected on what they are doing." [63]

For Steiner, the curriculum should aim to prepare the child for all eventualities in life, and it is only the mature, knowledgeable adult who is capable of judging what is in the interests of children while they are growing up.

Steiner is concerned both with providing an education which is in the interests of the child, as well as with interesting the child. However, he does not aim merely to fascinate, but rather to bring the whole child into activity in each lesson. The artistic approach aims to arouse the physical body through rhythmic movements of the limbs, and the mind and feelings are involved both through the cultivation of the body as well as through fantasy, imagination and music (see 4.5 *et seq.*). Therefore Steiner identifies the mode of presentation, rather than content alone, as the means towards interesting the child.

Steiner does not try to encourage individuality by allowing pupils to pursue personal interests rather than a prescribed curriculum. He rather accepts the individuality of each child and provides a means towards harmonizing imbalances of temperament (see 4.6). After puberty the child's individuality is allowed free expression, on the basis of the harmony achieved earlier.

Despite advocating a prescriptive curriculum, Steiner claims that he does not simply overlay on the child a model of what he thinks man ought to be. This seeming contradiction is resolved by giving the child "artistic concepts", which are in keeping with his or her own inner nature. Thus education brings the child's natural faculties into realisation using pictorial and musical content with symbolic rather than abstract value. After puberty, children are helped to develop their own abstract conceptions of the "artistic concepts" given them in childhood (see 4.4.2.3 and 4.4.2.4).

The question that arises from this is whether it is possible to find grounds to evaluate Steiner's perceptions of the natural capacities and needs of children. It may seem that it could be done quite easily by simply comparing Steiner's stages with empirically based research. However, the problem is compounded because the features that Steiner sees as important in any one stage are not excluded from any other stage. For Steiner, it is not a matter of whether certain faculties are present or not, but whether they are ready for development. Premature stimulation of qualities of the Soul which are still "in embryo" (see 4.3 and 4.4) may harm the individual for the whole of life, and educators must have deep insight into the inner life of the child if they are to avoid such mistakes.

The fact that Steiner links changes in the child's Soul life to observable, physical changes at the change of teeth and puberty, adds credence to his model of development.

Psychologists who structure stages in accordance with their perceptions of the faculties that exist among most children at a particular age, face a dual problem.

Not only may their constructions of stages be out of keeping with what is really in the nature of the child, but their experiments themselves have been so structured as to test predicted results.

Nevertheless, Steiner's work bears comparison with the developmental studies which have become important to education in recent decades. For example, he finds extensive support in Arnold Gesell's work. Gesell (1880-1961) traced the young child's attraction towards stories (especially concerning animals), songs, poems with strongly marked rhythms and rhymes, and, by the age of seven, fairy tales, myths and legends[64].

Space does not allow for comparison between Steiner's thought and that of researchers such as Piaget and Erikson. Such comparisons would require close examination of the concepts each uses in order to find common reference points. However, one researcher, Jerome Bruner, has integrated much of modern development theory into a comprehensive theory of education, and interesting comparisons can be made between this and Steiner's work.

Bruner postulated that the principle of Readiness was misunderstood and that it was causing unnecessary delays in education.

> "We begin with the hypothesis that any subject can be taught effectively
> in some intellectually honest form to any child at any stage of development." [65]

In fact, all Bruner's work concedes the importance of Readiness through its emphasis that an "intellectually honest form" consists of presenting material in accordance with the child's way of viewing things. Bruner's analysis of the child's way of viewing things is given in a later work in which he postulates three main "storage systems" whereby the child builds his "model of the world". Each storage system utilises its own "mode of representation" to encode experience.

Firstly, there is the *enactive mode* of representation in which one "learns by doing". Secondly, the *iconic mode* of representation is a process of gaining an "image" of something which then organises visual and other sensory stimuli. Finally, words and language become the *symbolic mode* of representation, and are capable of representing actions and images for purposes of cognition[66].

According to Bruner, intellectual development seems to follow these three modes of representation sequentially, culminating with their integration in adulthood. The first stage of development is characterised by attempts to "know how to do". The second involves reflective functioning with internal representation of the child's world through images (the model here is enactive and iconic), which reaches a "high point" between five and seven years of age. Then around adolescence, "... something very special happens ... when language becomes increasingly important as a medium of thought." The child develops the ability to consider propositions and combinations of alternatives[67].

In Bruner's view, education should follow the three modes of representation both sequentially in the course of the child's development, and sequentially in the learning of any specific task. Symbolic thought is most sound when it is based on both iconic and enactive modes of representation[68].

Like Steiner, Bruner argues that these stages are not very clearly linked to age. However, he also questions whether they are linked to physiological changes, since equally sharp changes occur in the years before puberty without corresponding hormonal change.

This argument does not necessarily contradict Steiner if one remembers Steiner's point of view that physical changes at the change of teeth and puberty are the results, and not the causes, of changes in the Soul. Steiner points to several changes in the Soul-life which have no observable physical manifestations (see 4.3 *et seq.*).

Bruner's stages of development and the modes of representation which give them their character have close similarities to Steiner's. Steiner points to the Limb System as being most active and receptive to imitative influences before the "change of teeth" (see 4.2 *et seq.*). Between the change of teeth and puberty the Rhythmic System dominates the child and pictorial thinking or imagination is liberated (see 4.3.2). After adolescence, abstract thinking develops (see 4.4.1). Furthermore, Steiner's theory of instruction is to proceed from the Will (Limb System; activity), to Feeling (Rhythmic system; imagination) and then to Thinking (Head system; intellect) (see 4.5 *et seq.,* and 6.4). The psychological bases to Steiner's and Bruner's theories of instruction are therefore closely related, although they differ over their view of knowledge. Steiner has an artistic, or aesthetic epistemology, whereas Bruner's is rational, so that their respective applications of the theory of stages of development diverge.

Both Steiner (see 4.4.2.1) and Bruner[69] believe in the educational value of a "spiral curriculum", whereby knowledge that is to be relevant in adulthood should be first introduced in earlier stages of childhood, transformed into modes of representation appropriate to each stage. Although Steiner takes an aesthetic view of knowledge and Bruner a rational one, both believe that knowledge should be generative or alive, and not merely inert and factual. This theme runs through all Bruner's work, beginning with a paper published in 1957 called On Going Beyond the Information Given[70]. For Steiner, an essential value of aesthetic education is that "artistic concepts" with pictorial or musical form can evolve throughout life as the individual's perception of them deepens (see 4.4.2.4). This is the context in which Steiner emphasises the value of "discovery learning": the adolescent should never be given moral instruction but should experience an awakening to the moral content of imagery that he or she has absorbed in childhood through imitation and stories. This awakening is a vital stimulant to the adolescent's sense of independence.

By contrast, Bruner follows the line of thought begun by Montessori, and promotes the value of discovery learning throughout education. Steiner's belief in the value of Imitation and Authority relationships before puberty puts him strongly at variance with all theorists who advocate the value of discovery learning as a central principle of education during those early stages.

189

Even after puberty Steiner's view of discovery learning is very different to Bruner's. For Steiner, discovery is an intimate, moral awakening within the Soul, whereas Bruner externalises it as a process to do with objective knowledge. Bruner is interested in ensuring that the intellect is brought to full power by whatever external stimuli are necessary to effect this development[71]. Steiner is much more interested in the moral qualities of the Soul and Spirit, emphasizing that the intellect will develop best when it has an artistic foundation (see 5.3.1.3 and 4.5 *et seq.*).

Many more comparisons could be made between Bruner and Steiner, but the above account must suffice here in order to indicate the close parallels between their insights into the nature of child development.

In the field of Sociology there have been extensive developments since Steiner's time. Steiner's rejection of Marxism was on the grounds that it consisted of a theoretical construction imposed upon social events instead of being drawn out of the nature of human life (see 1.2.4), and he would have rejected the work of many modern theorists on similar grounds.

However, some aspects of Steiner's approach to the curriculum can be seen within the context of Basil Bernstein's analysis of the control of knowledge within schools. Bernstein's work is rooted in Durkheim's hypothesis, which postulates that in the course of industrialisation, social institutions tend to undergo a change from "Mechanical Solidarity" with traditional and hierarchical structures for social control, to "Organic Solidarity" in which social roles become more diverse but at the same time more interdependent due to specialisation. Interdependence leads to an integration and decentralisation of social control[72]. This forms the context in which Bernstein analyses the "message systems" through which educational knowledge is "realised".

He deals first with the relationships between contents of the subjects of the curriculum. When subjects are separated as in the traditional curriculum, each with a clearly defined status, he says they are "strongly classified" and organised by a "Collection Code". When there is a weakening of classification the subjects become more interrelated and they are organised by an "Integrated Code" [73].

Bernstein also looks at the degree of control that teachers and pupils have over the knowledge that is to be transmitted in education. When teachers and pupils have little control over what is taught and learned, "Framing" of educational knowledge is said to be "strong". As they gain more control over knowledge, Framing weakens[74].

Steiner's thought on education attempts to institutionalise balanced "classification" and "framing" of knowledge. He accepts subject divisions while emphasizing the importance of integrating the content of the curriculum (see especially 5.3.2.8 Geography), and he gives control over much of curriculum design (Framing) to the teacher, who must learn to respond to the needs and interests of pupils when deciding the curriculum (see 5.3.1.1).

In addition, Steiner's plan of a College of Teachers (see 5.3.1.2) ensures a power structure which cannot become entrenched in the hands of a few individuals, so averting what he calls "fanaticism". There is a rotating chair, equal pay among all teachers (with allowance made for extra dependants), and every member of staff must be prepared to discuss his or her work openly with the other teachers. The occult foundation for this attempt to balance the control structures within schools may be found in 1.2.1, which describes Steiner's view of man's tasks in the modern age (*cf.* Ahriman and Lucifer).

Further comparisons may be made between Steiner and thinkers who support the idea that Art in its broad sense should play a central role in education. In this regard an interesting contributor is the philosopher of science, Michael Polanyi, who bridges the gap between empirical and existential epistemologies with his concept of "personal knowledge", which is a fusion of the personal and the objective. This to some extent reflects Steiner's view of knowledge (see 2.2.3 and 3.1.4). Polanyi also argues that "... what is comprehended has the same structure as the act which comprehends it" [75] a view which corresponds with Steiner's claim that the Etheric Body, which has a sculpting, formative influence in the young child, becomes the medium of pictorial thinking after the change of teeth, and can only be properly understood by developing a sense of form through sculptural activities (see 3.2.2.1). Steiner makes similar links between the Astral Body and music (see 3.2.2.2), and between the Ego and language (see 3.2.2.3).

Like Steiner (see 4.5.3 and 5.3.1.4 respectively), Polanyi sees Art and authority as being fundamental to education[76].

An existentialist who has made a great impact on education through his spiritual perspective is Martin Buber, who, like Steiner, sees human relationships as being of central importance to education. His concept of authority in education is bound up with his description of the "I-Thou" relationship, which is characterised by a feeling of personal responsibility towards others.

"Genuine responsibility exists only when there is real responding.

Responding to what?

... We respond to the moment .... A dog has looked at you, you answer for its glance, a child has clutched your hand, you answer for its touch...." [77]

This relationship is called "inclusion", and in it the educator finds he or she is able to perceive the inner needs of his or her pupil, "... the wholly concrete spirit of this individual and unique being who is living and confronting him ..." [78]

"The educator who practises the experience of the other side and stands firm in it, experiences two things together, first that he is limited by otherness, and second that he receives grace by being bound to the other. He feels that 'over there' the acceptance and rejection of what is approaching (that is, approaching from himself, the educator) — of course often only in a fugitive mood or uncertain feeling; but this discloses the real need and absence of need in the soul." [79]

This spiritual relationship, which seems to be similar to Steiner's description of the early stages of "Spiritual Sight" (see 3.1.3 and 5.3.1.3), enables a teacher to give moral education without externalising it into any form of ethical instruction, but purely through the power of his authority.

> "Yet the master remains the model for the teacher. For if the educator of our day has to act consciously he must nevertheless do it 'as if he did not'. That raising of the finger, that questioning glance, are his genuine doing. Through him the selection of the effective world reaches the pupil. He fails the recipient when he presents this selection to him with a gesture of interference. It must be concentrated in him; and doing out of concentration has the appearance of rest. Interference divides the soul in his care into an obedient part and a rebellious part. But a hidden influence proceeding from his integrity has an integrating force." [80]

This profound insight into the nature of authority is present in Steiner's thought in the form of his aesthetic education through parables and pictures instead of in abstract concepts (see 4.3.4). Through such an education, knowledge becomes a fusion of the subjective and objective, just as Polanyi sees it. In Buber's words,

> "We do not find meaning lying in things, nor do we put it into things, but between us and things it can happen." [81]

Knowledge, therefore, becomes a living thing, not inert but as alive as the knower is able to make it. (*cf.* 3.1.3).

> "Whoever unlocks it and beholds it again as present, fulfils the meaning of that act of knowledge as something that is actual and active between men." [82]

Another concept which Buber investigates is the "originator instinct" which is man's impulse to make things: "... by one's own intensely experienced action something arises that was not there before" [83]. This seems to be what Steiner calls the Will, which is an expression of the Spirit (see 4.5.3).

Buber's work is similar to Steiner's insofar as he leads one into experiences of the soul rather than into information or rational arguments. Only by entering into his ideas with an open mind as well as open feelings can one understand what he is speaking about. In Keats' words, "... for axioms in philosophy are not axioms until they are proved upon our pulses ...." [84]

A disciple of Buber's, whose book Education through Art (1958) has become a classic, is Sir Herbert Read. His book covers many of the concepts that Steiner speaks about: Art, perception, imagination, temperament, unconscious processes, the "natural form of Education", the "aesthetic basis of discipline and morality", the teacher, the child and the environment.

Unfortunately, Read made only a fleeting reference to Steiner's work[85], but he has provided a framework to show that Steiner's thought on education stands very much within the context of "education through Art", and further research will reveal the degree to which Steiner draws together and parallels the work of other thinkers in this regard.

Steiner's insights into the life of Feeling are similar in some respects to Robert Witkin's[86]. Witkin points out that "knowing" is itself an "action" which uses symbols to organise experience and behaviour[87]. He considers the relationship between subjective and objective experience, explaining that sensation is "known-in-Being" through a "subject-reflexive act which recalls it."

> "The reciprocation of a sensate impulse (subject response) is a feeling-idea just as the reciprocation of an object is a concept. Being is made up of feeling-idea. It has an order and a logic of its own. The structured and adaptive characteristics of Being are what is meant here by an intelligence of feeling. Feeling is quite distinct from mood or emotion. It is the reflexive component of the affective life. It is the fabric of Being. Mood and emotion are simply disturbance unknowing." [88]

These ideas are related to Bruner's and Polanyi's mentioned earlier, and they merit closer attention. From the above, it can be seen that Witkin's account of the role of action and feeling in the process of "knowing" may be linked to Steiner's description of the "logical process" in which the whole being, and not only the "head" is involved (see 4.4.1). Like Steiner, Witkin has drawn attention to aspects of being that are often ignored in education, and has pointed to Art as the means by which this inner life may be cultivated.

This completes the comparisons between Steiner's thought and that of some other educational theorists. It only remains to draw together the conclusions reached in this book.

7.4 SUMMARY AND CONCLUSIONS

At the beginning of this book descriptions of Steiner's life and interests were given because so little is known of him except among the circle of his followers. It was shown that Steiner was a man of exceptional qualities and formidable energy who turned his attention to many fields of human life, of which education was one. Some of his perspectives of subjects distinct from education were described, both by way of introduction as well as to establish a context from which the holism in Steiner's thought could be indicated.

In Chapter 2, *Review of the Literature,* some characteristics of the most important books on Steiner were described. The review of Galbreath's thesis on Steiner outlined the occult context to Steiner's thought (see 2.2.4), and the summary of Barfield's view of Steiner's epistemology provided a concise foundation for later references to this aspect of Steiner's thought (see 2.2.3). The conclusions to be drawn from these reviews were that Steiner's thought was part of a strong trend towards an interest in the occult in his day, and that Steiner had a firm grounding in orthodox philosophy before developing his Spiritual Science. He was, therefore, very much a "man of his times". However, since his death his thought has become isolated, and little mention is made of him outside publications by his followers.

The fact that this is the first formal and comprehensive analysis of his educational thought reveals the neglect that has been shown towards him, despite the world-wide expansion of the Waldorf Schools Movement.

The extent of public knowledge about Waldorf Schools is generally restricted to brief summaries such as the following one.

"The Schools are co-educational, taking children from 6 to 18, following a pre-school Nursery Class. Most of them are equipped for boarders as well as day children.

Children are admitted mainly on interview. They are grouped according to chronological, rather than mental, age, as the aim is not only to feed the intelligence but to strengthen feeling and will, and to provide for the harmonisation of all three. The appeal is to the maturing forces of character based on normal organic development.

The Schools are Christian in outlook but non-denominational. Throughout the twelve years of school life, the teaching of Science, Art and Religion is so integrated that it may lead to a unity of experience in the understanding of man. To this end all children are introduced equally to the Humanities and Sciences as well as to languages, and all receive training in music and the arts and crafts. The education is thus comprehensive in character and specialisation is deferred for as long as conditions allow. There are no internal examinations. Special provision is made, however, in the latter years of school life for those pupils who need to take the General Certificate of Education." [89]

The main reason for the isolation of Steiner's thought appears to be its complex and unorthodox foundations, which this analysis has attempted to organise and clarify in order to integrate it and make it more easily accessible.

Chapter 3 began with an introduction to Steiner's Spiritual Science. It was shown that Steiner's philosophical work provided an epistemological foundation for his occultism, and that Spiritual Science could be "proved" by anyone who was prepared to rigorously discipline and develop his Thought, Feelings and Will along strictly moral lines.

Thereafter, Steiner's analysis of man, based on his Spiritual Sight, was outlined. The Soul consisted of two "Soul Bodies" the Etheric and Astral which were united with the Ego, or Spirit, and with the physical body. The physical body could be analysed into three "systems" which were also fully integrated. The Nervous or Head System was responsible for Thinking, and in it the physical body dominated the Soul Bodies and Ego. The Rhythmic or Chest System was responsible for Feeling, and was dominated by the Etheric Body. The Metabolic and Limb System was responsible for Willing, and it was dominated by the Astral Body and Ego. Man's senses were linked to these three Systems, so that some senses were mainly to do with Thinking, some with Feeling, and some with Willing.

Chapter 4 revealed Steiner's reasons for maintaining that an understanding of the Soul Bodies and Ego were essential for understanding child development and thence education.

Firstly, Steiner's belief in Reincarnation and Karma were described in order to show what it was that Steiner considered the child to already possess from birth. Then the three major stages of development were outlined. The first, from physical birth to the Change of Teeth, consisted of the main period of growth for the inherited physical organism. The Soul Bodies and Ego remained "in embryo" during this stage, and the Ego was absorbed in its environment so that children could not separate themselves from those around them, and they reproduced within themselves (imitated) whatever happened in their environment. Because the Soul Bodies and Ego were still in embryo, the child's senses were not differentiated into the Nervous, Rhythmic and Limb Systems, and they pervaded the whole body, so that even the limbs expressed the experience of feeding.

The most important means of education at this stage was example, and the child was said to be able to imitate not only physically discernible behaviour, but also the thoughts, attitudes, feelings and will of others. Therefore the educator's task was to be the sort of person he or she wished the child to become.

The first stage moved gradually into the second stage when the Etheric Body was "born". The outward, most noticeable physical sign of this was the emergence of the permanent teeth. The birth of the Etheric Body effected two main changes in the child's being as far as education was concerned. Firstly, the process of imitation became increasingly externalised so that children no longer reproduced their environment within themselves, but followed the authority of others. Secondly, the birth of the Etheric caused the Rhythmic system and all its associated qualities to dominate the child's being. The means towards educating the Rhythmic System was Art which had to be free from intellectuality or abstraction, and all subject matter had to be presented in the form of pictures, imagery and music.

Three sub-stages were evident during this period, and they merged gradually into the change which took place at puberty with the "birth" of the Astral Body. This birth was the first stage of the emancipation of the child's Will from the influences of others, a process which was only fulfilled after the age of twenty when the Ego was "born".

For education to be successful after puberty, the child had to have absorbed a rich store of the examples of others, as well as information in the form of imaginative pictures and imagery. The Astral Body was able to work upon these "aesthetic concepts" and transform them into a more abstract content, not with the instruction of a teacher, but as an act of free discovery and inner realisation. This was essential for the fulfilment of the child's developing Will, because it gave a feeling of secure independence which would be of value to the whole of life. Once youths had a firm foundation for their moral and personal life, education had to introduce them to the Social and Economic Life before they left school.

The education of the whole child could be achieved in each lesson when the relationship between body and Soul was properly understood. The Will could be educated through the Limb System, the Feelings through the Rhythmic System, and Thinking through the Head System. When these three integrated Systems were engaged by the teacher he or she was able to educate the whole child in a balanced way. The teacher could also help to balance the development of each individual through an understanding of the temperaments, and, given such balance, freedom or "spiritual activity" was attainable.

Chapter 5 outlined the aims that Steiner held for education, but went on to show his insistence that education should never be reduced to a list of principles. For Steiner, education was a matter for life and living. Any true method had to be in keeping with human nature, and not transformed into abstract rules for practice. Nevertheless, he gave many suggestions of how schools should be run and subjects taught so as to meet the needs of children and teachers.

Steiner's curriculum was wide and without provision for specialisation. His suggestions for teaching were drawn directly from his perception of the child's nature, so that presentation was pictorial, rhythmical and always followed the direction of moving from the "whole" to its parts.

Steiner's educational thought was then shown in practice through descriptions of lessons observed in South Africa and Britain. These were chosen to illustrate the fundamental methods of Waldorf education. It was noticed that Steiner's ideas were carried out faithfully in most junior classes, but the method of working from the Limb to the Rhythmic and Head Systems was not always achieved so success-fully with older pupils.

This chapter has compared Steiner's educational thought with that of some other theorists. It appeared that he had much in common with ancient Greek thought, yet his aims for education included preparation for modern social, eco-nomic and spiritual conditions. Though a "child-centred theorist" himself, Steiner held many contrasting viewpoints with such thinkers. Locke and Herbart began their education with the intellect, a course of action which Steiner considered to have long-term harmful effects on the whole person, including the physical body. Kant's principle of morality was the opposite of Steiner's, and Montessori's em-phasis on discovery learning was shown to be in conflict with Steiner's belief in the value of authority in the education of children between the change of teeth and puberty.

Steiner's educational beliefs are similar in some respects to the thought of Froebel, A.N. Whitehead and William James, but again, Steiner was at variance with Nunn's views on the education of the Will.

Among more recent thinkers, Steiner finds confirmation of his perception of the way a child learns in the work of J.S. Bruner. Whatever differences Bruner and Steiner may have, their views of child development strongly coincide with respect to Bruner's analysis of the enactive, iconic and symbolic modes of repre-sentation as compared to Steiner's method of working from the Limb to the Rhythmic and Head Systems.

Buber, like Steiner, based his educational ideas on the direct relationship between teacher and pupil. Buber's insights bear close similarities to Steiner's and reveal his awareness of the powerful influences at work when an adult feels real responsibility for a child.

Read's work revealed how far Steiner's thought is related to that of thinkers such as Polanyi and Witkin, as well as Buber. For them, education is essentially a human process in which human values are put before ideological or economic interests. Art is the one medium which can be freed from such interests, and Steiner shows how this ought to be done. In music it is the harmony of the notes; in sculpture and painting the beauty of form and colour; and in language it is the experience of sound that provide the educative value of Art. Analysis and abstraction of content only destroy such aesthetic value, whereas imagery such as is possible through the use of parables allows the individual to awaken to an understanding of the world in his or her own time and freedom.

In general this book has shown that Steiner's thought is complex and integrated. It has provided detailed textual references as well as a structure for the theory. It has therefore tackled the problems of analysis and organisation of a large number of lectures, each of which revealed additional material on Steiner's overall thought.

Considering that the Waldorf School Movement is expanding rapidly throughout the world, it seems timely that such a study should be done, both as an attempt to inform orthodox educationists about the subject, as well as to clarify and further the insights of those attempting to practise Steiner's methods.

With regard to the occult nature of Steiner's thought, it is clear that unqualified support for Steiner's insights is just as naïve as unqualified rejection, unless such judgements are made on the basis of profound insights. In Keats' words,

" ... for axioms in philosophy are not axioms until they are proved upon our pulses: We read fine things but never feel them to the full until we have gone the same steps as the Author." [90]

Exception should not be taken to the terminology Steiner used; indeed, the reader who wishes to understand Steiner should employ the utmost patience and sympathy for the problems facing someone who is trying to describe intangible experiences. In Steiner's own words,

"It is not easy to describe these perceptions, for our language has been created for the physical world alone and only approximate terms can be found for what simply does not belong to that world. Yet such terms must be used to describe the higher worlds and this is possible only by the free use of simile; but since everything in the world is interrelated, this can be done. The things and beings of the higher worlds are related to those of the physical world closely enough to ensure that with a measure of good will some conception of these higher worlds can be formed, even though words suitable for the physical world have to be used. Only it must be kept in mind that much of these descriptions of supersensible worlds is bound to be in the nature of simile and symbol." [91]

Steiner's insights may seem to many people to be so far beyond everyday perceptions of life that, for the most part, the student can do no better than adopt a non-judgemental attitude towards the occult aspects of Steiner's thought and examine the less controversial areas in order to decide on its merits. However, those who are willing to study his spiritual insights and strive to understand them will find ample evidence that he was a man of great spiritual qualities. Steiner brings to education a richness of life which is at once idealistic, aesthetic and practical. His thought on education was based on many years of teaching experience, as well as a life lived among turbulent social change in which the foundations of much current thought took root.

Steiner's message for education is clear: that no education will come of the pursuit of knowledge alone, but that the human being has inner qualities of the Soul and Spirit which it is possible to awaken and nourish once one knows how. The human being is not reducible to a number of faculties which may be trained; he is a living being with constant potential for spiritual expression.

> "The riddle of the universe should not be stated as a thing to be solved and done away with: the solution of it should give one power to make a new start. And if world problems are rightly understood this comes about. The world presents many problems to us. So many, that we cannot at once even perceive them all .... What then is the real answer to all these problems? The real answer is none other than: man himself. The world is full of riddles and man confronts them. He is a synthesis, a summary, and from man comes to us the answer to the riddle of the universe." [92]

FOOTNOTES

Introduction

1   See Chapter 1.
2   Galbreath, R.C. (1970) : <u>Spiritual Science in an Age of Materialism: Rudolf Steiner and Occultism.</u> See 2.2.4

Chapter 1

1   See Chapter 2, 2.2.1, <u>Review of the Literature; Biographical,</u> for a discussion of sources.
2   Steiner, R. (1928) : <u>The Story of My Life,</u> p 2.
3   *Ibid.*
4   *Ibid.* pp 2-3.
5   *Ibid.* p 6.
6   *Ibid.* p 3.
7   *Ibid.* p 7.
8   *Ibid.* p 11.
9   *Ibid.* p 12.
10 *Ibid.* pp 14-16.
11 *Ibid.* p 19.
12 *Ibid.* p 22.
13 *Ibid.* pp 23-25.
14 *Ibid.* p 26.
15 *Ibid.* pp 26-27.
16 *Ibid.* p 28.
17 *Ibid.*
18 *Ibid.* p 30.
19 *Ibid.* p 34.
20 *Ibid.* p 35.
21 *Ibid.* p 39.
22 *Ibid.*
23 *Ibid.* p 40.
24 Galbreath, R.C. (1970) : <u>Spiritual Science in an Age of Materialism: Rudolf Steiner and Occultism,</u> p 184.
25 *Ibid.* p 185.
26 *Ibid.* p 186.
27 Steiner, R. (1928) : <u>The Story of My Life.</u> pp 42-43.
28 *Ibid.* p 41.
29 *Ibid.* p 44.
30 *Ibid.* p 45.
31 *Ibid.* pp 46-47.
32 *Ibid.* p 69.
33 *Ibid.* p 71.
34 *Ibid.* pp 73-74.
35 *Ibid.* pp 71-72.

36   *Ibid.*   p 73.
37   *Ibid.*   p 73.
38   *Ibid.*   p 76.
39   *Ibid.*   pp 77-78.
40   *Ibid.*   p 78.
41   *Ibid.*   p 98.
42   *Ibid.*   p 102.
43   *Ibid.*   p 104.
44   *Ibid.*   p 109.
45   *Ibid.*   p 114.
46   Steiner, R. (1891) : Philosophy of Spiritual Activity, pp 277-382.
47   *Ibid.*   p 381.
48   Hemleben, J. (1975) : Rudolf Steiner, p 60.
49   Steiner, R. (1928) : The Story of My Life, p 135.
50   *Ibid.*   p 245.
51   Hemleben, *op. cit.*, p 73.
52   *Ibid.*   p 74.
53   *Ibid.*   p 76.
54   *Ibid.*
55   *Ibid.*   p 78.
56   *Ibid.*   p 79.
57   *Ibid.*   p 78.
58   *Ibid.*
59   *Ibid.*   p 79.
60   Steiner, R. (1928) : The Story of My Life, p 264.
61   Steiner, R. (1909) : Gospel of Luke, pp 26-27.
62   Steiner, R. (1928) : The Story of My Life, p 7 (Editor's inclusion).
63   *Ibid.*   p 87.
64   *Ibid.*   p 92.
65   *Ibid.*   pp 94-95.
66   *Ibid.*   p 103.
67   Steiner, R. (1909) : Education of the Child in the Light of Anthroposophy, p 5.
68   *Ibid.*   p 31.
69   Hemleben, *op. cit.*, pp 159-160.
70   Galbreath, *op. cit.*, p 216.
71   *Ibid.*   p 217.
72   *Ibid.*   pp 207-211.
73   *Ibid.*   p 212.
74   Hemleben, *op. cit.*, pp 110-111.
75   *Ibid.*   pp 107-109.
76   *Ibid.*   p 160.
77   *Ibid.*   p 121.
78   *Ibid.*   p 122.
79   *Ibid.*   p 161.
80   *Ibid.*
81   *Ibid.*
82   *Ibid.*   p 135.
83   *Ibid.*   pp 140-142.
84   *Ibid.*   pp 144-148.
85   *Ibid.*   p 162.
86   Galbreath, *op. cit.*, p 235
87   Hemleben, *op. cit.*, p 162.

88 *Ibid.* p 153.
89 Steiner, R. (1924) : The Kingdom of Childhood, p 41.
90 Hemleben, *op. cit.*, p 126.
91 Battersby, J. (1978) : Francis Edmunds, in *Odyssey*, Vol. 2, No. 5, p 8.
92 Steiner, R. (1919) : Practical Advice to Teachers, p 66.
93 Steiner, R. (1922) : The Younger Generation, p 9. "Man" refers to Modern European Man.
94 Steiner, R. (1922) : The Younger Generation, p 33 and p 66.
95 Steiner, R. (1910) : Occult Science, p 213.
96 Steiner, R. (1919) : Lucifer and Ahriman, p 11.
97 Steiner, R. (1922) : The Younger Generation, p 66.
98 Steiner, R. (1923) : Education and the Modern Spiritual Life, pp 72-73.
99 Steiner, R. (1908) : The Four Temperaments, p 14.
100 Steiner, R. (1919) : Lucifer and Ahriman, p 12.
101 Steiner, R. (1922) : The Younger Generation, p 20.
102 Steiner, R. (1919) : Education as a Social Problem, p 18.
103 Steiner, R. (1924) : Essentials of Education, p 37.
104 Steiner, R. (1910) : Occultism, p 35.
105 Steiner, R. (1919) : Study of Man, p 16.
106 Steiner, R. (1924) : Roots of Education, p 86.
107 Steiner, R. (1922) : The Younger Generation, p 136.
108 *Ibid.* pp 8-9.
109 *Ibid.*, pp 4-5.
110 *Ibid.* p 5.
111 *Ibid.* pp 8-9
112 Steiner, R. (1921) : Waldorf Education for Adolescence, p 75.
113 Steiner, R. (1922) : The Younger Generation, p 2.
114 Steiner, R. (1921) : Waldorf Education for Adolescence, p 76.
115 *Ibid.*
116 Steiner, R. (1922) : The Younger Generation, p 11.
117 *Ibid.* p 56.
118 Steiner, R. (1914) : The Riddles of Philosophy, p 3.
119 *Ibid.* p 434.
120 Steiner, R. (1891) : Truth and Science, in Philosophy of Spiritual Activity, p 379.
121 *Ibid.* Kant and Fichte are his main interests in this work.
122 Steiner, R. (1894) : The Philosophy of Spiritual Activity.
123 Steiner, R. (1919) : Study of Man, pp 54-55.
124 *Ibid.* p 54.
125 Steiner, R. (1921) : Education and the Science of Spirit, p 37.
126 Steiner, R. (1921) : Waldorf Education for Adolescence, p 94.
127 Steiner, R. (1919) : Education as a Social Problem, p 8.
128 Steiner, R. (1919) : Study of Man, p 154.
129 Steiner, R. (1891) : Philosophy of Spiritual Activity, p 253.
130 Steiner, R. (1921) : Waldorf Education for Adolescence, p 94.
131 *Ibid.* p 79.
132 *Ibid.* p 78.
133 Steiner, R. (1922) : The Younger Generation, p 9.
    This point is illustrated in Steiner's discussion of Einstein's Theory of Relativity, in Steiner, R. (1914) : The Riddles of Philosophy, pp 442-444. He argues that a conclusion such as that of relativity is only possible in a materialistic conception of the world. The spiritual perspective does not become "lost" in relativities but is "substantial in itself", and proves itself of value because of this.

134 Steiner, R. (1919) : <u>Practical Advice to Teachers</u>, p 96.
135 Steiner, R. (1921) : <u>Waldorf Education for Adolescence</u>, p 103.
136 Steiner, R. (1919) : <u>Lucifer and Ahriman</u>, p 24.
137 Steiner, R. (1902) : <u>Christianity as Mystical Fact</u>, p 4.
138 Steiner, R. (1919) : <u>Study of Man</u>, p 44 and p 56.
139 *Ibid.* p 56. Example given.
140 Steiner, R. (1922) : <u>Spiritual Ground of Education</u>, p 40.
141 Steiner, R. (1921) : <u>Waldorf Education for Adolescence</u>, p 104.
142 Steiner, R. (1921) : <u>Science of Spirit, Education and the Practical Life</u>, pp 53-54.
143 Steiner, R. (1919) : <u>Study of Man</u>, p 115.
144 Steiner R. (1928) : <u>The Story of My Life</u>, p 169.
145 *Ibid.* p 170.
146 1920.
147 Steiner, R. (1919) : <u>Education as a Social Problem</u>.
148 Steiner, R. (1922) : <u>Spiritual Ground of Education</u>, p 92.
149 Steiner, R. (1920) : <u>The Threefold State</u>, p 21.
150 *Ibid.* p 18.
151 *Ibid.* pp 18-19.
152 *Ibid.* p 24.
153 *Ibid.* p 20.
154 *Ibid.* p 29.
155 *Ibid.* p 35.
156 *Ibid.* p 30.
157 *Ibid.* p 32.
158 *Ibid.* p 25.
159 *Ibid.* p 34.
160 *Ibid.* p 104.
161 *Ibid.* pp 55-57. See note from translators, p vi : "GEIST (Old English 'Ghost') is <u>Spirit, in its primary sense</u>: that which inspires and directs thought and all forms of labour and action in a quite practical way." "RECHT ('<u>Right' in both the legal and moral sense</u>) contains the old ideas of Right and Justice; and hence it implies Law, Equity, and what a citizen is by Law entitled to: his 'Rights'."
162 *Ibid.* p 55.
163 *Ibid.* pp 56-57.
164 Steiner, R. (1921) : <u>The Science of Spirit. Education and the Practical Life</u>, pp 78-79.
165 Steiner, R. (1920) : <u>The Threefold State</u>, p 182.
166 Steiner, R. (1921) : <u>The Science of Spirit. Education and the Practical Life</u>. pp 72-73.
167 Steiner, R. (1919) : <u>Education as a Social Problem</u>, pp 56-59.
168 Galbreath, R.C. (1970) : <u>Spiritual Science in an Age of Materialism</u>, pp 144-145.
169 Hemleben, J. (1975) : <u>Rudolf Steiner</u>, p 154.
170 1917.
171 Steiner, R. (1921) : <u>Education and the Science of Spirit</u>, pp 20-21.
172 *Ibid.* p 36.
173 Steiner, R. (1923) : <u>Education and the Modern Spiritual Life</u>, p 118.
174 Steiner, R. (1924) : <u>The Kingdom of Childhood</u>, p 14.
175 Steiner, R. (1919) : <u>Education as a Social Problem</u>, p 46.
176 Steiner, R. (1923) : <u>Education and the Modern Spiritual Life</u>, p 187.
177 Steiner, R. (1922) : <u>The Younger Generation</u>, p 147.
178 Steiner, R. (1921) : <u>Waldorf Education for Adolescence</u>, p 67.
179 *Ibid.* p 82.
180 *Ibid.* p 104.
181 Steiner, R. (1919) : <u>Practical Advice to Teachers</u>, pp 182-183.

182 Steiner, R. (1924) : The Kingdom of Childhood, p 27.
183 Steiner, R. (1922) : Spiritual Ground of Education, pp 104-105.
184 Steiner, R. (1919) : Practical Advice to Teachers, p 188.
185 Steiner, R. (1919) : Education as a Social Problem, p 15.
186 Steiner, R. (1921) : The Science of Spirit. Education and the Practical Life. p 61.
187 Ibid. p 73.
188 Ibid.
189 Steiner, R. (1921) : Waldorf Education for Adolescence, p 40.
190 Steiner, R. (1919) : Practical Advice to Teachers, p 36.
191 Steiner, R. (1921) : Waldorf Education for Adolescence, p 40.
192 Ibid. p 72.
193 Steiner, R. (1902).
194 Ibid. p 237.
195 Steiner, R. (1909) : The Education of the Child in the Light of Anthroposophy. p 4.
196 Steiner, R. (1921) : Education and the Science of Spirit, p 21.
197 Steiner, R. (1919) : Practical Advice to Teachers, pp 170-171.
198 Steiner, R. (1919) : Education as a Social Problem, pp 109-110.
199 Ibid. p 109.
200 Steiner, R. (1919) : Practical Advice to Teachers, pp 166-168.
201 Steiner, R. (1919) : Education as a Social Problem, p 9.
202 Ibid. pp 38-39.
203 Ibid. p 10.
204 Steiner, R. (1924) : The Kingdom of Childhood, p 63.
205 Ibid. p 17.
206 Ibid. p 53.
207 Steiner, R. (1919) : Education as a Social Problem, pp 24-25.
208 Hemleben, op. cit., pp 166-176, lists 41 books and a survey of about 6000 lectures.
209 Wachsmuth, G. (1955) : The Life and Work of Rudolf Steiner, p 475.
210 Ibid. p 570.
211 Ibid. p 569.
212 Ibid. p 571.
213 Ibid. p 572.
214 Ibid. p 573.
215 Ibid.
216 Ibid. p 371.
217 Steiner, R. (1928) : The Story of My Life, p 334.
218 (1924).
219 Ibid. p 217.

Chapter 2

1   Hemleben, J. (1975) : Rudolf Steiner, pp 166-170.
2   Ibid. p 170.
3   Steiner, R. (1919) : Study of Man, p 188.
4   Lecture courses which belong together are those given at the start of the Waldorf School, from 21st August - 6th September, 1919. They are published as Study of Man, Practical Advice to Teachers and Discussions with Teachers.
5   (1909) : The Gospel of St. Luke, and (1919) : Lucifer and Ahriman.
6   (1894) Truth and Science, and The Philosophy of Spiritual Activity; (1904) : Theosophy; (1904-1909) : Knowledge of the Higher Worlds; (1910) : Occult Science.
7   Steiner, R. (1918) : Preface to Revised Edition of The Philosophy of Spiritual Activity, p xiii.

8   Steiner, R. (1925) : Preface to the 1925 Edition of <u>Occult Science</u>, p 9.
9   *Ibid.* p 10.
10   *Ibid.* pp 10-12.
11   Steiner, R. (1909) : Preface to the First Edition of <u>Occult Science</u>, p 23.
12   Steiner, R. (1913) : Preface to the 1913 Edition of <u>Occult Science</u>, p 17.
13   Steiner, R. (1925) : Preface to the 1925 Edition of <u>Occult Science</u>, p 11.
14   *Ibid.* p 12.
15   Steiner, R. (1918) : Preface to the Revised Edition of <u>The Philosophy of Spiritual Activity</u>, p xv.
16   Steiner, R. (1904) : <u>Theosophy</u>, p 14.
17   Steiner, R. (1909) : Preface to First Edition of <u>Occult Science</u>, pp 23-24.
18   Galbreath, R.C. (1970) : <u>Spiritual Science</u>, p 177.
19   *Ibid.* pp 175-176.
20   Steiner, R. (1928) : <u>The Story of My Life</u>, p 1.
21   Steiner, R. (1928) : <u>The Story of My Life</u>, p 322.
22   *Ibid.* p 323.
23   *Ibid.* p 322.
24   *Ibid.* p 323.
25   Steiner, R. (1909) : <u>The Education of the Child in the Light of Anthroposophy</u>. This lecture was revised and developed into a short book, and contains in seminal form much of the information that he was to develop during and after 1919.
26   One important course of public lectures was given at Ilkley, Yorkshire, in 1923, and is published as <u>Education and the Modern Spiritual Life</u>. Steiner does not assume previous knowledge of Anthroposophy in this course, or in single public lectures, such as <u>The Science of Spirit</u>. <u>Education and the Practical Life</u> (1921), and <u>Education and the Science of Spirit</u>, (1921).
27   Steiner, R. (1928) : <u>The Story of My Life</u>. Quoted in the Preface to <u>The Gospel of St. Luke</u>, p 5.
28   Steiner, R. (1919) : <u>Practical Advice to Teachers</u>, p 50.
29   Steiner, R. (1921) : <u>Waldorf Education for Adolescence</u>, p 107.
30   Steiner, R. (1925) : Preface to the 1925 Edition of <u>Occult Science</u>, p 10.
31   Obviously, complete isolation would have been a negative strategy, since experience and time render Anthroposophists superior in certain understandings. The many contacts the author had with Anthroposophists proved invaluable and he attended Society play readings and workshops by invitation. Visits to the Waldorf Schools were also of the utmost value to his research.
32   The teachers are not necessarily Anthroposophists. Membership of the Society requires a special induction.
33   Steiner, R. (1928) : <u>The Story of My Life</u>, p 7.
34   Steiner, R. (1909) : <u>Knowledge of the Higher Worlds</u>, p 112.
35   See for example the first paragraph of Steiner's Preface to the 1925 edition of <u>Occult Science</u>, p 7, where he describes the gradual process by which his perceptions of the spiritual world were completed and formulated into writing.
36   Hemleben., *op. cit.*, p 152.
37   Wachsmuth, G. (1955) : <u>The Life and Work of Rudolph Steiner</u>.
38   Hemleben, J. (1975) : <u>Rudolf Steiner</u>.
39   Galbreath, R.C. (1970) : <u>Spiritual Science in an Age of Materialism: Rudolf Steiner and Occultism</u>, Ph.D. Thesis, University of Michigan.
40   Hemleben, *op. cit.*, p 173.
41   First published 1972 and translated into English in 1975.
42   *Ibid.* p 204.
43   © 1975.
44   1967.

45   © 1958.
46   March 23, 1973.
47   Vol. 81, No. 3, Spring 1980. pp 322-370.
48   Vol. 57, No. 972. 2 July 1981. pp 7-10.
49   *Ibid.* p 10.
50   1969.
51   1970.
52   A list appears in Carlgren, F. (1976) : Education Towards Freedom, p 204.
53   © 1978.
54   © 1974.
55   © 1977.
56   1980.
57   1973.
58   1968.
59   1975.
60   Wilkinson, R. (1975) : The Curriculum of the Waldorf School. Editor's Note.
61   Von Heydebrand, C. (1977) : The Curriculum of the First Waldorf School, pp iv and v.
62   *Ibid.* p iii.
63   "Rudolf Steiner", Encyclopaedia Britannica, 15th ed., (1973) Micropaedia, Vol. ix, p 549.
64   *Ibid.* Macropaedia, Vol. 4, p 530.
65   Blishen, E. (ed.), (1969) Blond's Encyclopaedia of Education, p 726.
66   Harwood, A.C. (1957) : Rudolf Steiner Schools, in The Year Book of Education, Bereday, G. (ed.), (1957) : p 483.
67   Galbreath, *op. cit.*, pp 248-293.
68   Barfield, O. Rudolf Steiner's Concept of Mind, in The Faithful Thinker, (1961) Harwood, A.C. (ed.), p 11.
69   Galbreath, *op. cit.*, p 282.
70   *Ibid.*
71   Barfield, *op. cit.*, p 12.
72   *Ibid.* p 14.
73   *Ibid.* p 13.
74   *Ibid.*
75   *Ibid.* p 11.
76   *Ibid.* p 16.
77   *Ibid.* p 15.
78   *Ibid.* p 17.
79   *Ibid.* p 18.
80   *Ibid.* p 19.
81   *Ibid.* p 20.
82   *Ibid.*
83   *Ibid.* p 21.
84   *Ibid.*
85   Galbreath, *op. cit.*, p 293.
86   *Ibid.*
87   Shepherd, A.P. (1975) : A Scientist of the Invisible. An Introduction to the Life and Work of Rudolf Steiner.
88   Hemleben, *op. cit.*, pp 174-176.
89   Galbreath, *op. cit.*, p 4.
90   *Ibid.* p 10.
91   *Ibid.* p 46.

92   *Ibid.* p 51.
93   *Ibid.* p 49.
94   *Ibid.* p 51.
95   *Ibid.* p 49.
96   *Ibid.* p 50.
97   *Ibid.* p 52.
98   *Ibid.* p 53.
99   *Ibid.*
100 *Ibid.* p 55.
101 Both terms are derived from roots implying secrecy, of something hidden. The Greek word *mystes* means an initiate of the Mysteries, one who has vowed to keep silence, and the Latin word *occulere* means to cover over, hide or conceal. *Ibid.* p 47.
102 *Ibid.* p 46.
103 *Ibid.* p 65.
104 *Ibid.* p 66.
105 *Ibid.*
106 2 volumes; Paris: Librairie Ancienne Honore Champion, 1928.
107 Galbreath, R.C. *op. cit.,* p 67.
108 *Ibid.*
109 *Ibid.* p 70.
110 *Ibid.* p 93.
111 *Ibid.* p 84.
112 *Ibid.* p 105.
113 *Ibid.* p 108.
114 *Ibid.* pp 112-113.
115 *Ibid.* p 113.
116 *Ibid.*
117 *Ibid.* p 117.
118 *Ibid.* p 119.
119 *Ibid.* p 121.
120 *Ibid.* p 129.
121 *Ibid.* p 124.
122 *Ibid.* p 140.
123 *Ibid.* pp 140-146.
124 *Ibid.* pp 147-149.
125 *Ibid.* p 151.
126 *Ibid.* pp 152-157.
127 *Ibid.* p 160.
128 *Ibid.* p 176.
129 *Ibid.* pp 248-293.
130 *Ibid.* pp 299-319.
131 *Ibid.* pp 320-376.
132 *Ibid.* pp 383-460.
133 *Ibid.* pp 476-481.
134 *Ibid.* p 482.
135 *Ibid.* p 483.
136 *Ibid.* p 484.
137 *Ibid.* p 485.
138 *Ibid.*
139 *Ibid.* p 486.
140 *Ibid.* p 487.
141 *Ibid.*

142 *Ibid.* pp 488-489.
143 *Ibid.* p 491.
144 *Ibid.* p 490.
145 *Ibid.* p 491.
146 *Ibid.* p 492.
147 *Ibid.* p 493.
148 *Ibid.* p 494.

Chapter 3

1 For Steiner's description see Theosophy, pp 71-109.
2 Steiner, R. (1921) : The Science of Spirit. Education and the Practical Life, p 68.
3 Steiner, R. (1919) : Lucifer and Ahriman, p 47.
4 Steiner, R. (1909) : The Gospel of St. Luke, p 154.
5 Steiner, R. (1922) : The Younger Generation, p 129.
6 Steiner, R. (1908) : The Four Temperaments, p 9.
7 Steiner, R. (1909) : The Gospel of St. Luke, p 27.
8 *Ibid.* p 30.
9 Steiner, R. (1909) : Knowledge of the Higher Worlds, pp 66-67.
10 *Ibid.* pp 68-69.
11 Steiner, R. (1904) : Thesophy p 15.
12 Steiner, R. (1909) : The Gospel of St. Luke, p 201.
13 Steiner, R. (1921) : The Science of Spirit. Education and the Practical Life, p 50.
14 Steiner, R. (1910) : Occult Science, p 27.
15 *Ibid.*
16 Steiner, R. (1921) : The Science of Spirit. Education and the Practical Life, p 50.
17 Steiner, R. (1921) : Education and the Science of Spirit, p 20.
18 Steiner, R. (1910) : Occult Science, p 104
19 Steiner, R. (1910) : Occult Science, p 71.
20 Steiner, R. (1902) : Christianity as Mystical Fact, p 8.
21 Steiner, R. (1904) : Theosophy, p 17.
22 *Ibid.* pp 18-19.
23 Steiner, R. (1910)   Occult Science, pp 36-38.
24 *Ibid.* pp 245-247.
25 *Ibid.* p 248.
26 *Ibid.* p 245.
27 *Ibid.* p 248.
28 *Ibid.* pp 262-263.
29 Steiner, R. (1909) : Knowledge of the Higher Worlds, p 203.
30 Steiner, R. (1910) : Occult Science, p 242.
31 Steiner, R. (1909) : Knowledge of the Higher Worlds, p 31.
32 *Ibid.* pp 209-210.
33 *Ibid.* p 70.
34 *Ibid.* pp 22-24.
35 *Ibid.* pp 74-76.
36 *Ibid.* p 114.
37 Steiner, R. (1910) : Occult Science, p 235.
38 *Ibid.* p 242.
39 *Ibid.* p 244.
40 *Ibid.* p 250.
41 *Ibid.* p 253.

42   *Ibid.* p 228.

43   Steiner, R. (1904) : Theosophy, p 59.

44   Steiner, R. (1909) : Knowledge of the Higher Worlds, p 105.

45   *Ibid.* p 119.

46   *Ibid.* pp 67-68.

47   Steiner, R. (1904) : Theosophy, p 34.
       Steiner, R. (1910) : Occult Science, p 290.

48   *Ibid.* p 33. See also Steiner, R. (1904) : Theosophy, p 156.

49   Steiner, R. (1910) : Occult Science, p 28.

50   *Ibid.* p 288.

51   *Ibid.* p 22.

52   "Inspiration" is a special term used by Steiner to denote perception of, though not entry into, the spiritual world. See Occult Science, p 263.

53   *Ibid.* p 277. See also Steiner, R. (1902) : Christianity as Mystical Fact, p 15.

54   *Ibid.* p 15.

55   "Imagination" here is quite different from the normal use of the term and refers to the first stage in the development of spiritual sight. See Occult Science, p 235.

56   *Ibid.* p 9.

57   Steiner, R. (1904) : Theosophy, pp 13-14.

58   *Ibid.* p 50.

59   Steiner, R. (1909) : Knowledge of the Higher Worlds, p 16.

60   Steiner, R. (1910) : Occult Science, p 13.

61   *Ibid.* p 72.

62   *Ibid.* pp 30-31.

63   *Ibid.* p 18.

64   *Ibid.* p 290. "Intuition" is a special term with no relationship to the normal use of the word.

65   Steiner, R. (1904) : Theosophy, p 28.

66   Steiner, R. (1910) : Occult Science, pp 106-107.

67   Steiner, R. (1924) : Essentials of Education, p 30.

68   Steiner, R. (1909) : Knowledge of the Higher Worlds, p 17.

69   Steiner, R. (1910) : Occult Science, p 33.

70   Steiner, R. (1904) : Theosophy, pp 56-57.

71   Steiner, R. (1921) : The Science of Spirit. Education and the Practical Life, p 52.

72   Steiner, R. (1910) : Occultism, p 20.

73   *Ibid.* p 254.

74   *Ibid.* p 297.

75   *Ibid.* p 323.

76   *Ibid.* p 98.

77   Steiner, R. (1904) : Theosophy, p 14.

78   Steiner, R. (1909) : Knowledge of the Higher Worlds, p 20.

79   *Ibid.* pp 20-23.

80   Steiner, R. (1910) : Occult Science, p 10.

81   Steiner, R. (1919) : Study of Man, p 147.

82   Steiner, R. (1925) : The Roots of Education, p 47.

83   Steiner, R. (1910) : Occult Science, p 11.

84   *Ibid.* pp 39-40.

85   Steiner, R. (1904) : Theosophy, p 22.

86   *Ibid.* p 23.

87   *Ibid.* p 31.

88   *Ibid.* p 47.

89   *Ibid.* p 23.

90   *Ibid.* p 24.
91   *Ibid.* p 98.
92   *Ibid.* pp 80-81.
93   *Ibid.* p 43.
94   Steiner, R. (1924) : The Roots of Education, p 47.
95   Steiner, R. (1909) : Education of the Child in the Light of Anthroposophy, p 12.
96   Steiner, R. (1910) : Occult Science, p 41.
97   *Ibid.* p 43.
98   *Ibid.* p 41.
99   *Ibid.* pp 40-41.
100 *Ibid.* p 43.
101 Steiner, R. (1904) : Theosophy, pp 26-27.
102 Steiner, R. (1910) : Occult Science, pp 63-64.
103 Steiner, R. (1924) : The Roots of Education, p 48.
104 Steiner, R. (1909) : Knowledge of the Higher Worlds, pp 140-141.
105 Steiner, R. (1910) : Occult Science, p 68.
106 Steiner, R. (1910) : Occult Science, p 317.
107 *Ibid.* p 44.
108 Steiner, R. (1904) : Theosophy, p 32.
109 Steiner, R. (1910) : Occult Science, pp 63-64.
110 Steiner, R. (1904) : Theosophy, p 116.
111 *Ibid.* p 35.
112 *Ibid.* p 42.
113 Steiner, R. (1910) : Occult Science, p 44.
114 *Ibid.* p 68.
115 *Ibid.* p 48.
116 *Ibid.* p 320.
117 Steiner, R. (1924) : The Roots of Education, pp 51-52.
118 Steiner, R. (1904) : Theosophy, p 35.
119 *Ibid.* pp 29-45.
120 Steiner, R. (1910) : Occult Science, p 45. See also translator's note.
121 Steiner, R. (1891) : Philosophy of Spiritual Activity, p 217.
122 Steiner, R. (1910) : Occult Science, p 46.
123 *Ibid.* p 45.
124 *Ibid.* p 46.
125 *Ibid.* p 47.
126 *Ibid.* p 46.
127 *Ibid.* p 37.
128 Steiner, R. (1909) : Education of the Child in the Light of Anthroposophy, p 10.
129 *Ibid.*
130 *Ibid.*
131 *Ibid.*
132 Steiner, R. (1909) : Education of the Child in the Light of Anthroposophy, p 12.
133 Steiner, R. (1910) : Occult Science, p 48.
134 *Ibid.* p 49.
135 *Ibid.* p 50.
136 Steiner, R. (1904) : Theosophy, p 43.
137 Steiner, R. (1910) : Occult Science, pp 53-57.
138 Steiner, R. (1904) : Theosophy, p 37,
139 Steiner, R. (1919) : Practical Advice to Teachers, pp 68-69.
140 Steiner, R. (1919) : Study of Man, p 91.
141 Steiner, R. (1922) : Spiritual Ground of Education, p 47.

142 *Ibid.* p 110.
143 *Ibid.* pp 43-44.
144 *Ibid.* p 43.
145 Steiner, R. (1910) : Occult Science, pp 279-280.
146 Steiner, R. (1919) : Study of Man, pp 114-115.
147 Steiner, R. (1922) : Spiritual Ground of Education, pp 42-44.
148 Steiner, R. (1919) : Study of Man, p 37.
149 *Ibid.* p 146.
150 *Ibid.* p 37.
151 *Ibid.* pp 182-183.
152 *Ibid.* p 149.
153 Steiner, R. (1921) : Waldorf Education for Adolescence, p 20.
154 *Ibid.*
155 Steiner, R. (1924) : Curative Education, pp 18-19.
156 Steiner, R. (1923) : Education and the Modern Spiritual Life, p 90.
157 Steiner, R. (1919) : Study of Man, p 37.
158 *Ibid.* p 146.
159 Steiner, R. (1922) : Spiritual Ground of Education, p 42.
160 Steiner, R. (1919) : Education as a Social Problem, pp 73-74.
161 Steiner, R. (1922) : Spiritual Ground of Education, p 42.
162 *Ibid.* p 53.
163 Steiner, R. (1919) : Study of Man, p 145.
164 Steiner, R. (1921) : Waldorf Education for Adolescence, pp 20-21.
165 *Ibid.*
166 Steiner, R. (1922) : Spiritual Ground of Education, p 44.
167 Steiner, R. (1919) : Study of Man, p 146.
168 Steiner, R. (1922) : Spiritual Ground of Education, p 44.
169 Steiner, R. (1919) : Education as a Social Problem, pp 73-74.
170 Steiner, R. (1923) : Education and the Modern Spiritual Life. p 90.
171 *Ibid.*
172 Steiner, R. (1921) : Waldorf Education for Adolescence, p 21.
173 Steiner, R. (1919) : Study of Man, p 139 and pp 176-177.
174 *Ibid.* p 45.
175 Steiner, R. (1921) : Waldorf Education for Adolescence, p 21.
176 *Ibid.* p 22.
177 *Ibid.* p 19.
178 *Ibid.* p 21.
179 Steiner, R. (1919) : Study of Man, p 92.
180 Steiner, R. (1921) : Waldorf Education for Adolescence, p 34.
181 Steiner, R. (1919) : Study of Man, p 122.
182 *Ibid.* p 123.
183 *Ibid.* p 116.
184 *Ibid.* p 119.
185 *Ibid.*
186 *Ibid.* p 120.
187 *Ibid.* p 121.
188 *Ibid.* p 120.

Chapter 4

1   Steiner, R. (1909) : Gospel of St. Luke, p 77.

2   Steiner, R. (1924) : The Kingdom of Childhood, p 19.
3   Steiner, R. (1923) : Education and the Modern Spiritual Life, p 83.
4   *Ibid.* p 81.
5   Steiner, R. (1909) : Gospel of St. Luke, p 127.
6   Steiner, R. (1923) : Education and the Modern Spiritual Life, p 85.
7   Steiner, R. (1921) : Waldorf Education for Adolescence, p 69.
8   Steiner, R. (1922) : Spiritual Ground of Education, p 64.
9   Steiner, R. (1909) : Education of the Child in the Light of Anthroposophy, p 5.
10 Steiner, R. (1909) : The Four Temperaments, p 17.
11 Steiner, R. (1910) : Occult Science, p 205.
12 Steiner, R. (1904) : Theosophy, p 60.
13 *Ibid.* p 98.
14 *Ibid.* p 99.
15 *Ibid.* p 106.
16 *Ibid.* p 109.
17 Steiner, R. (1919) : Study of Man, p 58.
18 Steiner, R. (1910) : Occult Science, p 87.
19 *Ibid.* p 89.
20 Steiner, R. (1904) : Theosophy, p 83.
21 *Ibid.* p 67.
22 Steiner, R. (1910) : Occult Science, p 89.
23 Steiner, R. (1904) : Theosophy, p 98.
24 *Ibid.* p 67.
25 *Ibid.* p 103.
26 *Ibid.* p 107.
27 Steiner, R. (1924) : Curative Education, p 45.
28 *Ibid.* p 47.
29 *Ibid.* pp 46-47.
30 Steiner, R. (1919) : Practical Advice to Teachers, pp 19-20.
31 Steiner, R. (1904) : Theosophy, pp 52-54.
32 Steiner, R. (1910) : Occult Science, p 94.
33 *Ibid.* p 92.
34 Steiner, R. (1908) : The Four Temperaments, p 13.
35 Steiner, R. (1904) : Theosophy, p 59.
36 Steiner, R. (1924) : Curative Education, pp 21-22.
37 *Ibid.* p 33.
38 Steiner, R. (1921) : Waldorf Education for Adolescence, pp 22-23.
39 Steiner, R. (1924) : The Kingdom of Childhood, p 22.
40 Steiner, R. (1921) : The Science of Spirit. Education and the Practical Life. p 59.
41 Steiner, R. (1919) : Study of Man, p 18.
42 Steiner, R. (1909) : Education of the Child in the Light of Anthroposophy, p 13.
43 *Ibid.*
44 Steiner, R. (1919) : Study of Man, p 161.
45 Steiner, R. (1921) : Education and the Science of Spirit, p 30.
46 Steiner, R. (1923) : Education and the Modern Spiritual Life, p 106.
47 *Ibid.* pp 106-107.
48 Steiner, R. (1919) : Study of Man, p 151.
49 *Ibid.* pp 150-151.
50 *Ibid.*
51 Steiner, R. (1919) : Practical Advice to Teachers, p 110.
52 Steiner, R. (1921) : Waldorf Education for Adolescence, p 69.
53 *Ibid.* p 104.

54   Steiner, R. (1919) : <u>Practical Advice to Teachers</u>, p 110.
55   Steiner, R. (1919) : <u>Study of Man</u>, pp 150-151, and Steiner, R. (1923) : <u>Education and the Modern Spiritual Life</u>, p 107.
56   *Ibid.*
57   *Ibid.*
58   Steiner, R. (1919) : <u>Study of Man</u>, p 150
59   Steiner, R. (1924) : <u>The Roots of Education</u>, p 39.
60   Steiner, R. (1910) : <u>Education and the Modern Spiritual Life</u>, p 107.
61   Steiner, R. (1921) : <u>Waldorf Education for Adolescence</u>, p 99.
62   *Ibid.*
63   Steiner, R. (1910) : <u>Education and the Modern Spiritual Life</u>, p 106.
64   Steiner, R. (1909) : <u>Education of the Child in the Light of Anthroposophy</u>, p 13.
65   Steiner, R. (1910) : <u>Education and the Modern Spiritual Life</u>, p 110.
66   Steiner, R. (1919) : <u>Study of Man</u>, p 155.
67   *Ibid.* p 151.
68   Steiner, R. (1919) : <u>Study of Man</u>, pp 153-154.
69   Steiner, R. (1921) : <u>Waldorf Education for Adolescence</u>, pp 69-70.
70   Steiner, R. (1919) : <u>Study of Man</u>, pp 154-155.
71   Steiner, R. (1910) : <u>Education and the Modern Spiritual Life</u>, p 109.
72   *Ibid.* pp 110-111.
73   *Ibid.* p 111.
74   *Ibid.* p 112.
75   Steiner, R. (1919) : <u>Practical Advice to Teachers</u>, p 22.
76   *Ibid.* p 47.
77   *Ibid.*
78   Steiner, R. (1924) : <u>The Roots of Education</u>, p 41.
79   *Ibid.* p 85.
80   Steiner, R. (1922) : <u>Spiritual Ground of Education</u>, p 107.
81   Steiner, R. (1923) : <u>Education and the Modern Spiritual Life</u>. p 115.
82   *Ibid.* pp 114-115.
83   Steiner, R. (1919) : <u>Practical Advice to Teachers</u>, p 23-25.
84   Steiner, R. (1909) : <u>Education of the Child in the Light of Anthroposophy</u>, p 16.
85   Steiner, R. (1909) : <u>Education of the Child in the Light of Anthroposophy</u>, p 1
86   *Ibid.*
87   Steiner, R. (1923) : <u>Education and the Modern Spiritual Life</u>, p 55.
88   Steiner, R. (1924) : <u>The Roots of Education</u>, p 14.
89   Steiner, R. (1923) : <u>Education and the Modern Spiritual Life</u>, p 56.
90   *Ibid.* p 81.
91   Steiner, R. (1924) : <u>The Essentials of Education</u>, p 40.
92   Steiner, R. (1919) : <u>Study of Man</u>, pp 19-20.
93   Steiner, R. (1923) : <u>Education and the Modern Spiritual Life</u>, pp 55-56.
94   Steiner, R. (1921) : <u>Waldorf Education for Adolescence</u>, p 96.
95   Steiner, R. (1923) : <u>Education and the Modern Spiritual Life</u>, p 130.
96   *Ibid.* p 133.
97   Steiner, R. (1921) : <u>The Science of Spirit. Education and the Practical Life</u>, p 61.
98   Steiner, R. (1923) : <u>Education and the Modern Spiritual Life</u>, p 129.
99   Steiner, R. (1909) : <u>Study of Man</u>, p 126.
100   Steiner, R. (1923) : <u>Education and the Modern Spiritual Life</u>, p 131.
101   Steiner, R. (1924) : <u>The Essentials of Education</u>, p 40.
102   Steiner, R. (1923) : <u>Education and the Modern Spiritual Life</u>, p 80.
103   Steiner, R. (1921) : <u>The Science of Spirit. Education and the Practical Life</u>, p 55.
104   Steiner, R. (1909) : <u>Education of the Child in the Light of Anthroposophy</u>, p 21.

105 Steiner, R. (1924) : Roots of Education, p 65.
106 Steiner, R. (1921) : Education and the Science of Spirit, pp 34-35.
107 Steiner, R. (1924) : Roots of Education, p 74 (editor's footnote).
108 Steiner, R. (1921) : Education and the Science of Spirit, p 40.
109 Steiner, R. (1924) : Roots of Education, p 65.
110 Steiner, R. (1921) : The Science of Spirit. Education and the Practical Life, pp 60-61.
111 Steiner, R. (1921) : Education and the Science of Spirit, pp 40-41.
112 Steiner, R. (1924) : Kingdom of Childhood, p 124.
113 Steiner, R. (1921) : Education and the Science of Spirit, pp 40-41.
114 Steiner, R. (1924) : Kingdom of Childhood, p 35.
115 Steiner, R. (1921) : Education and the Science of Spirit, p 40.
116 Steiner, R. (1923) : Education and the Modern Spiritual Life. p 119.
117 *Ibid.* p 77.
118 Steiner, R. (1921) : Waldorf Education for Adolescence, p 102.
119 *Ibid.* p 104.
120 *Ibid.*
121 Steiner, R. (1921) : Education and the Science of Spirit, p 42.
122 Steiner, R. (1924) : Kingdom of Childhood, p 124.
123 *Ibid.* pp 44-45.
124 Steiner, R. (1919) : Practical Advice to Teachers, pp 115-116.
125 Steiner, R. (1921) : Waldorf Education for Adolescence, p 104.
126 Steiner, R. (1924) : Roots of Education, p 79.
127 Steiner, R. (1922) : The Younger Generation, p 135.
128 *Ibid.* pp 135-136.
129 Steiner, R. (1923) : Education and the Modern Spiritual Life, p 133.
130 Steiner, R. (1919) : Practical Advice to Teachers, p 110.
131 Steiner, R. (1922) : Spiritual Ground of Education, p 76.
132 *Ibid.* pp 76-77.
133 Steiner, R. (1924) : Kingdom of Childhood, p 124.
134 Steiner, R. (1922) : Spiritual Ground of Education, pp 76-77.
135 Steiner, R. (1924) : Roots of Education, p 81.
136 Steiner, R. (1919) : Practical Advice to Teachers, p 126.
137 Steiner, R. (1922) : Spiritual Ground of Education, pp 53-54.
138 *Ibid.* pp 55-56.
139 Steiner, R. (1924) : Kingdom of Childhood, p 124.
140 Steiner, R. (1921) : The Science of Spirit. Education and the Practical Life, p 67.
141 Steiner, R. (1924) : Kingdom of Childhood, p 47.
142 *Ibid.* p 46.
143 Steiner, R. (1924) : Essentials of Education, pp 85-86.
144 Steiner, R. (1922) : The Younger Generation, p 133.
145 Steiner, R. (1923) : Education and the Modern Spiritual Life, pp 135-137.
146 *Ibid.* p 138.
147 *Ibid.*
148 Steiner, R. (1922) : Spiritual Ground of Education, p 66.
149 Steiner, R. (1921) : Waldorf Education for Adolescence, p 104.
150 Steiner, R. (1919) : Practical Advice to Teachers, p 82.
151 *Ibid.* pp 89-90.
152 Steiner, R. (1924) : Roots of Education, p 85.
153 Steiner, R. (1924) : Kingdom of Childhood, p 124.
154 Steiner, R. (1919) : Practical Advice to Teachers, p 111.
155 Steiner, R. (1923) : Education and the Modern Spiritual Life, p 169.
156 *Ibid.*

157   Steiner, R. (1919) : Practical Advice to Teachers, pp 166-167.
158   Steiner, R. (1910) : Occult Science,   p 319.
159   Steiner, R. (1909) : Education of the Child in the Light of Anthroposophy, p 13.
160   Steiner, R. (1924) : Curative Education, p 22.
161   Steiner, R. (1919) : Practical Advice to Teachers, p 103.
162   Steiner, R. (1923) : Education and the Modern Spiritual Life, p 91.
163   Ibid. p 88.
164   Steiner, R. (1921) : Waldorf Education for Adolescence, p 104.
165   Steiner, R. (1921) : Education and the Science of Spirit, p 43.
166   Steiner, R. (1919) : Practical Advice to Teachers, pp 190-191.
167   Steiner, R. (1922) : Spiritual Ground of Education, p 41.
168   Steiner, R. (1922) : The Younger Generation, p 112.
169   Steiner, R. (1921) : Waldorf Education for Adolescence, p 58.
170   Ibid. p 59.
171   Ibid. p 21.
172   Steiner, R. (1919) : Study of Man, p 159.
173   Steiner, R. (1924) : The Roots of Education, p 85.
174   Steiner, R. (1919) : Study of Man, pp 126-127.
175   Ibid. p 131.
176   Ibid. p 126.
177   Ibid. pp 130-131.
178   Ibid. pp 131-132.
179   Ibid. p 132.
180   Steiner, R. (1921) : Waldorf Education for Adolescence, p 65.
181   Steiner, R. (1924) : Roots of Education, p 85.
182   Steiner, R. (1921) : Education and the Science of Spirit, p 44.
183   Steiner, R. (1909) : Education of the Child in the Light of Anthroposophy, p 21.
184   Steiner, R. (1923) : Education and the Modern Spiritual Life, p 201.
185   Steiner, R. (1921) : Waldorf Education for Adolescence, p 96.
186   Ibid. p 106.
187   Steiner, R. (1921) : The Science of Spirit. Education and the Practical Life, pp 61-62.
188   Steiner, R. (1921) : Waldorf Education for Adolescence, pp 59-60.
189   Ibid. pp 60-61.
190   Steiner, R. (1924) : Roots of Education, p 85.
191   Steiner, R. (1922) : Spiritual Ground of Education, pp 18-19.
192   Ibid. p 19.
193   Ibid.
194   Steiner, R. (1909) : Education of the Child in the Light of Anthroposophy, p 25.
195   Steiner, R. (1919) : Study of Man, p 104.
196   Steiner, R. (1922) : The Younger Generation, p 112.
197   Steiner, R. (1921) : Waldorf Education for Adolescence, p 66.
198   Steiner, R. (1909) : Knowledge of the Higher Worlds, pp 27-28.
199   Steiner, R. (1922) : Spiritual Ground of Education, p 56.
200   Ibid.
201   Ibid. p 57.
202   Steiner, R. (1921) : Waldorf Education for Adolescence, p 61.
203   Steiner, R. (1923) : Education and the Modern Spiritual Life, p 200.
204   Steiner, R. (1919) : Study of Man, p 136.
205   Steiner, R. (1921) : Waldorf Education for Adolescence, p 65.
206   Ibid.
207   Steiner, R. (1922) : The Younger Generation, p 75.
208   Ibid. p 77.

209 Steiner, R. (1921) : Waldorf Education for Adolescence, p 66.
210 Steiner, R. (1923) : Education and the Modern Spiritual Life. pp 170-171.
211 *Ibid.* p 172.
212 Steiner, R. (1921) : Waldorf Education for Adolescence, p 66.
213 Steiner, R. (1919) : Education as a Social Problem, p 16.
214 *Ibid.* p 40.
215 Steiner, R. (1921) : Waldorf Education for Adolescence, pp 74-75.
216 Steiner, R. (1919) : Education as a Social Problem, p 17.
217 Steiner, R. (1919) : Study of Man, p 57.
218 *Ibid.* p 72.
219 *Ibid.* p 75. These forces are not normally conscious.
220 *Ibid.* p 8. See editor's note.
221 *Ibid.*
222 *Ibid.* p 32.
223 *Ibid.* p 74.
224 *Ibid.* p 76.
225 *Ibid.* p 39.
226 *Ibid.*
227 Ibid. p 76.
228 *Ibid.* p 77.
229 *Ibid.* pp 44-45.
230 *Ibid.* p 151.
231 *Ibid.* pp 19-20.
232 Steiner, R. (1919) : Education as a Social Problem pp 82-85.
233 *Ibid.* p 85.
234 Steiner, R. (1919) : Study of Man, pp 108-109.
235 *Ibid.* p 110.
236 Steiner, R. (1923) : Education and the Modern Spiritual Life, p 122.
237 *Ibid.* p 123.
238 Steiner, R. (1924) : Kingdom of Childhood, pp 132-133.
239 *Ibid.* p 46.
240 Steiner, R. (1919) : Discussions with Teachers, p 23, (see editor's note).
241 Steiner, R. (1919) : Study of Man, p 101.
242 Steiner, R. (1909) : Education of the Child in the Light of Anthroposophy, p 28.
243 Steiner, R. (1922) : Spiritual Ground of Education, p 54.
244 Steiner, R. (1921) : Waldorf Education for Adolescence, pp 20-21.
245 Steiner, R. (1909) : Education of the Child in the Light of Anthroposophy, p 28.
246 Steiner, R. (1919) : Practical Advice to Teachers, pp 171-172.
247 *Ibid.* p 194.
248 Steiner, R. (1909) : Education of the Child in the Light of Anthroposophy, p 23.
249 Steiner, R. (1921) : Waldorf Education for Adolescence, p 7.
250 *Ibid.* p 8.
251 Steiner, R. (1909) : Education of the Child in the Light of Anthroposophy, p 23.
252 Steiner, R. (1919) : Practical Advice to Teachers, p 93.
253 Steiner, R. (1919) : Study of Man, p 68.
254 *Ibid.* p 113.
255 *Ibid.* pp 29-30.
256 *Ibid.* pp 60-66.
257 Steiner, R. (1923) : Education and the Modern Spiritual Life, p 88.
258 Steiner, R. (1904) : Theosophy, p 36.
259 Steiner, R. (1919) : Study of Man, p 69.
260 *Ibid.*

261 *Ibid.* p 70.
262 Steiner,R. (1919) : Practical Advice to Teachers, p 22.
263 Steiner,R. (1923) : Education and the Modern Spiritual Life, p 92.
264 Steiner,R. (1919) : Study of Man, p 70.
265 *Ibid.* p 104.
266 Steiner, R. (1909) : Education of the Child in the Light of Anthroposophy, p 26.
267 Steiner, R. (1921) : Waldorf Education for Adolescence, pp 104-105.
268 Steiner, R. (1919) : Study of Man, p 179.
269 Steiner, R. (1924) : Kingdom of Childhood, pp 148-149. Steiner taught that although sport had no great educative value, it should not be suppressed. Customs should be respected.
270 Steiner, R. (1923) : Education and the Modern Spiritual Life. p 127.
271 *Ibid.*
272 Steiner, R. (1921) : Education and the Science of Spirit, p 40.
273 Steiner, R. (1919) : Practical Advice to Teachers, p 45.
274 *Ibid.* p 49.
275 Steiner, R. (1923) : Education and the Modern Spiritual Life, p 127.
276 Steiner, R. (1919) : Practical Advice to Teachers, p 23.
277 Steiner, R. (1919) : Study of Man, p 179.
278 Steiner, R. (1923) : Education and the Modern Spiritual Life. p 123.
279 Steiner, R. (1922) : The Younger Generation, p 121.
280 Steiner, R. (1921) : The Science of Spirit. Education and the Practical Life. p 65.
281 Steiner, R. (1922) : Spiritual Ground of Education, p 85.
282 Steiner, R. (1908) : The Four Temperaments, p 10.
283 Steiner, R. (1922) : The Younger Generation, p 47.
284 Steiner, R. (1921) : Waldorf Education for Adolescence, p 51.
285 Steiner, R. (1922) : Spiritual Ground of Education, p 80. It is not necessary to research the ancient Greek origins of the concept of temperament here.
286 Steiner, R. (1910) : Occult Science, pp 54-55.
287 Steiner, R. (1924) : Curative Education, p 202.
288 Steiner, R. (1919) : Discussions with Teachers, pp 31-32.
289 *Ibid.* p 34.
290 *Ibid.* p 12.
291 *Ibid.* p 18.
292 *Ibid.* p 12.
293 Steiner, R. (1908) : The Four Temperaments, pp 32-33.
294 *Ibid.* p 33.
295 *Ibid.* pp 38-39.
296 *Ibid.* p 32.
297 *Ibid.* p 37.
298 *Ibid.* p 31.
299 *Ibid.* p 35.
300 *Ibid.* pp 35-36.
301 *Ibid.* p 29.
302 *Ibid.* pp 33-35.
303 Steiner, R. (1919) : Discussions with Teachers, p 22
304 *Ibid.* p 50.
305 *Ibid.* p 34.
306 See especially The Four Temperaments, pp 41-52; Discussions with Teachers, pp 15-32; and Spiritual Ground of Education, pp 80-85.
307 Steiner, R. (1922) : Spiritual Ground of Education, pp 81-82.
308 Steiner, R. (1919) : Discussions with Teachers, pp 17-18.

309 Steiner, R. (1922) : Spiritual Ground of Education, p 84.
310 *Ibid.*
311 Steiner, R. (1924) : Roots of Education, p 20.
312 *Ibid.* pp 21-22.
313 *Ibid.* p 19.
314 Steiner, R. (1922) : Spiritual Ground of Education, p 85.
315 Steiner, R. (1891) : Truth and Science, p 353.
316 *Ibid.* p vii, editor's note to the 1921 edition.
317 *Ibid.* p 250.
318 *Ibid.* p 253.
319 *Ibid.* pp 167-168.
320 *Ibid.* pp 169-170.
321 *Ibid.* p 200.
322 Steiner, R. (1921) : Waldorf Education for Adolescence, p 40.
323 Steiner, R. (1923) : Education and the Modern Spiritual Life, pp 129-130.
324 Steiner, R. (1921) : Waldorf Education for Adolescence, p 83.
325 Steiner, R. (1922) : Spiritual Ground of Education, p 64.
326 Steiner, R. (1909) : Education of the Child in the Light of Anthroposophy, p 5.

Chapter 5

1   Steiner, R. (1919) : Practical Advice to Teachers, p 13
2   Steiner, R. (1919) : Practical Advice to Teachers, p 13.
3   Steiner, R. (1922) : Spiritual Ground of Education, p 55.
4   Steiner, R. (1924) : Roots of Education, p 44.
5   Steiner, R. (1921) : Waldorf Education for Adolescence, p 34.
6   Steiner, R. (1923) : Education and the Modern Spiritual Life. p 92.
7   Steiner, R. (1922) : Spiritual Ground of Education, p 134.
8   Steiner, R. (1921) : Education and the Science of Spirit, p 44.
9   Steiner, R. (1922) : The Younger Generation, p 142.
10 *Ibid.* p 79.
11 *Ibid.* p 164.
12 *Ibid.* p 177.
13 *Ibid.* p 118.
14 *Ibid.* pp 142-143.
15 Steiner, R. (1919) : Practical Advice to Teachers, p 13.
16 Steiner, R. (1921) : Education and the Science of Spirit, p 23.
17 Steiner, R. (1924) : The Roots of Education, p 45.
18 Steiner, R. (1922) : The Younger Generation, p 23.
19 *Ibid.* p 11.
20 Steiner, R. (1921) : Waldorf Education for Adolescence, p 70.
21 *Ibid.* pp 40-41.
22 Steiner, R. (1923) : Education and the Modern Spiritual Life, p 211.
23 Steiner, R. (1921) : Waldorf Education for Adolescence, p 74.
24 Steiner, R. (1919) : Practical Advice to Teachers, p 142.
25 Steiner, R. (1921) : Waldorf Education for Adolescence, p 67.
26 Steiner, R. (1921) : Education and the Science of Spirit, p 22.
27 Steiner, R. (1923) : Education and the Modern Spiritual Life. p 104.
28 *Ibid.* pp 186-187.
29 Steiner, R. (1924) : Essentials of Education, pp 47-51.
30 Steiner, R. (1919) : Study of Man, p 18.

31 Steiner, R. (1922) : <u>Spiritual Ground of Education</u>, p 107.

32 Steiner, R. (1921) : <u>Waldorf Education for Adolescence</u>, p 31.

33 *Ibid.* p 16.

34 Steiner, R. (1924) : <u>Essentials of Education</u>, p 58.

35 Steiner, R. (1922) : <u>The Younger Generation</u>, p 163.

36 Steiner, R. (1921) : <u>Waldorf Education for Adolescence</u>, p 93.

37 Steiner, R. (1923) : <u>Education and the Modern Spiritual Life</u>, pp 201-202. See Chapter 4 for activities appropriate to each stage of development in childhood, and 5.3.2.8 <u>Geography</u> for the integration of the whole curriculum.

38 Steiner, R. (1909) : <u>Education of the Child in the Light of Anthroposophy</u>, p 12.

39 Steiner, R. (1919) : <u>Study of Man</u>, pp 158-159.

40 Steiner, R. (1921) : <u>Education and the Science of Spirit</u>, pp 23-24.

41 *Ibid.* p 35.

42 *Ibid.* p 24.

43 *Ibid.* p 23.

44 Steiner, R. (1919) : <u>Discussions with Teachers</u>, p 14.

45 Steiner, R. (1922) : <u>The Younger Generation</u>, p 178.

46 Steiner, R. (1919) : <u>Study of Man</u>, p 16.

47 Steiner, R. (1919) : <u>Practical Advice to Teachers</u>, p 172.

48 *Ibid.* p 194.

49 Steiner, R. (1921) : <u>Waldorf Education for Adolescence</u>, p 10.

50 Steiner, R. (1922) : <u>Spiritual Ground of Education</u>, p 88.

51 Steiner, R. (1919) : <u>Discussions with Teachers</u>, p 98.

52 *Ibid.* pp 93-94.

53 Steiner, R. (1919) : <u>Study of Man</u>, p 174.

54 Steiner, R. (1924) : <u>Curative Education</u>, p 100.

55 Steiner, R. (1923) : <u>Education and the Modern Spiritual Life</u>, pp 185-186.

56 *Ibid.* p 186.

57 Steiner, R. (1924) : <u>Roots of Education</u>, p 57.

58 *Ibid.*

59 Steiner, R. (1919) : <u>Study of Man</u>, p 157.

60 Steiner, R. (1923) : <u>Education and the Modern Spiritual Life</u>, pp 112-113, and Steiner, R. (1922) : <u>Spiritual Ground of Education</u>, pp 106-107.

61 Steiner, R. (1919) : <u>Study of Man</u>, p 156.

62 *Ibid.* p 157.

63 Steiner, R. (1919) : <u>Education as a Social Problem</u>, p 48.

64 Steiner, R. (1923) : <u>Education and the Modern Spiritual Life</u>, pp 161-162.

65 Steiner, R. (1924) : <u>Kingdom of Childhood</u>, p 84.

66 Steiner, R. (1922) : <u>Spiritual Ground of Education</u>, p 96.

67 Steiner, R. (1923) : <u>Education and the Modern Spiritual Life</u>, p 162.

68 Steiner, R. (1924) : <u>Kingdom of Childhood</u>, p 114.

69 Steiner, R. (1919) : <u>Practical Advice to Teachers</u>, p 11.

70 *Ibid.* p 164.

71 *Ibid.* pp 172-173.

72 Steiner, R. (1921) : <u>Waldorf Education for Adolescence</u>, p 49.

73 Steiner, R. (1919) : <u>Discussions with Teachers</u>, p 24.

74 Steiner, R. (1919) : <u>Practical Advice to Teachers</u>, p 93.

75 Steiner, R. (1922) : <u>Spiritual Ground of Education</u>, pp 112-113.

76 Steiner, R. (1919) : <u>Study of Man</u>, p 125.

77 Steiner, R. (1919) : <u>Discussions with Teachers</u>, p 137.

78 *Ibid.* p 143.

79 Steiner, R. (1924) : <u>Kingdom of Childhood</u>, p 92.

80   *Ibid.* p 86.
81   *Ibid.* p 125.
82   Steiner, R. (1923) : Education and the Modern Spiritual Life, pp 148-149.
83   *Ibid.* p 141.
84   Steiner, R. (1919) : Practical Advice to Teachers, p 160.
85   *Ibid.* pp 23-24.86 Steiner, R. (1921) : Waldorf Education for Adolescence, p 17.
87   Steiner, R. (1922) : Spiritual Ground of Education, p 72.
88   Steiner, R. (1919) : Discussions with Teachers, p 70.
89   Steiner, R. (1919) : Practical Advice to Teachers, pp 144-145.
90   Steiner, R. (1923) : Education and the Modern Spiritual Life, pp 187-188.
91   Steiner, R. (1922) : Spiritual Ground of Education, pp 112-113.
92   *Ibid.* p 65.
93   Steiner, R. (1919) : Study of Man, p 134.
94   Steiner, R. (1919) : Discussions with Teachers, p 19.
95   Steiner, R. (1922) : Spiritual Ground of Education, p 68.
96   *Ibid.* pp 29-30.
97   Steiner, R. (1919) : Study of Man, p 126.
98   Steiner, R. (1922) : The Younger Generation, p 148.
99   *Ibid.* p 78.
100 Steiner, R. (1919) : Practical Advice to Teachers, p 59.
101 *Ibid.* p 71.
102 Steiner, R. (1921) : The Science of Spirit. Education and the Practical Life, p 73.
103 Steiner, R. (1919) : Practical Advice to Teachers, p 163.
104 *Ibid.* p 100.
105 Steiner, R. (1922) : The Younger Generation, p 135.
106 *Ibid.* p 68.
107 Steiner, R. (1923) : Education and the Modern Spiritual Life, p 166.
108 Steiner, R. (1922) : Spiritual Ground of Education, p 110.
109 Steiner, R. (1919) : Practical Advice to Teachers, pp 134-135.
110 *Ibid.* p 146.
111 Steiner, R. (1921) : Waldorf Education for Adolescence, p 8.
112 Steiner, R. (1919) : Discussions with Teachers, p 64.
113 Steiner, R. (1919) : Practical Advice to Teachers, p 190.
114 Steiner, R. (1924) : Roots of Education, p 67.
115 Steiner, R. (1919) : Discussions with Teachers, p 69.
116 Steiner, R. (1909) : Education of the Child in the Light of Anthroposophy, p 25.
117 Steiner, R. (1919) : Practical Advice to Teachers, pp 129-131.
118 Steiner, R. (1923) : Education and the Modern Spiritual Life, p 172.
119 Steiner, R. (1919) : Study of Man, pp 180-181.
120 Steiner, R. (1922) : Spiritual Ground of Education, p 63.
121 Steiner, R. (1919) : Discussions with Teachers, p 23.
122 Steiner, R. (1919) : Practical Advice to Teachers, p 60.
123 Steiner, R. (1922) : Spiritual Ground of Education, p 111.
124 *Ibid.* p 112.
125 Steiner, R. (1924) : Kingdom of Childhood, p 138.
126 Steiner, R. (1922) : Spiritual Ground of Education, p 94.
127 *Ibid.* p 111.
128 Steiner, R. (1923) : Education and the Modern Spiritual Life, p 208.
129 Steiner, R. (1922) : Spiritual Ground of Education, p 93.
130 Steiner, R. (1921) : Waldorf Education for Adolescence, p 16.
131 Steiner, R. (1922) : Spiritual Ground of Education, p 134.
132 Steiner, R. (1921) : Waldorf Education for Adolescence, p 44.

133 Steiner, R. (1919) : Study of Man, p 41.
134 Steiner, R. (1922) : Spiritual Ground of Education, p 15.
135 Steiner, R. (1919) : Education as a Social Problem, p 64.
136 Steiner, R. (1923) : Education and the Modern Spiritual Life, p 99.
137 Steiner, R. (1919) : Education as a Social Problem, p 65.
138 Steiner, R. (1921) : Waldorf Education for Adolescence, p 74.
139 Steiner, R. (1919) : Practical Advice to Teachers, p 123.
140 Steiner, R. (1921) : Waldorf Education for Adolescence, p 104.
141 Steiner, R. (1924) : Curative Education, p 175.
142 Steiner, R. (1924) : Roots of Education, p 13.
143 Steiner, R. (1924) : Kingdom of Childhood, p 128.
144 Steiner, R. (1922) : Spiritual Ground of Education, p 30.
145 Ibid. p 28.
146 Ibid. p 29.
147 Ibid. pp 29-30.
148 Ibid. p 29.
149 Ibid. p 59.
150 Steiner, R. (1919) : Study of Man, p 41.
151 Ibid. pp 23-25.
152 Steiner, R. (1922) : Spiritual Ground of Education, p 58.
153 Steiner, R. (1919) : Practical Advice to Teachers, p 97.
154 Steiner, R. (1922) : Spiritual Ground of Education, p 126.
155 Steiner, R. (1919) : Discussions with Teachers, p 77 (Steiner's emphasis).
156 Steiner, R. (1924) : Curative Education, p 41.
157 Steiner, R. (1919) : Practical Advice to Teachers, pp 169-170.
158 Steiner, R. (1919) : Education as a Social Problem, p 104.
159 Steiner, R. (1923) : Education and the Modern Spiritual Life, p 211.
160 Steiner, R. (1924) : Kingdom of Childhood, p 77.
161 Steiner, R. (1922) : Spiritual Ground of Education, p 125.
162 Steiner, R. (1924) : Kingdom of Childhood, p 95.
163 Steiner, R. (1922) : Spiritual Ground of Education, p 59.
164 Steiner, R. (1924) : Curative Education, p 213.
165 Steiner, R. (1922) : The Younger Generation, p 42.
166 Ibid. p 58.
167 Ibid. p 56.
168 Ibid. pp 130-131.
169 Steiner, R. (1923) : Education and the Modern Spiritual Life, p 75.
170 Steiner, R. (1924) : Roots of Education, p 56.
171 Steiner, R. (1919) : Study of Man, p 70.
172 Steiner, R. (1919) : Practical Advice to Teachers, p 83.
173 Steiner, R. (1923) : Education and the Modern Spiritual Life, p 131.
174 Steiner, R. (1919) : Practical Advice to Teachers, p 17 and 82.
175 Steiner, R. (1924) : Kingdom of Childhood, p 73.
176 Steiner, R. (1919) : Practical Advice to Teachers, pp 24-25.
177 Steiner, R. (1922) : The Younger Generation, pp 115-117.
178 Ibid. p 118.
179 Steiner, R. (1919) : Practical Advice to Teachers, p 17.
180 Ibid. p 24.
181 Steiner, R. (1923) : Education and the Modern Spiritual Life, pp 130-131.
182 Steiner, R. (1909) : Education of the Child in the Light of Anthroposophy, p 21.
183 Steiner, R. (1924) : Kingdom of Childhood, p 74.
184 Steiner, R. (1919) : Discussions with Teachers, p 61.

185 *Ibid.* p 88.
186 Steiner, R. (1923) : Education and the Modern Spiritual Life, pp 113-114.
187 Steiner, R. (1924) : Roots of Education, p 88.
188 Steiner, R. (1922) : Spiritual Ground of Education, p 122.
189 Steiner, R. (1919) : Discussions with Teachers, p 62.
190 *Ibid.* p 61.
191 Steiner, R. (1909) : Knowledge of the Higher Worlds, pp 108-109.
192 Steiner, R. (1921) : Education and the Science of Spirit, pp 31-32.
193 Steiner, R. (1924) : Roots of Education, p 38.
194 Steiner, R. (1924) : Kingdom of Childhood, p 20.
195 Steiner, R. (1924) : Roots of Education, p 43.
196 Steiner, R. (1919) : Practical Advice to Teachers, p 145.
197 Steiner, R. (1919) : Discussions with Teachers, p 61.
198 Steiner, R. (1922) : Spiritual Ground of Education, p 80.
199 Steiner, R. (1924) : Kingdom of Childhood, p 67.
200 Steiner, R. (1922) : Spiritual Ground of Education, p 84.
201 Steiner, R. (1909) : Education of the Child in the Light of Anthroposophy, p 21.
202 Steiner, R. (1924) : Kingdom of Childhood, p 67.
203 Steiner, R. (1924) : Kingdom of Childhood, p 75.
204 Steiner, R. (1919) : Discussions with Teachers, pp 60-61.
205 Steiner, R. (1921) : Waldorf Education for Adolescence, p 64.
206 Steiner, R. (1919) : Practical Advice to Teachers, p 100.
207 Steiner, R. (1909) : Education of the Child in the Light of Anthroposophy, p 27.
208 Steiner, R. (1919) : Practical Advice to Teachers, p 189.
209 Steiner, R. (1924) : Kingdom of Childhood, p 43.
210 *Ibid.* p 32.
211 *Ibid.* p 154.
212 Steiner, R. (1919) : Practical Advice to Teachers, p 142.
213 *Ibid.* p 178.
214 Steiner, R. (1923) : Education and the Modern Spiritual Life, p 138.
215 Steiner, R. (1921) : Waldorf Education for Adolescence, pp 100-101.
216 Steiner, R. (1922) : The Younger Generation, p 133.
217 Steiner, R. (1924) : Roots of Education, pp 60-63.
218 Steiner, R. (1922) : The Younger Generation, p 134.
219 Steiner, R. (1921) : Waldorf Education for Adolescence, p 100.
220 Steiner, R. (1919) : Practical Advice to Teachers, pp 170-175.
221 *Ibid.* pp 76-77.
222 Steiner, R. (1923) : Education and the Modern Spiritual Life, p 137.
223 Steiner, R. (1922) : Spiritual Ground of Education, p 68.
224 Steiner, R. (1919) : Practical Advice to Teachers, pp 183-184.
225 Steiner, R. (1922) : Spiritual Ground of Education, p 65.
226 Steiner, R. (1921) : Waldorf Education for Adolescence, p 47.
227 Steiner, R. (1924) : Roots of Education, pp 54-55.
228 Steiner, R. (1919) : Practical Advice to Teachers, p 69.
229 Steiner, R. (1923) : Education and the Modern Spiritual Life, p 111.
230 Steiner, R. (1919) : Discussions with Teachers, p 54.
231 Steiner, R. (1919) : Practical Advice to Teachers, p 32.
232 *Ibid.* p 50.
233 *Ibid.* p 51.
234 Steiner, R. (1921) : Waldorf Education for Adolescence, p 51.
235 Steiner, R. (1919) : Practical Advice to Teachers, p 51.
236 *Ibid.* pp 88-89.

237 *Ibid.* p 49.
238 *Ibid.* p 179.
239 *Ibid.* pp 63-64.
240 *Ibid.* p 66.
241 Steiner, R. (1921) : Education and the Science of Spirit, p 28.
242 Steiner, R. (1919) : Practical Advice to Teachers, p 131.
243 *Ibid.* pp 133-134.
244 Steiner, R. (1924) : Roots of Education, p 90.
245 Steiner, R. (1919) : Practical Advice to Teachers, pp 147-149.
246 Steiner, R. (1924) : Kingdom of Childhood, pp 153-154.
247 Steiner, R. (1923) : Education and the Modern Spiritual Life, pp 174-175.
248 Steiner, R. (1922) : Spiritual Ground of Education, p 96.
249 Steiner, R. (1924) : Kingdom of Childhood, p 115.
250 *Ibid.* p 148.
251 Steiner, R. (1919) : Practical Advice to Teachers, pp 129-131.
252 *Ibid.* pp 137-138.
253 *Ibid.* p 187.
254 Harwood, A.C. (1958) : The Recovery of Man in Childhood, pp 147-157, and Raffé,
     M. *et al.,* (1974) : Eurythmy and the Impulse to Dance.
255 Steiner, R. (1919) : Practical Advice to Teachers, p 65.
256 Steiner, R. (1922) : Spiritual Ground of Education, p 117.
257 *Ibid.* p 118.
258 Steiner, R. (1923) : Education and the Modern Spiritual Life, p 203.
259 Steiner, R. (1922) : The Younger Generation, p 133.
260 Steiner, R. (1919) : Study of Man, pp 178-179.
261 Steiner, R. (1919) : Practical Advice to Teachers, p 182.
262 Steiner, R. (1921) : Waldorf Education for Adolescence, p 101.
263 *Ibid.* p 9.
264 *Ibid.* p 48.
265 *Ibid.* p 33.
266 *Ibid.* pp 27-28.
267 Steiner, R. (1923) : Education and the Modern Spiritual Life, p 206.
268 Steiner, R. (1924) : Kingdom of Childhood, pp 149-150.
269 Steiner, R. (1923) : Education and the Modern Spiritual Life, p 207.
270 Steiner, R. (1922) : Spiritual Ground of Education, p 88.
271 Steiner, R. (1923) : Education and the Modern Spiritual Life, pp 189-190.
272 Steiner, R. (1924) : Kingdom of Childhood, pp 81-83.
273 Steiner, R. (1922) : The Younger Generation, p 114.
274 Steiner, R. (1924) : Roots of Education, p 68.
275 *Ibid.*
276 Steiner, R. (1923) : Education and the Modern Spiritual Life, p 158.
277 Steiner, R. (1924) : Kingdom of Childhood, pp 86-88.
278 Steiner, R. (1919) : Discussions with Teachers, p 97.
279 Steiner, R. (1919) : Practical Advice to Teachers, p 16.
280 Steiner, R. (1924) : Kingdom of Childhood, p 96.
281 *Ibid.* pp 139-140.
282 Steiner, R. (1923) : Education and the Modern Spiritual Life, p 161.
283 Steiner, R. (1922) : Spiritual Ground of Education, pp 74-75.
284 Steiner, R. (1909) : Education of the Child in the Light of Anthroposophy, p 25.
285 Steiner, R. (1924) : Kingdom of Childhood, p 143. (See editor's footnote).
286 *Ibid.* pp 141-143.
287 Steiner, R. (1919) : Study of Man, p 53.

288 *Ibid.* p 121.
289 Steiner, R. (1919) : Discussions with Teachers, p 97.
290 Steiner, R. (1919) : Practical Advice to Teachers, p 143.
291 Steiner, R. (1923) : Education and the Modern Spiritual Life, p 154.
292 Steiner, R. (1924) : Kingdom of Childhood, p 80.
293 Steiner, R. (1923) : Education and the Modern Spiritual Life, p 154.
294 Steiner, R. (1919) : Practical Advice to Teachers, pp 150-152 and 185-186.
295 *Ibid.* p 143.
296 Steiner, R. (1922) : The Younger Generation, p 14.
297 Steiner, R. (1924) : Essentials of Education, p 41.
298 Steiner, R. (1922) : The Younger Generation, p 142.
299 Steiner, R. (1924) : Essentials of Education, p 43.
300 Steiner, R. (1909) : Education of the Child in the Light of Anthroposophy, p 26.
301 Steiner, R. (1923) : Education and the Modern Spiritual Life, pp 140-142.
302 Steiner, R. (1919) : Practical Advice to Teachers, p 54.
303 *Ibid.* p 118.
304 *Ibid.* pp 101-104. See also Steiner, R. (1924) : Kingdom of Childhood, p 107 for sculptural exercises in physiology.
305 Steiner, R. (1923) : Education and the Modern Spiritual Life, p 168.
306 Steiner, R. (1922) : Spiritual Ground of Education, pp 70-71.
307 *Ibid.* p 71.
308 Steiner, R. (1919) : Practical Advice to Teachers, pp 104-109.
309 Steiner, R. (1919) : Practical Advice to Teachers, p 112. The final sentence of this quotation is included to remind the reader of the strong influences of Goethe upon this aspect of Steiner's thought. See 1.1.
310 Steiner, R. (1921) : Waldorf Education for Adolescence, p 93.
311 Steiner, R. (1924) : Kingdom of Childhood, p 53-55.
312 Steiner, R. (1919) : Practical Advice to Teachers, pp 163-164.
313 *Ibid.* pp 120-121.
314 Steiner, R. (1924) : Kingdom of Childhood, p 126.
315 Steiner, R. (1919) : Practical Advice to Teachers, pp 124-125.
316 Steiner, R. (1921) : Waldorf Education for Adolescence, pp 25-26.
317 *Ibid.* p 34.
318 Steiner, R. (1919) : Practical Advice to Teachers, p 143.
319 Steiner, R, (1923) : Education and the Modern Spiritual Life, pp 170-171.
320 Steiner, R. (1919) : Practical Advice to Teachers, p 163.
321 Ibid. p 162.
322 *Ibid.* p 143.
323 *Ibid.* pp 156-159.
324 *Ibid.* pp 155-156.
325 *Ibid.* p 161.
326 *Ibid.* pp 159-160.
327 Steiner, R. (1921) : Waldorf Education for Adolescence, p 38.
328 Steiner, R. (1919) : Practical Advice to Teachers, pp 160-161.
329 Steiner, R. (1919) : Discussions with Teachers, p 97.
330 *Ibid.* p 137.
331 Steiner, R. (1922) : Spiritual Ground of Education, p 77.
332 Steiner, R. (1919) : Study of Man, p 187.
333 Steiner, R. (1909) : Education of the Child in the Light of Anthroposophy, pp 20-21.
334 Steiner, R. (1923) : Education and the Modern Spiritual Life, p 164.
335 Steiner, R. (1921) : Waldorf Education for Adolescence, pp 38-39.
336 Steiner, R. (1919) : Practical Advice to Teachers, pp 116-117.

337 *Ibid.* p 143.
338 Steiner, R. (1919) : Discussions with Teachers, p 77.
339 *Ibid.* p 78.
340 Steiner, R. (1923) : Education and the Modern Spiritual Life, pp 165-166.
341 *Ibid.* p 166.
342 Steiner, R, (1919) : Practical Advice to Teachers, p 11.
343 Steiner, R. (1924) : Kingdom of Childhood, p 113.
344 Steiner, R. (1919) : Practical Advice to Teachers, pp 12-13.
345 *Ibid.* p 89.
346 Steiner, R. (1909) : Education of the Child in the Light of Anthroposophy, p 10.
347 Steiner, R. (1910) : Occult Science, p 55.
348 Steiner, R. (1922) : The Younger Generation, pp 119-120.
349 *Ibid.* p 118.
350 Steiner, R. (1919) : Discussions with Teachers, p 19.
351 Steiner, R. (1921) : Waldorf Education for Adolescence, p 9.
352 Steiner, R. (1919) : Practical Advice to Teachers, pp 40-41.
353 *Ibid.* p 52.
354 *Ibid.* p 49.
355 *Ibid.* pp 52-53.
356 *Ibid.* p 41.
357 *Ibid.* pp 51-52.
358 *Ibid.* pp 44-45.
359 Steiner, R. (1924) : Kingdom of Childhood, pp 143-148.
360 Steiner, R. (1919) : Practical Advice to Teachers, pp 43-44.
361 *Ibid.* p 70.
362 *Ibid.* p 61.
363 Steiner, R. (1922) : Spiritual Ground of Education, p 102.
364 *Ibid.* p 54.
365 Steiner, R. (1922) : The Younger Generation, p 139
366 Steiner, R. (1922) : Spiritual Ground of Education, p 105.
367 Steiner, R. (1909) : Education of the Child in the Light of Anthroposophy, p 16.
368 *Ibid.* p 28.
369 Steiner, R. (1923) : Education and the Modern Spiritual Life, p 192.
370 *Ibid.*
371 Steiner, R. (1922) : Spiritual Ground of Education, pp 98-99.
372 Steiner, R. (1919) : Practical Advice to Teachers, pp 46-47.
373 Steiner, R. (1924) : Roots of Education, p 50.
374 Steiner, R. (1924) : Kingdom of Childhood, p 107.
375 Steiner, R. (1922) : Spiritual Ground of Education, p 103.
376 Steiner, R. (1919) : Practical Advice to Teachers, p 48.
377 *Ibid.* p 182.
378 Steiner, R. (1921) : Waldorf Education for Adolescence, p 50.
379 Steiner, R. (1924) : Kingdom of Childhood, pp 112-113.
380 Steiner, R. (1919) : Practical Advice to Teachers, p 182.
381 *Ibid.* pp 61-62.
382 *Ibid.* p 49.
383 Steiner, R. (1919) : Discussions with Teachers, p 102.
384 Steiner, R. (1924) : Roots of Education, pp 52-53.
385 Steiner, R. (1921) : Waldorf Education for Adolescence, p 48.
386 Steiner, R. (1922) : Spiritual Ground of Education, p 97.
387 Steiner, R. (1921) : Waldorf Education for Adolescence, p 36.
388 *Ibid.* p 53.

389   Steiner, R. (1923) : Education and the Modern Spiritual Life, pp 196-197.
390   *Ibid.* p 198.
391   Steiner, R. (1922) : Spiritual Ground of Education, p 103.
392   Steiner, R. (1919) : Practical Advice to Teachers, p 45.
393   Steiner, R. (1921) : Waldorf Education for Adolescence, pp 65-66.
394   Steiner, R. (1924) : Kingdom of Childhood, pp 136-137.
395   Steiner, R. (1922) : Spiritual Ground of Education, p 40.
396   Steiner, R. (1921) : Waldorf Education for Adolescence, pp 66-67.
397   Steiner, R. (1919) : Practical Advice to Teachers, pp 166-167.
398   *Ibid.* p 168.
399   Steiner, R. (1921) : Waldorf Education for Adolescence, p 61.
400   Steiner, R. (1909) : Education of the Child in the Light of Anthroposophy, p 27.
401   Steiner, R. (1919) : Practical Advice to Teachers, pp 170-172.
402   Steiner, R. (1922) : Spiritual Ground of Education, p 116.
403   *Ibid.* p 114.
404   Steiner, R. (1923) : Education and the Modern Spiritual Life, p 178.
405   Steiner, R. (1924) : Kingdom of Childhood, p 153.
406   *Ibid.* pp 151-153.
407   Steiner, R. (1923) : Education and the Modern Spiritual Life, pp 179-180.
408   *Ibid.* pp 178-179.
409   Steiner, R. (1922) : Spiritual Ground of Education, p 114.
410   *Ibid.*
411   Steiner, R. (1923) : Education and the Modern Spiritual Life, p 181.
412   Steiner, R. (1924) : Kingdom of Childhood, p 152 (see editor's note).
413   Steiner, R. (1923) : Education and the Modern Spiritual Life, p 180.
414   Steiner, R. (1921) : Waldorf Education for Adolescence, p 29.
415   Steiner, R. (1921) : The Science of Spirit. Education and the Practical Life, p 67.
416   Steiner, R. (1919) : Practical Advice to Teachers, p 174.
417   *Ibid.* p 197.
418   *Ibid.*

Chapter 6

1   For further descriptions of the starting of Waldorf Schools see Hayn, G. (1975) : The Bristol Waldorf School, in Child and Man, Vol. xi, No.1.   Bell, N. and D. (1976): The Vancouver Waldorf School Steps Out, in *Child and Man*, Vol. xi, No. 4.   Blom, A. (1978) : The Miracle of Michael House, in *Child and Man*, Vol. xiii, No. 1.

Chapter 7

1   Steiner, R. (1921) : Waldorf Education for Adolescence, p 25 and pp 70-92; *and* Steiner, R. (1923) : Education and the Modern Spiritual Life, pp 40-63, p 76 and p 128.
2   Quoted by Cubberley, E.P. (1920) : Readings in the History of Education, p 5. From The Protagoras, Plato.
3   Steiner, R. (1928) : Story of My Life, pp 140-142.
4   Steiner, R. (1902) : Christianity as Mystical Fact, p 65.
5   Plato. (380 B.C.) : The Republic, X, 614.
6   *Ibid.* 615.
7   Steiner, R. (1919) : Study of Man, pp 154-155. (See 4.2.3).
8   Plato, *op. cit.*, VII, 518.

9   *Ibid.* III, 396.

10 *Ibid.* III, 402.

11 Boyd, W. (1921) : The History of Western Education, pp 40-41.

12 *Ibid.* pp 43-44.

13 "History of Medicine," Encyclopaedia Britannica, 15th ed., Vol. 11, p 824.

14 Read, H. (1958) : Education through Art, pp 73-106.

15 Rusk, R.R. (1965) : Doctrines of the Great Educators, p 153.

16 Russel, B. (1946) : History of Western Philosophy, p 634.

17 Rusk, R.R. *op. cit.,* p 133.

18 Boyd, W. (1917) : From Locke to Montessori, p 26.

19 Rusk, R.R. *op. cit.,* p 139.

20 Lawrence, E. (1970) : The Origins and Growth of Modern Education, pp 157-158.

21 *Ibid.* p 159.

22 *Ibid.* p 185.

23 Steiner, R. (1894) : Philosophy of Spiritual Activity, p 161.

24 *Ibid.* p 5.

25 Steiner, R. (1909) : Knowledge of the Higher Worlds, pp 170-178.

26 Lawrence, E. *op. cit.,* pp 188-201.

27 Galbreath, R.C. (1970) : Spiritual Science in an Age of Materialism, p 185 notes that Steiner's occult Master frequently referred to Fichte's writings. In Steiner's introduction to Theosophy (1904), p 11, he quotes from Fichte's Introduction to the Science of Knowledge, (1813) to prove that Fichte was aware of the faculty of "Spiritual Sight".

28 Boyd, W. (1921) : The History of Western Education, pp 353-354.

29 *Ibid.* p 405.

30 *Ibid.* p 364.

31 Steiner, R. (1921) : Waldorf Education for Adolescence, pp 36-37.

32 Rusk, R. (1951) : A History of Infant Education, p 67.

33 Lawrence, E. *op. cit.,* pp 244-246.

34 *Ibid.* p 251.

35 Dewey, J. (1961) : Democracy and Education, p 235.

36 Rusk, R. (1951) : A History of Infant Education, pp 70-71.

37 *Ibid.* p 85.

38 Whitehead, A.N. (1962) : The Aims of Education, p 43.

39 *Ibid.* p 28.

40 *Ibid.*

41 *Ibid.* p 31.

42 *Ibid.* p 50.

43 *Ibid.* p 59.

44 *Ibid.* p 29.

45 *Ibid.* p 54.

46 *Ibid.* p 58.

47 *Ibid.* p 57.

48 *Ibid.* p 44.

49 *Ibid.* p 50.

50 *Ibid.* p 35.

51 *Ibid.* p 36.

52 Nunn, P. (1920) : Education. Its Data and First Principles, p 64.

53 James, W. (1899) : Talks to Teachers, p 71. Emphases his.

54 *Ibid.* p 49.

55 Nunn, P (1920) : Education. Its Data and First Principles, p 37.

56 *Ibid.* p 100.

57 *Ibid.* p 12.
58 *Ibid.* pp 102-103.
59 Buhler, C. (1971) : Basic Theoretical Concepts of Humanistic Education, p 437.
60 Rogers, C.R. (1969) : Freedom to Learn, p 304.
61 Holt, J. (1972) : Freedom and Beyond.
62 Postman, N. and Weingartner, C. (1969) : Teaching as a Subversive Activity.
63 Dearden, R.F. (1972) : Education and the Development of Reason, p 81.
64 Durham, K. (1969) : The Problems of Teaching Poetry, pp 70-73.
65 Bruner, J.S. (1960) : The Process of Education, p 33.
66 Bruner, J.S. (1966) : Towards a Theory of Instruction, pp 10-11.
67 *Ibid.* pp 37-38.
68 *Ibid.* pp 49-50.
69 Bruner, J.S. (1960) : The Process of Education, p 52.
70 Bruner, J.S. (1973) : Beyond the Information Given, in Anglin, J.M. (ed.) p 129.
71 Bruner, J.S. (1966) : Towards a Theory of Instruction, p 29.
72 Bernstein, B. (1975) : Class, Codes and Control, Vol. III, p 67-68.
73 *Ibid.* Vol. I, p 230.
74 *Ibid.* p 231.
75 Polanyi, M. (1966) : The Tacit Dimension, p 55.
76 Allen, D. (1980) : English Teaching since 1965, pp 105-108.
77 Buber, M. (1947) : Between Man and Man, pp 16-17.
78 *Ibid.* p 100.
79 *Ibid.* p 101.
80 *Ibid.* p 90.
81 *Ibid.* p 36.
82 Buber, M. (1970) : I and Thou, p 90.
83 Buber, M. (1947) : *op. cit.,* p 85.
84 Page, F.(ed.), *op. cit.,* p 113.
85 Read, H. (1958) : Education through Art, p 226.
86 Witkin, R. (1974) : The Intelligence of Feeling.
87 *Ibid.* p 9.
88 *Ibid.* p 21.
89 Burton, M.A. (ed.) (1968) : The Independent Schools Association Year Book, p xxvi.
90 Letter to John Reynolds, May 1818, in Page, F. (ed.) (1954) : Letters of John Keats, p 173.
91 Steiner, R. (1909) : Knowledge of the Higher Worlds, p 172.
92 Steiner, R. (1922) : Spiritual Ground of Education, p 131.

BIBLIOGRAPHY

This bibliography includes all the sources which have been directly referred to in this book. It does not include all the sources which may be relevant to the subject.

Allen, D. (1980) : English Teaching since 1965. How Much Growth. Heinemann Educational Books.

Anglin, J.M. (ed.) (1973) : J.S. Bruner. Beyond the Information Given: Studies in the Psychology of Knowing. W.W. Norton & Co.

Barfield, 0. (1961) 'Rudolf Steiner's Concept of Mind', in: The Faithful Thinker. Centenary Essays on the Work and Thought of Rudolf Steiner, Hodder and Stoughton, London.

Barnes, H. (1980) : 'An Introduction to Waldorf Education', in: Teachers College Record, Vol.81, No.3, Spring 1980.

Battersby, J. (1978) : 'Francis Edmunds', in: Odyssey, Vol.2, No.5, Aug/Sep, 1978.

Bell, N. and D. (1976) : 'The Vancouver Waldorf School Steps Out', in: Child and Man, Vol.XI, No.4, July, 1976.

Bernstein, B. (1973) : Class, Codes and Control. Vol.I. Paladin.

Bernstein, B. (1975) : Class, Codes and Control. Vol.III. Routledge and Kegan Paul.

Blishen, E. (ed.) (1969) : Blond's Encyclopaedia of Education. Blond Educational, London.

Boos-Hamburger, H. (1973) : The Creative Power of Colour. Rudolf Steiner's Approach to Colour in Art. The Michael Press, Temple Lodge, London.

Bowen, J. (1975) : A History of Western Education. Vol.I, 1972; Vol.II, 1975, Methuen and Co., London.

Boyd, W. (1921) : A History of Western Education. A. and C. Black Ltd.,, London.

Boyd, W. (1917) : From Locke to Montessori. George Harrap and Co., London.

Blom, A. (1978) : 'The Miracle of Michael House', in: Child and Man, Vol.XIII, No.1.

Bruner, J.S. (1960) : The Process of Education. Vintage.

Bruner, J.S. (1966) : Towards a Theory of Instruction. Belknap Press.

Buber, M. (1970) : I and Thou. Translation and Prologue by Walter Kaufman. T. and T. Clark, Edinburgh.

Buber, M. (1947) : Between Man and Man. Translated by R.G. Smith. Keegan Paul, London.

Buhler, C. (1971) : 'Basic Theoretical Concepts of Humanistic Psychology' in: American Psychologist, Vol.26, 1971.

Burton, M.A. (1968) : The Independent Schools Association Yearbook. Adam and Charles Black, London.

Carlgren, F. (1976) : Education Towards Freedom: A Survey of the Work of Waldorf Schools throughout the World. English edition by Joan and Siegried Rudel, Lanthorn Press, East Grinstead, England.

Cubberley, E. P. (1920) : Readings in the History of Education. Houghton Mifflin Co., Cambridge, Mass.

Davy, J. (1973) : Child Centred Education. The Ideas of Rudolf Steiner. Reprinted from *Times Educational Supplement*, March 23, 1973. Rudolf Steiner Publications, South Africa.

Davy, J. (1980) : 'The Social Meaning of Education', in: *Teachers College Record*, Vol.81, No.3, Spring, 1980.

Dearden, R.F. (1972) : Education and the Development of Reason. Routledge and Kegan Paul.

Dewey, J. (1961) : Democracy and Education. Macmillan, New York.

Dinnage, R. (1981) : 'Benign Dottiness : The World of Rudolf Steiner', in: *New Society*, Vol.57, No.972, 2 July 1981.

Durham, K. (1969) : A Critical Investigation of the Problems of Teaching Poetry to English-Speaking Pupils in South African Senior Schools. Unpublished M.A. dissertation, Rhodes University, Grahamstown.

Edmunds, F. (1975) : Rudolf Steiner's Gift to Education – The Waldorf Schools. Rudolf Steiner Press, London.

Galbreath, R.C. (1970) : Spiritual Science in an Age of Materialism: Rudolf Steiner and Occultism. Unpublished Ph.D. dissertation, University of Michigan.

Good, C.V. (ed.) (1945) : Dictionary of Education. McGraw Hill.

Harwood, A.C. (1957) : 'Rudolf Steiner Schools', in: The Year Book of Education. Bereday, G. (ed.)

Harwood, A.C. (1958) : The Recovery of Man in Childhood. A Study in the Educational Work of Rudolf Steiner. Hodder and Stoughton, London.

Harwood, A.C. (ed.) (1961) : The Faithful Thinker. Centenary Essays on the Work and Thought of Rudolf Steiner, 1861-1925. Hodder and Stoughton, London.

Harwood, A.C. (1967) : The Way of the Child. Rudolf Steiner Press, London.

Hayn, G. (1975) : 'The Bristol Waldorf School, in: *Child and Man*, Vol.XI, No.1, January 1975.

Hemleben, J. (1975) : Rudolf Steiner. A Documentary Biography. Translated from the German edition by Leo Twyman. Henry Goulden Ltd.

Heydebrand, C. Von (1970) : Childhood : A Study of the Growing Soul. Second edition. Rudolf Steiner Press, London.

Heydebrand, C. Von (1977) : The Curriculum of the First Waldorf School. Translated by Eileen Hutchins. Steiner Schools Fellowship, Michael Hall School, Forest Row, Sussex, England.

Holt, J. (1972) : Freedom and Beyond. Pelican.

Howard, A. (1980) : 'Education and our Human Future', in: *Teachers College Record*, Vol.81, No.3, Spring 1980.

James, W. (1905) : The Will to Believe. First published 1897. Longman's, Green & Co.

James, W. (1911) : Talks to Teachers on Psychology, and to Students on some of Life's Ideals. First published 1899. Longman's, Green and Co.

König, K. (1969) : The First Three Years of the Child. Anthroposophic Press, New York.

Leichter, H.J. (1980) : 'A Note on Time and Education', in: *Teachers College Record*, Vol.81, No.3, Spring 1980.

Lund, K.A. (1978) : Understanding our Fellow Man. The Judgement of Character through Trained Observation. Translated by B.J. Klitgaard. New Knowledge Books, East Grinstead, Sussex, England.

McAllen, A.E. (1977) : Teaching Children to Write. Its Connection with the Development of Spatial Consciousness in the Child. Distributed by Rudolf Steiner Press, London. Printed by Downfield Press Ltd.

Meyer, A.E. (1939) : The Development of Education in the Twentieth Century. Prentice-Hall Inc., New York.

Nunn, P. (1945) : Education. Its Data and First Principles. Third Edition. First Published 1920. Edward Arnold.

Ogletree, E.J. (1968) : A Cross Cultural Exploratory Study of the Creativeness of Steiner and State School Pupils in England, Scotland and Germany. Unpublished Ph.D. dissertation, Wayne State University.

Page, F. (ed.) (1954) : Letters of John Keats, Oxford University Press.

Peterson, A.D.C. (1960) : A Hundred Years of Education. First published 1952. Gerald Duckworth and Co. Ltd., London.

Plato (c 360 B.C.) : The Republic. Translated and Introduced by Desmond Lee. Second edition, revised. Penguin Classics, 1974.

Polanyi, M. (1966) : The Tacit Dimension. Routledge and Kegan Paul Ltd.

Postman, N. and Weingartner, C. (1971) : Teaching as a Subversive Activity. First published 1969. Penguin.

Raffé. M., Harwood, C. and Lundren, M. (1974) : Eurythmy and the Impulse to Dance. Rudolf Steiner Press, London.

Read, H. (1958) : Education through Art. First Published 1943. Faber and Faber.

Rogers, C.R. (1969) : Freedom to Learn. Charles E. Merril.

Ross, J.S. (1962) : Groundwork of Educational Theory. First Published 1942. George G. Harrap and Co. Ltd., London.

Rusk, R.R. (1933) : A History of Infant Education. University of London Press.

Rusk, R.R. (1965) : Doctrines of the Great Educators. Third Edition. Macmillan.

Russell, B. (1946) : History of Western Philosophy. George Allen and Unwin.

Selleck, R.J.W. (1972) : English Primary Education and the Progressives. Routledge and Kegan Paul.

Shepherd, A.P. (1975) : A Scientist of the Invisible. An Introduction to the Life and Work of Rudolf Steiner. Eighth impression. Hodder and Stoughton.

Skidelsky, R. (1969) : English Progressive Schools. Pelican.

Steiner, R. (First published 1891) : The Philosophy of Spiritual Activity. A Modern Philosophy of Life Developed by Scientific Methods. An enlarged and revised edition of Philosophy of Freedom, together with the original thesis on Truth and Science. Authorised translation by Prof. and Mrs R.F. Alfred Hoernle. G. P. Putnam's Sons, London and N.Y. Second edition, 1922.

Steiner, R. (First published 1902) : Christianity as Mystical Fact, Translated by H. Collison. G. P. Putnam's Sons, London and N.Y. Third edition, 1914.

Steiner, R. (First published 1904) : Theosophy. An Introduction to the Supersensible Knowledge of the World and the Destination of Man. Translated from the German text (28th edition) in the Complete Centenary Edition of the works of Rudolf Steiner. Rudolf Steiner Press, London. Fourth edition, 1970.

Steiner, R. (First published 1909) : Knowledge of the Higher Worlds. How is it Achieved? Translated by D.S.O. and C.D. Rudolf Steiner Press, London. Sixth edition, second impression, 1973.

231

Steiner, R. (From lecture, 1908) : The Four Temperaments. Lecture delivered in the winter of 1908-1909. Previously published with the title The Mystery of the Human Temperaments. Translated by Frances E. Dawson. Anthroposophic Press Inc., Second Edition Revised, 1968.

Steiner, R. (First published 1909) : The Education of the Child in the Light of Anthroposophy. A lecture re-cast in essay form with additional footnotes. Translated by Mary and George Adams. Rudolf Steiner Press, 1965.

Steiner, R. (From lectures 1909) : The Gospel of St Luke. Ten lectures given in Basle in Sept. 1909. Translated by D.S. Osmond, assisted by Owen Barfield. Rudolf Steiner Press, London. Fourth edition, 1964.

Steiner, R. (First published 1910) : Occult Science. Translated by George and Mary Adams from the 26th Edition of the German Text entitled Die Geheimwissenschaft im Umriss. Rudolf Steiner Press, London. Second impression, 1972.

Steiner, R. (First published 1914) : The Riddles of Philosophy. Authorised translation. Anthroposophic Press, N.Y., 1973.

Steiner, R. (From lectures 1917) : Behind the Scenes of External Happenings. Two lectures given in Zurich in Nov. 1917. Rudolf Steiner Publishing Co., London, 1947.

Steiner, R. (From lectures 1919) : Education as a Social Problem. Six lectures given in Dornach, Aug. 1919. Anthroposophic Press, 1969.

Steiner, R. (From lectures 1919) : Discussions with Teachers. Fourteen lectures given in Stuttgart, Aug/Sept 1919. Translated by Helen Fox. Rudolf Steiner Press, London, 1967.

Steiner, R. (From lectures 1919) : Study of Man. Fourteen lectures given in Stuttgart in Aug/Sept 1919. Translated by Daphne Harwood and Helen Fox, revised by A.C. Harwood. Rudolf Steiner Press, London, 1966.

Steiner, R. (From lectures 1919) : Practical Advice to Teachers. Fourteen lectures given in Stuttgart in Aug/Sept 1919. Translated by Johanna Collis. Rudolf Steiner Press, London, 1976.

Steiner, R. (From lectures 1919) : The Influences of Lucifer and Ahriman. Man's Responsibility for the Earth. Five lectures given in Nov. 1919. Authorised translation by D.S. Osmond. Rudolf Steiner Press, London, 1954. Second impression by Steiner Book Centre, N. Vancouver, Canada, 1976.

Steiner, R. (1920) : The Threefold State. The True Aspect of the Social Question. Authorised translation. George Allen and Unwin Ltd., London.

Steiner, R. (From lecture, 1921) : 'The Science of Spirit. Education and the Practical Life'. Lecture at the Hague, Feb. 1921. Translated by Michael and Elizabeth Tapp. In: Education as an Art, edited by Paul M. Allen. Rudolf Steiner Publications, N.Y., 1970.

Steiner, R. (From lectures, 1921) : Waldorf Education for Adolescence. Eight lectures given in Stuttgart, June, 1921. Authorised translation. Kolisko Archive Publications, for the Steiner Schools Fellowship Publications, U.K., 1980.

Steiner, R. (From lecture 1921) : 'Education and the Science of Spirit'. Lecture given in Aarau, Switzerland, in Nov. 1921. Translated by Michael and Elizabeth Tapp. In: Education as an Art, edited by Paul M. Allen. Rudolf Steiner Publications, N.Y., 1970.

Steiner, R. (From lectures 1922) : The Spiritual Ground of Education. Nine lectures given at Oxford in Aug. 1922. Anthroposophical Publishing Co., London, 1947.

Steiner, R. (From lectures 1922) : The Younger Generation. Educational and Spiritual Impulses for Life in the Twentieth Century. Thirteen lectures given at Stuttgart, Oct. 1922. Translated by R.M. Querido. Anthroposophic Press, Inc., N.Y., 1967.

Steiner, R. (From lectures 1923) : Education and Modern Spiritual Life. Twelve lectures given at Ilkley, Yorkshire in August 1923. Revised translation by J. Darrell with an additional lecture translated by George Adams. Anthroposophical Publishing Co., London, 1954. Also published under the title A Modern Art of Education, Rudolf Steiner Press, London, 1972.

Steiner, R. (From lectures 1924) : The Essentials of Education. Five lectures given in Stuttgart in April 1924. Rudolf Steiner Press, London, 1968.

Steiner, R. (From lectures 1924) : The Roots of Education. Five lectures given in Berne in April 1924. Translated by Helen Fox. Rudolf Steiner Press, London, 1968.

Steiner, R. (From lectures 1924) : Curative Education. Twelve lectures given in Dornach in June/July 1924. Translated by Mary Adams. Rudolf Steiner Press, London, 1972.

Steiner, R. (From lectures 1924) : The Kingdom of Childhood. Seven lectures given in Torquay in Aug. 1924. Translated by Helen Fox. Rudolf Steiner Press, London, 1974.

Steiner, R. (1928) : The Story of My Life. Translated by O.D. Wannamaker. Anthroposophical Publishing Co.

Stockmeyer, E.A.K. (1969) : Rudolf Steiner's Curriculum for the Waldorf Schools. Rudolf Steiner Press, London.

Wachsmuth, G. (1955) : The Life and Work of Rudolf Steiner from the Turn of the Century to His Death. Translated by O.D. Wannamaker and R.E. Raab from the volume published in 1941 under the title Die Geburt der Geisteswissenschaft (The Birth of Spiritual Science). Second edition. Whittier Books Inc., N.Y.

Whicher, 0. (1980) : Projective Geometry. Creative Polarities in Space and Time. Second impression. Rudolf Steiner Press, London, 1980.

Whitehead, A.N. (1962) : The Aims of Education and Other Essays. C.T. North Whitehead.

Wilds, E.H. (1936) : The Foundations of Modern Education. Rinehart and Co. Inc., N.Y.

Wilkinson, R. (1973) : Rudolf Steiner Education. Teaching Geography. ©Roy Wilkinson, Forest Row, Sussex, England.

Wilkinson, R. (1973) : Rudolf Steiner Education. Teaching History. The Ancient Civilisations of India, Persia, Egypt/Babylonia. ©Roy Wilkinson, Forest Row, Sussex, England.

Wilkinson, R. (1975) : The Curriculum of the Waldorf School. ©Roy Wilkinson, Forest Row, Sussex, England.

Wilkinson, R. (1975) : Rudolf Steiner Education. Studies in Practical Activities. Farming, Gardening, Housebuilding for the age groups 9 and 10. ©Roy Wilkinson, Forest Row, Sussex, England.

Wilkinson, R. (1975) : Rudolf Steiner Education. Plant Study - Geology. For the age groups 11 and 12. ©Roy Wilkinson, Forest Row, Sussex, England.

Wilkinson, R. (1976) : Rudolf Steiner Education. Teaching English. ©Roy Wilkinson, Forest Row, Sussex, England.

Wilkinson, R. (1976) : Rudolf Steiner Education. Teaching Mathematics to age 14. ©Roy Wilkinson, Forest Row, Sussex, England.

Wilkinson, R. (1977) : Rudolf Steiner Education. The Physical Sciences I. For age groups 12/13/14. ©Roy Wilkinson, Forest Row, Sussex, England.

Wilkinson, R. (1977) : Rudolf Steiner Education. The Temperaments in Education. ©Roy Wilkinson, Forest Row, Sussex, England.

Wilkinson, R. (1978) : Commonsense Schooling Based on the Indications of Rudolf Steiner. Henry Goulden, East Grinstead, Sussex, England.

Wilkinson, R. (1978) : Rudolf Steiner Education. The Physical Sciences II. For age groups 13/14. Chemistry. ©Roy Wilkinson, Forest Row, Sussex, England.

Wilkinson, R. (1978) : Rudolf Steiner Education. Nutrition/ Health/Anthropology for classes 7/8 (ages 13/14). ©Roy Wilkinson, Forest Row, Sussex, England.

APPENDICES

The Von Hardenberg Foundation (The Novalis Institute).... 237

Brief: UNESCO International Commission on
Education for the Twenty-first Century................... 241

THE VON HARDENBERG FOUNDATION

The Von Hardenberg Foundation (which operates as The Novalis Institute) was established in Durban, South Africa, in 1982 as a vehicle for contributing to social and cultural change, by a group of people inspired by the Austrian scientist, educationist and spiritual researcher, Dr Rudolf Steiner. The Section 21 Company (Not For Gain) was registered and Novalis became a legal entity in 1984.

The founding group — Yvonne Oates (interior designer), Carol Ross (chartered accountant), Brian Johnson (architect) and Ralph Shepherd (businessman) — sought to offer their various professional talents in the development of innovative and creative processes for the educational, social and cultural problems of the day. This group was supported by many others including Stan Maher, now an active member of The Novalis Institute's management team. Although based firmly upon the Systems or Holistic thinking[1] of Rudolf Steiner, the founding group was also inspired by contemporary thinkers such as Fritjof Capra, Maurice Berman, Stephen Covey, Peter Senge, Vaclav Havel and South African Adam Small, all of whom have overcome the Cartesian or western materialistic view of the world.

Members of The Novalis Institute believe that social and cultural transformation from the current model based upon Western materialism to a more human-centred model must be preceded by individual change. Social change either in the individual or the community requires a paradigm shift in consciousness and not merely the adoption of another ideology, dogma or world view — political, religious or philosophical. A total change in the way in which we see the world or in the way in which we think is required. Such transformation can only be experienced and described in retrospect. The process employed to initiate such a change is based upon personal introspection and contemplation in which personal and human values and principles are considered against the destructive effects of Western materialism. All those people mentioned above, in particular Rudolf Steiner, have written extensively about the exercises and processes involved in acquiring this change in consciousness.

Until recent years, such processes were considered to be the 'suspect' domain of (sometimes dubious) Eastern gurus and of hippies, and were not thought to be worthy of serious consideration. However with the debunking of the atomic theory brought about by modern scientific discovery, together with the continuing collapse of the Darwinian theory of evolution for the same reason, mankind is increasingly released from the thought prison of the Cartesian mindset in which the universe was seen as an immense machine, and human beings (plus all living things) as

---

1 Also called Goetheanistic thinking after Wolfgang von Goethe, who, together with Frederich von Hardenberg (Novalis) and William Blake, stood in opposition to the materialistic philosophy of Descartes, the science of Newton and the economics of Malthus.

chance chemical phenomena within a meaningless time/space continuum.

With this background of Systems or Holistic thinking the first Novalis team addressed a series of projects relating to cultural and social issues. However it soon became apparent that education would become the major focus of The Novalis Institute's work. This also meant the establishment of a teacher training programme in which adult educators would be introduced to Systems or Goetheanistic thinking. This would happen through the founding of a new college, for in the words of Albert Einstein, "The significant problems we face cannot be solved at the same level of thinking we were at when we created them" [2]. In a similar vein we cannot expect the social, cultural and economic problems of our time to be solved by thinking coming from the same institutions — universities or research institutes — who themselves have come into being out of the same thinking or paradigm that created these problems in the first place. Experience has shown that most established institutions can only consider "those innovations that might logically evolve out of the current system" [3]; they seem incapable of considering a radical change in the system itself, that is, the possibility of operating under a different paradigm altogether. Hence the need for entirely new institutions that can operate out of new thinking, new paradigms, uncluttered by the past.

Since 1986 the main work of Novalis has developed in the Western Cape Province and KwaZulu/Natal regions in South Africa, the main office being situated in Cape Town, with a full-time staff of approximately 12, supported by many part-time teacher trainers. A small office is also being established in Natal to facilitate the development of programmes there, and it is also expected that an office will open in Gauteng. In addition, Novalis can call upon support from professional consultants in the artistic, architectural and organisational development spheres who share and support the aims and objectives of the Novalis Institute.

The Novalis Institute has a membership for which application may be made. The membership elects a Board of Directors (trustees) who in turn have the support of an international Board of Advisors. The Novalis Institute is a signatory to the Treaty of Innovative Teacher Trainers of the European Forum for Freedom in Education. This treaty embraces fifteen European universities and four major teacher training colleges (this includes major universities such as the University of Bielefeld in Germany, and the University of St Petersburg in Russia).

In 1994 the Novalis programmes reached over 1400 state school teachers who were introduced to innovative primary and senior primary courses. These programmes were designed to make education more meaningful for teachers and pupils and relevant to social and vocational needs. During the same period seventy school principals attended the Head Teachers Support Programme that enhances democratic processes, attitudinal change and community development programmes within the school and local community.

Plans are currently being formulated for Novalis to respond to a request from

---

2 *The Seven Habits of Highly Effective People*, p.42, by Stephen Covey. Simon & Schuster 1994.
3 *The Different Drum*, p.8, by M. Scott Peck. Rider, 1990.

238

the Department of Education in KwaZulu/Natal region, to take over the Bechet Teachers College in Durban, in order to develop and offer pre-service and in-service programmes.

Over the next 10 years Novalis hopes to establish colleges of Adult Education in the main centres of South Africa offering creative programmes that will contribute to a new culture of learning in this country.

Over the past two decades thousands of new non-Government organisations — NGOs — have come into being with many innovative ideas and ways to work with the social, educational and economic problems of South Africa. The very existence of these NGOs and the fruitful work that has sprung from them is confirmation of the need for new institutions unburdened by traditional or old thinking to deal with today's problems. Novalis is one of these institutions working out of a new cultural/social paradigm.

ESCO Commission internationale sur l'education pour le vingt et unième siècle
International Commission on Education for the Twenty-first Century

IEF - EN BREF - *BRIEF* - EN BREF - *BRIEF* - EN BREF

January 1994

EDUCATION FOR FREEDOM AND SOCIAL RESPONSIBILITY: THE RUDOLF STEINER SCHOOLS (WALDORF PEDAGOGY)

n school the question is not of receiving a complete education, but rather of preparing oneself receive it from life". (R.Steiner)

teiner Schools try to advocate a new spirit in a rapidly changing world; a purely materialistic onception of the world and of the human being is no longer sufficient to respond to questions osed in our industrial society. The future requires a fundamental change in our way of thinking: e human individual as an independent spiritual entity should be the starting point for all efforts iming at the renewal of our society. Based on a profound knowledge of human nature, the rinciples of the pedagogy of Rudolf Steiner (also called Waldorf pedagogy) can be summarized s follows:

All human faculties - Intellectual, artistic, moral - are developed in an equal manner. The urriculum of each school is individually devised, and there is always a balance between theory nd practice. Arts and science subjects are given equal importance. At secondary school level, ractical courses on agriculture, forestry, surveying, and internships in industrial and social nvironments are included in the curriculum.

Teaching is considered and practised as an art. The teachers act like artists whose aims re to help the child to discover and love the world surrounding him or her. Their aim is not to ram the child with knowledge, but to awaken at the right moment certain faculties of the soul, of e inner self. In everyday practice the question is not "what is possible?" or "what goes down ell?" but rather "what is challenging and what may best stimulate the pupil at the present state f development?" Therefore children stay together in age groups; there is no selection or early pecialization and no repetition. The diversity in every class reflects the diversity of humanity as fundamental basis for social education. This philosophy is in keeping with the 1966 _O-UNESCO Recommendation on the status of teachers (in particular provision III).

he teachers' roles are to **awaken** the child's **latent faculties** and allow its **profound ndividuality** to emerge and develop: they thus help the children to find the appropriate relation etween their individuality and physical being, their environment and the present-day society to which they are to integrate. It is this relation which will enable them to make the appropriate se of their freedom. Young people are then able to enter into society not as passive pectators, but as conscious sensitive citizens, ready to tackle the challenges of our times by aking an active part in the transformation of our world.

Organisation and management of the school

Steiner Schools are self-governing and have no school head or director, but are run by the eachers, who all have equal rights and decide on all administrative matters (teaching concept, mployment of teachers, buildings, finances, etc.). Based on mutual trust and comprehension, he bonds between parents and teachers are cultivated through frequent meetings. Parents lso participate in important decisions and take an active part in school life. This sets an xample of democracy to the pupils.

Steiner Schools are private schools, financed partially by the state or the local community, as well as by parents who contribute in a spirit of mutual aid, enabling low-income families to enrol their children also.

In 1993 there exist, worldwide, over 600 Rudolf Steiner schools, 1000 kindergartens, and 50 institutions for remedial education and social therapy. Some Steiner schools are members of the international network of UNESCO's Associated Schools Project.

In France, Steiner Schools can be visited at the Fédération des Ecoles Steiner en France, 5 rue Georges Clemenceau, 78400 Chatou, France, telephone no. (33-1) 3952 6917.

Education in critical environments

The originality of this educational approach and its longstanding practical application all over the world have recently proved to be particularly interesting and fruitful in such disadvantaged environments as slums, refugee camps or in conflict situations, conditions where alternative channels of education often prove to be more efficient than official school systems. The following pilot projects are outstanding examples of the success of this alternative method and they might be of great benefit to other situations and countries:

- Soweto and Alexandra (South Africa): schools in various black townships;
- Shati refugee camp (Gaza strip): Kindergarten and remedial education for Palestinian children;
- Zagreb (Croatia): Kindergarten;
- Favela Monte Azul, Sao Paolo (Brazil): schooling and work with marginal groups and street children using the principles of Steiner education;
- Holywood, Belfast (Northern Ireland): Protestant and Catholic children are taught together;
- Pine Ridge Reservation, South Dakota (U.S.A.): school for Sioux Indian children.

FURTHER READING

Carlgren, F. Eduquer vers la liberté, La pédagogie de Rudolf Steiner dans le mouvement international des écoles Waldorf, Les Trois Arches, Paris, 1992.
Craemer, U. Die Favel-Kinder, Sozialarbeit am Rande der Gesellschaft, Stuttgart, 1987.
Edmunds, F. Rudolf Steiner Education, The Waldorf Schools, R. Steiner Press, London, 1992.
Geraets, T. Stars and Rainbows over Alexandra, Heidenheim, 1990.
Kiersch, J. Die Waldorfpädagogik. Eine Einführung in die Pädagogik Rudolf Steiners, Stuttgart 1992.
Krampen, I. Self--governed Schools. Case studies. E.Fuchs (ed,), Frankfurt, 1992.
Steiner, R. L'art de l'éducation, Méthode et pratique, (conférences), Triades, Paris, 1993.
 (Specialized bookstore: PENTAGRAM, 15 rue Racine, 75006 Paris)

Commission Secretariat :

7 place de Fontenoy
75352 Paris 07 SP
France
tel : (33-1) 45 68 11 23
fax : (33-1) 43 06 52 55
E-Mail : EDXXI@FRUNES21.BITNET

Prepared by :

Ms. Sigrid Niedermayer-Tahri
Assistant Programme Specialist
Section for Humanistic, Cultural and
International Education
UNESCO

REPRODUCTION LIBRE, VEUILLEZ CITER LA SOURCE ET L'AUTEUR / FREE OF COPYRIGHT, PLEASE ACKNOWLEDGE SOURCE AND AUTHOR